Why Cows Need Names

Why Cows Need Names

and More Secrets of Amish Farms

Randy James

Black Squirrel Books™ TM

an imprint of The Kent State University Press

Kent, Ohio 44242   www.KentStateUniversityPress.com

🐿™ BLACK SQUIRREL BOOKS™
Frisky, industrious black squirrels are a familiar sight on the
Kent State University campus and the inspiration for Black
Squirrel Books™, a trade imprint of The Kent State University Press.
www.KentStateUniversityPress.com

© 2013 by The Kent State University Press, Kent, Ohio 44242
Library of Congress Catalog Card Number 2012043636
ISBN 978-1-60635-168-0
Manufactured in the United States of America

Library of Congress Cataloging-in-Publication Data
James, Randy, 1955–
Why cows need names : and more secrets of Amish farms / Randy James.
pages cm
Sequel to: Why cows learn Dutch. 2005.
ISBN 978-1-60635-168-0 (hardcover) ∞
1. Farm life—Ohio—Geauga County. 2. Farms—Ohio—Geauga County.
3. Amish farmers—Ohio—Geauga County—Biography. 4. Dairy farmers—
Ohio—Geauga County—Biography. I. James, Randy, 1955– Why cows learn
Dutch. II. Title.
S521.5.O3J36 2013
636'.0109771336—dc23
2012043636

17 16 15 14 13   5 4 3 2 1

*Dedicated to the people of
the Geauga Settlement*

Contents

Preface and Acknowledgments

The Geauga Amish settlement is a real community centered in Geauga County in northeast Ohio. The stories in this book are true, though most of the names, farm locations, and some other details have been changed to preserve the anonymity of the Amish farm families. Much of the dialogue is verbatim. However, the dialogue is reconstructed from notes since any recording device would be a major impediment to a free-flowing conversation with Amish people. Some of the conversations and a few of the characters are composites of various conversations and individuals in the settlement. Some of the dialogue and sentence structure may seem somewhat formal, or even a little archaic. Without a constant barrage of TVs, radios, computers, and cell phones, the syntax of Amish conversation often varies slightly from the larger non-Amish community. In addition, nearly everyone in the community is bilingual, with Pennsylvania Dutch being the language of the home and family.

While the Amish faith traces its origins to central Europe, all of the approximately 300 Amish settlements existing today are in the United States and Canada. Both the number of Amish people and the number of settlements are rapidly increasing, and the Geauga settlement—with over 2,500 households—is the fourth largest of all Amish settlements.

The farming practices and other customs discussed in this book are specific to the Geauga settlement and do not reflect all Amish settlements. Specific customs and practices between, and even within, settlements vary widely and change over time. For example, farmers in some settlements use tractors for fieldwork; in other settlements, tractors can only be used as stationary engines in the barnyard; and still other settlements forbid tractors altogether. In a compendium of settlements arranged from liberal to conservative by the number of modern farm technologies allowed, the Geauga settlement would be placed near the conservative end.

This book simply would not have been possible without the support of my wife and cheerleader, Barbara. She has read and reread every word and helped to shape the work by listening to my ideas and challenges and occasionally nudging me gently back to the computer. A big thank-you goes out to my dear friend Linda Jones for taking the time to rein in my wayward commas, run-on sentences, and overly creative punctuation. Much appreciation goes to Bill Pappas for using his considerable expertise and equipment to produce the author's photo and to Claude Clayton Smith, author of *Ohio Outback: Learning to Love the Great Black Swamp,* for his immensely helpful review of the manuscript. Thanks also to Joyce Harrison and all of the other wonderful folks at the Kent State University Press who have somehow managed once again to make publishing a warm, friendly, and exciting process. And a special thank-you to my copy editor, Rebekah Cotton, for her thoughtful review and many suggestions that helped to craft the final manuscript.

It is beyond my ability to explain how deeply indebted I am to the hundreds of Amish people in the Geauga settlement, who for over 30 years have opened their farms and homes to patiently teach a "Yankee" about the plain life. Their openness and friendship is a privilege I cherish each day. Finally, I need to especially thank the Gingerich family (name changed) for inviting me along on their five-year journey to start a new farm.

1

A Bumpy Road Ahead

"We're thinking about starting to farm, and my cousin Mahlon said I should talk to you."

It's a cold, gray, late winter day in March of 2005, and Eli Gingerich is on the line. The full round texture of his voice rearranges the cobwebs of my memory until a 30-something, bearded face comes dimly into focus.

Here we go again. Another young Amish couple who want to make a living on their own farm. Don't these people read the papers? Haven't they heard about the plight of the American farmer? Nearly every other county agent, farmer, and university professor I know would laugh and tell this foolish young man that it cannot be done. It's a modern, efficient, huge factory farm world, and the idea of starting up a new small family farm, well, it just sounds silly.

But it's not silly, and Eli knows it. His cousin Mahlon is a young Amish man who went out on a financial limb and bought his father's farm a few years back. Things were pretty tight for a year or so, but he's doing fine now. More than fine: the family works and plays together every day, and the farm generates enough income to pay off the debt and support Mahlon, his wife, and now four children.

Since February of 1980 I've had the honor of being the county agricultural agent in Geauga County, Ohio. The county is located in the heart of the snowbelt, just east of Cleveland, and is the center of the fourth largest Amish settlement in the world. Over the past 30 years or so, Ohio has lost roughly one-third of all its farms. Yet in Geauga County, where small family farms are the rule, not the exception, new farms are reasonably common.

Farm numbers have almost doubled here during those same three decades. The USDA Census of Agriculture tells us that the county went from a little over 500 farms back in the 1970s to over 1,000 now. Around half, or a little more, of the farms in the county are Amish; the rest are non-Amish small family farms. Perhaps surprisingly, in recent years both the Amish and non-Amish areas of the county have seen similar robust increases in local farm numbers. So the bottom line around these parts is, whether you're Amish or not, the idea of starting a new small family farm isn't silly at all.

"Well, Eli, what kind of a farm are you thinking about?"

There are a few moments of silence until he hesitantly says, "Dairy, I think. I mean, that's what I think we'd like to do."

"Okay, what part of it do you want to talk over with me?"

"Finances and stuff—well, everything really. I guess the big question is: do you think there's any way we can make a go of it?"

Yeah, that is the "big question" and as always it makes me profoundly uncomfortable when it is pointed in my direction. There are no canned answers. Each family, and each farm, faces its own unique set of challenges and opportunities. The simple truth is some new farms make it and others don't. The hard part is trying to predict which one is likely to flourish and which one will probably fail.

Like all of the other county agricultural agents around the state, I work for the College of Agriculture at the Ohio State University. A county agent takes research results from universities and morphs them into something that farmers in the real world might actually be able to use. Unfortunately, while no one wants to fess up to it, a lot of the researchers at the major colleges of agriculture around the country are just enamored with super-large farms and big agriculture. Therefore, much of the research, along with the educational programs and materials, is geared toward those large farms, and it often takes near Herculean efforts to make the results relevant for very small farms. This is especially true on a small Amish farm where there might be only 50 acres or less of cropland, a few cows, and a main power source that isn't a monster tractor but is rather a group of living, eating, snorting, biting, kicking, defecating, and sweating gentle draft horses. So, as always, predicting the success of someone like Eli can be a bit of a challenge.

We settle on next Wednesday morning at 10:00 for our first meeting at his farm. As we're talking, I'm trying to recall where his farm might be, but I just have no idea, so I'll have to ask and that can get real complicated. "All right, Wednesday morning it is. Now, where's your farm, Eli?"

"Oh, it's the third farm south of Ervin Byler's on the east side of the road."

"Are you talking about the Ervin A. out on Hayes Road?"

"No, no, Ervin J., the one down here in Parkman."

There are at least seven Ervin Bylers in the settlement, and it's not even a particularly common name. There are well over 30 John Millers. With this much name duplication, it really helps to know a person's middle initial. And it is just an initial; the Amish in the settlement usually don't have middle names. The middle initial for all of the children in a family is the first letter of the father's first name. Now if, as often happens, there are two people in the settlement with the same first name and middle initial, then they simply add the first letter of the grandfather's first name to the middle initial, so you end up with names like John J. G. or Mose E. L. In any case, I happen to know the Ervin J. that Eli is talking about, and I'm getting close to pinpointing his farm.

"Eli, who has the farm just to the south of you?"

"Well, that's a Yankee farm. Albert Smith owns it and lives there, but he has the land rented out to another Yankee farmer and I really can't think of his name." ("Yankee" simply means anyone who is not Amish in this settlement.)

After a few more minutes of comparing familiar landmarks, people, farms, and crossroads, I'm pretty sure I have a bead on where Eli's farm actually is. It sounds like it might be one of the few farms in the settlement that I've never been on. Eli describes the barn and other outbuildings, and I write down his address for good measure. No real sense in getting his phone number. He'll be in the house waiting for me on Wednesday, but in this settlement the phone won't be in the house. It will be in a little wooden phone booth somewhere in the farmyard, so if I get lost, calling for directions won't do me any good.

This whole geography puzzle about crossroads, farms, people, and directions could probably have been avoided by simply opening up Google Maps and letting the program exactly pinpoint where Eli lives. That would of course be the simple thing to do. On the other hand, these few moments have given me a chance to think about three farmers I haven't seen in quite a while and to better understand just where Eli's property rests in the larger Amish community. Google Maps can stay up there on the toolbar for another day and a less important meeting.

A little more interviewing reveals that Eli would like to milk 25 to 30 cows and that in his church district it's okay to use a milking machine.

That's good to know because some of the church districts in this settlement still require hand milking, and that really cuts back on the number of cows a farmer can milk.

"Well, looks like we're all set, Eli. I'll stop by next Wednesday morning."

"Okay, I'll be waiting."

Hanging up the phone, I'm not sure why but I have a really good feeling about this farm. Starting a new farm, or any business for that matter, is seldom easy. Eli will face a heaping, steaming manure-spreader load of decisions before he milks the first cow. Next week we will start to pull together an outline of a business plan that will guide this farm's development. Some of the plan will be written down, and some will be stored in Eli's head. If it becomes a reality, the new farm will immediately be buffeted by a wide variety of ever-changing and often unforeseen factors and circumstances. Some of these things are totally in his control, but many are not. Ultimately the success or failure of this new farm business will hinge on the ability of Eli and his family to react quickly to whatever obstacles—or opportunities—bubble out of the local and international agricultural marketplace, the national economy, government programs and regulations, as well as the living world of farm plants and animals and the randomly pernicious weather.

This new farm will have no control over the price of milk or other commodities and only very limited control over the price of any specialty agricultural products, like maple syrup, honey, or vegetables. Likewise, the farm will have almost no control over the price of inputs such as fertilizer, feed, and seed. However, small farms like this one have a great deal of control over many other things, like hay, silage, or grain that is grown on the farm, equipment costs, profitable use of the manure, and to some extent animal health. These are real, and routinely overlooked, competitive advantages that very small farms are able to capture. In addition, unlike large farms, this small farm will use little to no hired labor. Eli's farm will be specifically sized so that he and his family, with occasional traded labor among the neighbors, will supply all of the labor for both the crops and the livestock. When carefully employed these are but a few of the secrets that allow Amish farms to quietly prosper and grow in the heart of a factory-farm world.

Can the Gingeriches start a new farm? Yes. Should they start a new farm? I don't know. Would it be successful? Well, maybe yes . . . and maybe no. Next Wednesday, we'll just have to see. Although, in truth, even if the business plan we develop looks good, it will take a few years to really know if Eli and his family have what it takes to squeeze a profit out of their own small farm. Can they overcome the minor bumps and major setbacks that will surely come their way? Only time will tell.

2

A New Farm . . . Just Think of the Possibilities

It's Wednesday morning, barely a week after Eli first called. Our meeting isn't until 10:00, so I'll swing by the Extension office first and get a few things done. Usually National Public Radio would be my companion in the car, but soft, nondistracting, music is tuned in this morning. The drive to work is about 12 miles of paved, hilly, rural roads. Not a lot of houses and almost no traffic. Most of the way is wooded on both sides with an occasional clearing for a house, pasture, or farm field. The biggest danger is hitting a deer, wild turkey, raccoon, possum, squirrel, rabbit, chipmunk, coyote, goose, or any other critter that wanders onto the road. When the sun's out, it's a pretty drive, but like all too often in March the windshield wipers are busy intermittently flailing away at an ugly, gray, bone-chilling mixture of snow, sleet, and rain.

Winter is hard on these roads. The freezing and thawing breaks up the asphalt and leaves a fresh crop of potholes each spring. Between the wayward wildlife and omnipresent potholes, it's silly to drive fast. So I generally slow down and try to enjoy the ride. There's a road kill deer in the ditch on the left. Poor thing, she wasn't there yesterday, must have been hit some time last night, or early this morning. It's a fresh kill, the buzzards haven't even moved in yet. She's pretty big, and more than likely a pickup truck or car is limping its way toward the body shop this morning. Hope no one was hurt.

I can see a small pod of large black birds in the middle of the road about a quarter of a mile ahead. Can't tell if they're buzzards or crows from this distance. They won't leave whatever's dead up there until I almost hit them. Each one is afraid to leave because their flock-mates might make off with the really juicy parts. Close enough to see them now; they're crows. Looks like breakfast this morning is what's left of a good-sized raccoon. Must have been hit hard or twice. It's pretty well smashed, broke open and smeared over about three feet of asphalt. From a crow's perspective, this is an ideal presentation, not much digging and tearing needed. They should have it cleaned up in a few hours. By tonight, all that will be left are a little pile of hair, teeth, and bones, matted and framed by saucer-sized puddles of soupy, white bird droppings, slowly mingling filth through E. coli–contaminated, chalky rivulets, pulsing in the cold drizzle.

Well, that was a cheery drive. Almost into Burton now, hopefully this morning's carnage is behind me. Nope, not quite, there is a flat cat that was obviously just one step too slow. The cars in the village circle are slowly weaving their way around the guinea hens again. The hens' home is sup-posed to be on the County Historical Society's farm on the southeast end of the circle, but they like to wander. Guinea hens aren't cute, and they don't appear to be over smart. However, at least they are alive, and this particu-lar morning that's good enough.

Finally in the office I flip on the little electric space heater under my desk and walk back to the workroom to microwave myself a cup of bitter decaffeinated coffee. Like almost every morning, the microwave beeps, I pull the cup out and promptly cauterize the inside of my mouth with the nearly boiling liquid.

Back at the desk a glowing computer screen shows 31 messages in my inbox. Oh goody. The first 14 are all the same spam message. It managed to slip through the university's sophisticated spam blocker system 14 times, even though the words in the subject line are so filthy they would fetch an R rating in any movie. A couple messages are agricultural newsletters. Three are important administrative memos from important managers on the main campus in Columbus. I delete the first two without reading them, based solely on the relative value of the managers who sent them. The third one proves to be equally worthless and gets deleted half read. It's like these people slept through Enron and don't understand that the best thing managers can do is keep quiet and stay out of the way before some-one recognizes what a truly unnecessary expense they are to an otherwise productive system.

Four of the messages are from colleagues sharing information on spe-cific educational programs. Another is from a researcher answering some questions I had about the latest studies on hoof health in dairy cows. One is from a county agent in Indiana asking about some Amish farm economics work we've done. The rest are a hodgepodge of spam.

Staring out of the office window into an ashen sky as the computer quietly hums itself to sleep, I silently admit that so far this has not been the most upbeat of mornings, and my mood could be better. Turning back to the desk, I slip a large yellow pad of paper and a #2 pencil with an oversized eraser into my old leather briefcase. That's all the technology I'll need or want for my visit with Eli Gingerich. I suppose I could pack up my computer and haul it along, but there's real thinking to be done this morning, and a computer would just get in the way. Magically, in the short walk from the office door to my car, the day is transformed. It is immeasurably better. A new farm; just think of the possibilities!

Distinctly unlike my earlier drive to the office, the sojourn to Eli's house is restful and pleasant. The sun is still nowhere to be found, but the sky looks a bit brighter. Farms along the way seem to be slowly waking up and shaking winter's heavy mantle off of the barns, fields, and pastures. Eli lives only about eight or nine miles from the office. The buildings are easily recognizable from his description, and the address is even on the mailbox in large block-style green and white numerals. The barn off to the right looks to be in good repair, at least on the outside, and has a reasonably fresh coat of white paint. Same is true for the equipment shed. The corn crib looks okay—of course there's no corn in it. Most folks driving by would call this a farm—but it's not. It *was* a farm. Someday it might be a farm again, but right now it's just vacant buildings and some old fields. To be a farm, this place would need to get back into the business of growing and selling agricultural products. Currently the U.S. Census would simply, and correctly, classify all of this as a "rural residence."

My little silver Corolla crunches onto the gravel driveway and rolls between two spotless white houses. The larger two-story one on the left appears to be the main farmhouse. The one-story house on the right probably is, or at least was, a *daadihaus,* or small retirement home that Grandpa and Grandma would usually move into after the farm is passed on to the next generation. However, in this case I have the sense from Eli's discussion that he is starting a new farm and not necessarily taking it over from his father. Still, my guess is Eli and his family are in the larger house, so I park the car and head that way on foot. A medium-sized dog runs up before I get halfway to the house. He doesn't bark. In fact, his whole frantic, tail-wagging demeanor proclaims his timidity. After a couple of friendly pats on the head his muscles relax and he falls in a few paces behind, panting openmouthed and begging for my attention one more time.

Eli opens the side door that passes directly into the kitchen before I can knock twice. I have the distinct feeling that he watched me pull in and has been patiently waiting on the other side of the door. As he welcomes me in, I recognize his husky build and round face, ringed with black hair and a beard. We had talked several different times but only briefly.

He points to the kitchen table in the middle of the room and says, "I thought we'd sit right here and talk if that's okay."

"That'll be just fine." I bend down and start to take off my shoes on the rug in front of the door.

"Oh, don't worry about it," Eli says. "You can leave your shoes on."

"No, these shoes have cleats in them that hold dirt, and it's pretty muddy out. I don't mind slipping them off." It's only as I'm sliding across the floor in stocking feet that I catch sight of Eli's dark haired wife working quietly over by the sink.

Motioning in her direction Eli says, "This is my wife, Katie."

She turns, smiles, and says, "Hello." She's wearing a pale blue dress, with the traditional white apron in front. The small pleated white cap on her head accents an expressive face and bright eyes that seem both welcoming and sincere. I know I've met her before, but I can't remember where.

"Hi, Katie. Haven't we met at least one other time?"

"Yes, I was at one of the farm meetings over at Levi Miller's maybe a year or so ago."

"Yeah, now I remember."

Eli sits down on one side of the table with a pad of paper and ballpoint pen in front of him. I sit in the chair across the table and unload the yellow pad and pencil from the briefcase and lay them on the table. Katie quietly works with some dough on the counter a few feet away. We exchange pleasantries about the weather for a very few moments, but I think we're all eager to get down to the business at hand.

"Well, Eli, why don't you tell me a little bit about what you're planning to do with this farm." With that I lean back in the chair, slide the yellow notepad into my lap and pick up the pencil, ready to take notes.

With a slightly nervous laugh Eli asks, "What would you like to know?"

This is a big discussion for Eli and Katie and for me. If things work out, Eli will change his career as a carpenter midstream and begin working full-time at home. Things will likely change even more for Katie. She'll suddenly become a "farm wife," and she'll add a hundred new things into her routine. Mornings won't just be a time to get everybody off to school or work. Mornings will also be a time to help feed and milk cows and a time to teach the children how to feed milk replacer to the baby heifers. Her days will be filled with new barn chores and occasional fieldwork. When the milking is done in the morning, each breakfast will become a mini-business meeting, where she, the children, and Eli will plan what most urgently needs to be done on the farm that day. It is a big discussion we're starting this morning, and it will take a little time to get it flowing. I remind myself to slow down, for we do have all the time we need to talk these things over, and then talk them over again.

"Well, let's start with how many cows you're planning to milk."

"I'm thinking maybe 25 or 30. I've got a cousin over in Guys Mills and he's been milking about that many for three or four years now. He seems to think that's about what you need to make a go of it."

Guys Mills is a small Amish settlement just across the Ohio line into Pennsylvania. It's a daughter settlement of Geauga. I'm not sure when it got started, but it's been there quite a while. I think it was started before I became the county agent here in 1980, so I'm guessing it must be at least 30 years ago.

"Well, then, let's start, at least for planning purposes, to look at 30 cows." This would be considered an extremely small herd on a Yankee farm, where milking hundreds or even thousands of cows is the norm. But by Amish standards, here in the Geauga settlement, 30 cows is a big herd. If Eli goes ahead with this plan, it will be one of the largest herds in the settlement.

"Are you planning on raising your own replacement heifers?" Replacement heifers are female calves that are raised and bred to replace an older cow in the milking herd. The older cow will then be sold into the low quality beef market, butchered, and turned mostly into hamburger.

"I'm not sure, but I'd like to." Eli looks down at the floor and almost sheepishly confesses, "I probably got way ahead of myself, but actually I've got 15 heifers right now and nine of them will freshen by this December. If things work out, I'd like to be milking by this fall so I can keep them." He takes a deep breath and pauses a moment, before proceeding in a markedly more serious tone, "But I could sell them, if after we're done here it looks like there's no way we can make a go of it. I mean, I could sell them if I have to."

"No harm done, Eli. Like you say, you can always sell them. On the other hand, if you do start farming they will give you a real jump start."

Eli nods. "That's kind of what I was thinking. Some of the guys around here say it's better to buy heifers when you need them, rather than raising them. But I thought I'd like to start off at least raising a few. What do you think? Does it pay to raise your own heifers or should I buy them?"

"Well, each farm is different. A lot of larger farms buy all their heifers and concentrate just on milking. I guess there is nothing wrong with that, but it seems to me there are some real advantages to raising your own. It allows you to control the genetics and feeding. But also—this is just a personal opinion—the more you can raise on your own farm, including heifers, the better off you are. It's one of the secrets that make small farms work."

With a pronounced single nod of his head and a suddenly authoritative voice, Eli says, "Yes, that's how I've always looked at it too."

In heavy, plodding, block letters I write on the clean yellow pad, "Start milking in September? 15 heifers—9 fresh by December."

"So in total you want to have 30 cows, Eli. And about how many heifers?"

"Probably around 20, I think."

I quietly add 30 cows and 20 heifers to my notes, and remember that he has yet to identify the breed of dairy cow he'd like to milk. Most farms have Holsteins. They are the big, docile, black-and-white cows. They usually weigh in somewhere around 1,200 to 1,400 pounds or more, and they eat a lot. On the other hand, they make more milk than any other breed. Good Holstein cows routinely produce over 100 pounds—or about 9 or 10 gallons—of milk a day during their peak. The butterfat content of the milk is lower than other dairy breeds. That's important because farmers are paid a premium for higher butterfat milk. Still, most farmers think the total gallons of milk produced by a Holstein more than makes up for the lower percentage of butterfat—and most of the time that's probably right. So in general, Holsteins are big docile cows that eat a lot, and make a lot of low butterfat milk. Almost all the large Yankee dairy farms use Holsteins.

Another breed Eli might be considering is Jersey. They're originally from the Isle of Jersey in the English Channel, and they are much smaller than Holsteins. They generally weigh around 1,000 pounds or less and are light brown or tan—about the color of a white-tailed deer—with a darker face, tail, and feet. They are fine boned with a dainty face surrounding two huge, soft, brown eyes, and a temperament that is almost universally described as gentle. They eat less and give less milk than Holsteins, but the milk they give is worth more per gallon because it is much higher in butterfat.

Jerseys are also more "rangy." That is, they are better able to stay in good flesh and keep healthy, while foraging in the pasture for a good part of their diet. This trait is unimportant for a Holstein cow on a factory farm, since she will probably never see a pasture anyway. On a very large-scale farm, she would normally be kept in confinement, milling around on concrete for her entire life.

In stark contrast, cows on Amish family farms like Eli's can usually be found outside grazing on the pasture any time the weather is good enough. Some Amish and smaller non-Amish farms are beginning to rediscover the value of being "rangy." They're not the best for all farms, but in some situations farmers are starting to take a second look at Jerseys and some of the other small dairy breeds. So I'd better see what Eli has on his mind.

"What breed are you planning on getting, Eli?"

"Holsteins. Well, actually the heifers are Holsteins already, and I figure anything I buy would be Holstein too."

"Okay, that's fine." I really don't have a strong preference as to which breed of dairy cattle farmers should have. A good herdsman will bring out the strengths of any of the popular breeds and be successful. A poor herdsman will struggle regardless of the breed.

"Now if you do start milking this fall, are you planning on buying some cows or just slowly starting up by milking the heifers, as they come fresh?"

"I thought I'd buy some cows because I really want to stay here and work on the farm pretty much full-time, and if I'm just milking a few heifers there won't be enough money coming in."

"Yeah, that's right, Eli. So how many cows are you thinking about buying?"

With no hesitation, he says, "Probably 20." I like the confidence in his voice. It shows that he's done quite a bit of homework and has spent some real time thinking through the possibilities and challenges this new farm will pose.

"Alright, I'm sure you know that the local price of mature dairy cows has been jumping all over the place. I'm going to need to come up with a price per cow that you're comfortable with in order to make up a budget. Do you have any idea in mind of what you might have to pay for these cows?"

"I'd like to get them for $1,500 each, or maybe as high as $1,800."

"That may be a little low, Eli. I mean, that's about where they're selling now. Most of the economists are saying that milk price will likely strengthen this summer, and that always drives up the price of cows a little. You might get them for around $1,500. I'd be more comfortable if we penciled them in around $2,000 apiece. But it's your call. What number do you want me to use?"

"Go ahead and use $2,000. Then if I do manage to get them cheaper, it just works to my favor, right?"

"Sure. The reality is you might get them cheaper, but in working with this initial budget I think it's best to be real conservative where we can."

I pick my #2 yellow pencil up off the table and scratch "20 cows @ $2,000/cow = $40,000." It's a big number, and Eli's demeanor has gotten a little more serious, more intense. So has mine. All of a sudden the nuts and bolts of this possible new farm are taking shape. We are in the middle of coming up with real numbers, which will try to predict the survivability of this family's new farm enterprise. Forty thousand is the first big number of this morning, but there will be more in very short order. My shoulders are tense, and suddenly I am tired.

"Does anyone want some coffee?" As if on cue, Katie is standing there with her hand ever so lightly resting on Eli's left shoulder. "I just made it." She's been so quiet. Busy in the kitchen just a few feet away and listening to every word. It's her future too that we are talking about—hers and her children's.

"Katie, I would absolutely love some coffee. Thank you. Black is good for me."

Eli tips his head to the left, smiles up at her, and says, "Yes, coffee would be very, very good."

She turns and retraces the five steps back to the kitchen area, pulls two white mugs out of the cabinet, and sets them on the countertop next to the gleaming, wood-fired kitchen stove. The coffee is steaming on one of the burners, and it smells heavenly. Katie fills the cups, adds cream and sugar to Eli's, and brings them back to the table.

Hot coffee aroma and steam rise out of the cup and waft over my face. My shoulders relax with the first sip. "Thank you, Katie. You know you're more than welcome to sit here with us and discuss this."

"No, that's okay. I've got work to do in the kitchen—but I'm listening real close." Her face brightens and she half laughs. Then she strolls back over near the stove.

One of the biggest misconceptions outsiders have of the Amish community is that it is male dominated. That simply is not the case. In many areas women rule the roost. In others they may or may not defer to the menfolk. Relationships between husband and wife seem to be about as varied as those in the Yankee world. Any big decision like the one we're talking about here will need the agreement of both people. Katie may not ask a lot of questions while I'm here, but I'm sure she and Eli will spend a fair amount of time at this same table after I leave. They'll talk about what sounds good and what sounds troubling. After a midday break to do some chores around the farm and have dinner, they'll talk about it again and again and again.

It is critical that both of these young people are equally committed, comfortable, and excited about the prospect of turning their lives upside down, to go about the business of starting a new family farm. If they decide to go forward, Eli will face a ton of new challenges—and rewards. So will Katie. I know they are *both* at least interested or Eli would have never called me in the first place.

Time to get back to work. "Eli, do you have an idea about what it's going to cost to remodel the barn?"

Eli slides some notes across the table. "I'm doing a lot of the work myself, so it's not going to cost as much as it would if I were to hire it done. Anyway here are the estimates I've worked out. These aren't exact, but I think they're pretty close to what it will end up being."

Eli is a carpenter, so he's used to estimating jobs, and I trust his estimate will be very close to the actual final expense. "Okay, what's your estimate on the remodeling?"

"Well, I figure expanding the barn—that is, the actual walls, roof, windows, doors, and cement—is going to be right at $20,000."

I nod and write down $20,000 in my notes. "Alright, do you have any idea on the milking system?"

"Yeah, actually I had a guy out and he said it would probably be no more than $6,000."

I write down $6,000 and ask, "What kind of housing are you planning for the cows?" Eli looks a little perplexed, so I add, "Are you thinking about tie stalls or stanchions or loose housing and a milking parlor?" Tie stalls hold the cows in place for milking with a loose chain or rope clipped to their halter. Stanchions do roughly the same thing with a long metal and wood loop that fastens loosely around the cow's head to hold her in place. A lot of older barns—and, for all I know, the one sitting across this driveway—already have stanchions that can be used. Loose housing is just what it says. The cows aren't tethered at all until the last minute before they're milked in a small multi-cow room called a milking parlor. Each of the systems has pros and cons. Ultimately, Eli will need to design the barn and pastures to provide the best possible conditions for the health and comfort of each animal; for it is the well-being of individual animals that will make or break this farm. But right now I need to know which one Eli plans on using so I can put it in the budget.

Finally, a light seems to come on in his eyes. "Oh, I'm going to put in tie stalls, unless you think that's not good for some reason."

"No, tie stalls are just fine. Do you have an estimated cost for all of them?"

"Yeah, again I talked to the same man who gave me the estimate on the milking system, and he said it should only be around $2,000 for all of them."

"Okay, anything else?"

"Right now I'm planning on using rubber mats under the cows." He pauses for a moment and slowly shakes his head, like he's still not sure about this decision. "The mats are really expensive. Actually I'll be paying more for the mats than I will for the tie stalls. It's probably going to end up costing about $3,000 for all of them."

"I know the mats are expensive, Eli, but I think you'll really like them. They keep the cows cleaner, you don't have to use as much bedding, and they are great for cow comfort." Eli leans back a little in his chair and nods his head in agreement. "Now is there anything else that you know of as far as the barn remodeling project?"

"No, far as I know that should be about it."

I total up my notes and write down, "Barn remodeling total = $31,000." It's the second big number of the morning, and I think I hear a quiet sigh coming from Katie. She doesn't say anything, and neither does Eli. Experience tells me that it's best not to get too hung up on these individual numbers, no matter how large, so I press right on with the next question.

"I probably should've asked this first thing, but how many acres do you have on this place?"

"Not too much really, only 28 acres of crop ground and another 11 acres of pasture, and there's about 12 acres of woods."

"That's going to be tight, Eli. With 30 cows and only 28 acres of crop ground, you're probably not going to be able to grow all the hay, silage, and corn you'll need. So you should plan on buying some feed. Is there any farmland nearby that you can rent?"

"No, I haven't found any yet, but I have let the neighbors know that I'm interested, if any land becomes available."

"Even five or 10 acres would help. So keep your eyes open for any land that might open up. In the meantime we'll plan on buying some feed."

If this were a non-Amish farm with tractors and pickup trucks, finding five or 10 acres to rent wouldn't be all that hard; the fields could easily be anywhere within a 15- or 20-mile radius of the farm. But with horses, those acres need to be right here in the immediate neighborhood. At best, draft horses can maintain a sustained walk of about 5 mph. Therefore, a field that's 10 miles away takes two hours to get there and two hours to get back. The average draft horse workday is about six hours, so after transportation that leaves about two hours for fieldwork, and that's just not worth it.

Unfortunately, the nearby available land has all been leased by local cash grain farmers. These are relatively larger non-Amish farmers, often controlling well over a thousand acres, who work a few weeks in the spring, planting field corn, or soybeans, or occasionally wheat. Then they come back for a few weeks in the fall to harvest the fields. Most of the rest of the year there really is not a lot to do on a cash grain farm. After the grain is harvested, the farmer delivers it to a grain elevator/dealer and sells it for cash. Then almost all these guys will also receive a large U.S. government subsidy payment, which over time tends to drive small farms, like the one Eli and Katie are contemplating, out of the marketplace. The end result is Eli is going to have a very hard time finding the few acres he needs to rent. Any way you slice it, the subsidy payments are just flat-out wrong, but we can't solve that over this table, this morning, so we may as well move on.

"You mentioned there's 12 acres of woods on the place. Are there enough mature maples for you to make maple syrup?" A lot of the farms here in Geauga make and sell maple syrup if they have a sugar woods. It's a great high-value crop, and it's made in February and March, which is a time when the other farm work is relatively slow, so it fits in beautifully with a small dairy farm.

Eli shakes his head and says, "No, the woods was cut off for timber somewhere around 15 years ago, and there's no trees even close to big enough."

"That's unfortunate. Maple syrup is a good way to diversify the farm and add another source of income. But if you don't have the trees, you don't have the trees. What about field equipment for the crops, Eli, do you own any yet?"

"Actually, this is one place where I think I'm a little ahead of the game. I've been buying equipment for the last three or four years, and I have pretty much a full line of farm equipment already. I don't think I'll need to buy anything else really. Oh, maybe a pitchfork or something, but all of the major equipment is already bought."

"Okay, that's good, so we won't have to budget anything more for equipment." It generally costs somewhere in the neighborhood of about $25,000 for all of the major equipment needed to do fieldwork on an Amish farm. On a large non-Amish farm, $25,000 is a trivial amount of equipment. However, it's a major investment for this small Amish farm. He must've been using off-farm income from his carpentry job to buy this stuff. That's good. Essentially he has been gradually investing in the farm start-up for the last three or four years.

"How are you set for horses?"

"Well, I've got four good draft horses and one buggy horse."

"That's fine. That should be enough to get you started. Down the road you may want to add one or even two more draft horses, but right now you should be fine. I won't put anything in the budget to buy more horses."

"What about the farm itself? Do you have any kind of a mortgage on it?"

"Yes, I'm buying it from my dad."

That answers a question. Apparently, Eli's father stopped farming some years ago, and now Eli wants to bring the place back to life as a new, working farm.

"In order for me to do a budget and a cash flow statement, I'll need to know what your monthly payments are."

"Six hundred dollars a month for four more years. Then we'll own it outright."

Now I am impressed. Eli and Katie appear to be maybe in their mid to late 30s. Not too many of us in the larger world can say we own our home, farm, or business free and clear at that age. I'm sure they paid at or near the fair-market value for this place, so they must've really concentrated on making payments. I really don't know what the place would be valued at, surely well over $200,000. I would kind of like to ask him what he paid for the farm, but there really is no reason for me to know. All I need to know is the monthly payments, and that goes into my notes.

"Is there anything else in terms of debt, or income for that matter, that I need to know about?"

Eli doesn't hesitate and says, "Yes, there is a natural gas well on the place. Of course, we have no idea how long it will continue to produce, but right now we get between $3,000 and $4,000 a year from it."

"Great, an extra few thousand dollars a year coming out of the ground sure can't hurt. I think that's about it in terms of what I need. Oh, wait, do you have any money saved to invest in the farm?"

"We have around $15,000 in the bank, but I was thinking I'd like to hold that in reserve, as much as possible. In case something comes up."

"Good idea. It is always good to keep a cushion available for the unplanned stuff that will happen." With a serious look about his eyes, Eli nods in emphatic agreement, so I go on. "We have been moving pretty fast here"—actually we have been at this for the better part of an hour—"but I think the only other thing I need to get started is for us to agree on a projected milk price, to use on the revenue side of this budget. It's your call. What would you like me to use?"

Suddenly, Eli looks both startled and maybe a little nervous. In an almost pleading voice he says, "Oh, I don't know. What would you use?"

I'm really not surprised. In fact, I fully expected him to give the question back to me. Milk price is notoriously hard to predict, yet it is the factor that will make or break this budget. If we use a number that is too low the budget will predict a loss, and Eli and Katie might decide the risk is just too great. If the number is too high the budget will generate unrealistic profit, and in the long run they will likely be disappointed. Ultimately, I want to suggest a price that is reasonable and conservative. Most importantly, it has to be a price that Eli and Katie are fully comfortable with.

"Just like you, Eli, I don't know either. Here's what we have to go by. Right now dairy farmers are getting around $16 per hundredweight [100 pounds of milk sold]. However, that is almost a record-high price. It could stay up there, but who knows? Last year's average was about $12 per hundredweight. If it were me, I think I would like to budget this out at $12 per hundredweight. But you are the one in the hot seat, so what would you like me to use?"

"Let's go with $12."

"Okay, $12 it is. Now I want to look over my notes here very carefully and see if everything looks right. Then, if you don't have any other questions now, I'll go ahead and take these notes back to the office and start to play around with the numbers. I'm guessing I'll be able to get something pulled together and back to you in about a week and a half to two weeks. Is that okay, or do you really need this sooner?"

Eli nods much more slowly this time as he starts to study my notes. Absently, he mutters, "Two weeks will be just fine. We have plenty of time." If Eli weren't Amish, I'd simply call when I was ready to meet again. But he is Amish, so the family probably shares a phone with several other families in the neighborhood. Somewhere beside Eli's barn or one of the neighbors, there's a small wooden phone booth with a single phone that everybody shares. Eli is a contractor so it is at least possible that he has a cell phone for his business. However, often the cell phone, if there is one, is left outside of the house at night. The end result is that it is just devilishly difficult to set up a meeting on short notice, so I drag out my calendar and we choose a morning, about two weeks from now, to sit down over this kitchen table again.

Notes for Eli & Katie Gingerich Farm

—Start milking in September.
—Owns 15 heifers—9 fresh by December.
—Goal—30 cows +20 heifers—Holsteins.
—Wants to buy—20 cows @ $2,000/cow = $40,000.
—Barn expansion—$20,000.
—Milking system—$6,000.
—Tie stalls—$2,000.
—Rubber mats—$3,000.
—Barn remodeling total—$31,000.
—Land—28 acres crop ground +11 acres pasture.
—12 acres Woods—no mature maples.
—Owns full line of field equipment.
—5 horses—4 draft + 1 buggy.
—Mortgage—$600/month—paid off in 4 years.
—Gas well—$3,000 to $4,000 per year.
—Reserve funds in the bank—$15,000.
—Estimated milk price = $12/cwt.
—Four children—girl-2, boy-3, boy-6, girl-9.

3

Who Are These Amish Folks?

Driving back to the office past miles of tidy Amish farms, I can't help thinking back to 1980 when I first started as the brand-new—and very green—county agricultural agent for the Geauga Amish settlement. Even though I grew up near an Amish community and was quite used to seeing their buggies on the road, I knew practically nothing about these people. I've been riding on a very steep and rewarding learning curve for nigh on 25 years now; and it's still fun. Especially when the job calls on me to spend the morning peering into a future that could be, all the while sitting in the kitchen of good folks like Katie and Eli Gingerich.

Coming to the edge of the settlement now, I see the first Yankee farm up ahead. *Yankee.* Now there's a word you don't hear every day, unless, of course, it's baseball season. But it's used every day in and around this Amish community.

"Yankee" is just anyone who is not Amish. Both the Amish and the non-Amish people in this area use the term to distinguish between the two groups. It's not derogatory. It's simply easier to say than "everybody who's not Amish." There are over 300 Amish settlements in the United States and Canada, and almost all of them use the term "English" to describe their non-Amish neighbors. The few other settlements that use "Yankee" are all daughter settlements of Geauga.

It is only very recently that I learned the origin of the term. After giving a talk to a group of about 80 people and confidently saying that no one knows why we use the term "Yankee," an older Amish man from Huntsburg Township shuffled to the front and explained why. This area of Ohio is known as the Connecticut Western Reserve. It was originally owned by Connecticut through a land grant by King Charles II, and then bought by the Connecticut Land Company shortly after the Revolutionary War. This group of investors divided the land into smaller parcels and sold them to the hardy souls willing to move into what was then the Western frontier. When the Amish started moving here in the 1880s, almost all of their neighbors were "Connecticut Yankees" or other New Englanders. The term stuck, and the rest of us to this day are still "Yankees."

The roots of the Amish faith date back to the early years of the Protestant Reformation. In 1525, about eight years after Martin Luther kicked off the Reformation in Wittenberg, a man named Felix Manz started the first Anabaptist group in Zurich, Switzerland. The Anabaptists believe in adult baptism. In 1536 a priest in the Netherlands named Menno Simons organized a new Anabaptist group that called themselves Mennonites. Somewhere around 160 years later, in the 1690s, near the banks of the Rhine River in Germany, Jacob Ammann came on the scene. Believing that the Mennonites had grown far too liberal, he and some followers broke away and formed yet another Anabaptist group—the Amish.

All of these Anabaptist groups suffered severe religious persecution. They were burned at the stake, drowned, hung, or whatever other happy thing their neighbors could think of that week. Almost uniquely, the Anabaptists had the distinction of being hated by both the Catholics and other Protestants. So if a town was controlled by Catholics, they hunted down and tortured the Anabaptists. If some time later the town was taken over and controlled by Protestants, they also attacked the Anabaptists, even though the Anabaptists were clearly Protestant.

Why? What is there about adult baptism that would so enrage your neighbors that they would be moved to kill you? The word Anabaptist literally means to re-baptize. In Europe, in the early days of the Reformation, everyone was by law baptized as an infant. Therefore, if a person was baptized as an adult, it had to be a second baptism. The act of being baptized as an adult was an affront to law and the government.

At the time, there were Catholic governments and Protestant governments across Europe. Control of the government in any town or region could switch from Protestant to Catholic and back again, but the government and the church were always linked. The Anabaptists demonstrated their discontent with the church/government alliance partially through the act of adult baptism. In the parlance of today, the new, probably seditious, idea that the Amish and other Anabaptists were toying around with might be called separation of church and state. Does that have purchase? Is it relevant today?

This radically new Anabaptist ideal, which decoupled the church from the state, has come to define our American understanding of the proper relationship between these now separate institutions. It is part of our national social fabric, and we owe a great deal to the early Anabaptists who were so cruelly persecuted for their beliefs.

As the persecutions continued and intensified, the early Amish people became farmers and moved out into the European countryside. Not a hard choice there: either stay in the village and get burned at the stake or become a farmer and get left alone. Most of these early Amish people were not farmers. They became farmers as a vehicle to establish self-contained communities away from the larger, violent world.

The Amish truly value tradition, and they carry lessons learned in the distant past into today's world. Given their history, it should be no surprise that they continually strive to maintain some distance between themselves and the larger world, that they particularly avoid close contact with the government, and that a small farm is considered a community asset and one of the best possible businesses for an Amish family.

But starting any small farm is rarely easy, and the one Eli and Katie are contemplating brings with it a uniquely Amish set of challenges. Amish farms need to structure their business to deal not only with the economic realities of the agricultural industry but also with the spoken church rules, or *Ordnung*. From an Amish farm and business standpoint, it is extremely important to understand that each church district, or congregation, has its own *Ordnung* covering what is or is not acceptable. The Geauga Old Order Amish settlement is growing rapidly and currently has a little over 90 church districts. Districts are geographically defined. So if you live on dead-end Shed Road, you are in one church district; but if your house is over on Swine Creek Road, you're automatically in another, and you have a different set of church rules. Each district has about 25 to 40 families who meet every other Sunday for worship. There are no church buildings. Services are held in members' homes and rotate around the community. Therefore, the size of a district is limited by house size. If a district gets too many families to comfortably fit into an average house, the congregation will divide into two districts.

The clergy for each district consists of a bishop, one or two ministers, and what is essentially a deacon. Each of the men in these unpaid positions is selected by lot. They serve for life, and they can't turn down the position. Among other duties, they help interpret and refine the *Ordnung*. There are no archbishops to normalize the rules across all of the church districts. However, within a settlement, the rules tend to be somewhat similar, but not identical. Between settlements, the rules differ wildly. As the county agricultural agent here in Geauga, my job will be to try to help Eli and his family create a farm that is not only economically viable but also conforms to their particular *Ordnung*. What makes the task harder is that the *Ordnung* is the spoken rules of each church district. They are never written down, and they quietly change over time.

One of the first and most profound decisions Eli will make is how specialized or diverse the new farm will be. Will the dairy cows be the only major source of income for this farm? Or will they—like many of their Amish neighbors—have, in addition to the cows, income from a few pigs, draft horse colts, or beef, or vegetables, or chickens, or maple syrup, or any number of other agricultural products?

Even within the dairy herd portion of the new farm enterprise, the Gingeriches will need to decide just how specialized it should be. Will they raise their own heifers (female calves)? Will they raise all of the feed for the cows or part of it or none? Will they feed out some of the bull calves and sell them as beef? Or sell them to a veal farm when they're only a few days old?

The decision of whether or not to use milking machines and bulk refrigeration tanks on their proposed dairy farm has already been made for the Gingeriches by their church district. This has been one of the most difficult decisions each church district in the Geauga settlement has struggled with in the last several years. Even now there's nothing resembling a uniform decision. A farmer on one side of the road may have 30 cows, along with both the bulk refrigeration tank to cool the milk and a mechanical milking machine to milk the cows. On the other side of the road, a farmer in a different church district might be allowed the bulk refrigeration tank but no milking machine. That means he'll have to milk by hand and probably can't handle much over 15 cows. Because of the bulk refrigeration tank, at least both of these families can sell their milk as grade "A" and make much more money than their neighbor one road over. On that farm, they have to milk their 12 cows by hand and ship the milk to the cheese factory in old-style milk cans. Because it's not refrigerated on the farm, this is grade "B" milk, and they'll only get about two-thirds as much money as their grade "A" neighbors.

Now over in Pennsylvania in the Lancaster Amish settlement, those wild and crazy guys started using bulk tanks and milking machines back in the 1950s. Of course, that's Lancaster, where they even have refrigerators in the kitchen. They are powered by propane gas, but they are there. Here in Geauga County, everyone uses an icebox. You can get ice delivered by Yoder Ice, or you can cut it from ponds in the winter. But things are a little more conservative here than in Lancaster, so you *will* have an icebox.

It's not that the people in Geauga are ignorant of milking machines, bulk refrigeration tanks, or the Lancaster decisions; they have just needed a little more time—40 or 50 years—to very carefully weigh the benefits, or harm, these innovations may bring to the community. Time to ponder whether this or that change coming down the road will add to—or take away from—the cohesiveness of the community and the well-being of the people who live in it.

Fortunately, Eli's church district, like many in the settlement, changed its rules a few years ago, allowing farmers to ship grade "A" milk and make more money. As a result, it is easier to pencil out a positive cash flow for a new small farm, and the big question about surviving on a new family farm comes up a lot more often than it did before the change in rules. It is thrilling to see young carpenters, sawyers, craftsmen, and shop workers put down their lunch buckets and start new farms. However, predicting each farm's chances of long-term economic survival is at very best a well thought-out . . . guess.

4

The Budget Numbers

Eli's new farm start-up budget was pretty much done four days after our last visit. Two weeks have passed now and I'm in the car this morning headed for the meeting to go over the numbers. Each new farm is unique, but I've done enough of these in the last few years that it is getting a little easier. Some, but not all, of the new farm ideas will pencil out with a potential profit. When the numbers are good, it's fun to go over them with the prospective new farmer. When the numbers are bad, it is not fun. This morning the numbers are close. There's some profit, but not a lot, and I really don't know how Eli and Katie will react.

Getting ready for this meeting, I talked to a local banker to find out the likely interest rate for the needed loan. I also talked to two different state specialists on the main OSU campus in Columbus. One helped with the long-term milk price projections, and the other fine-tuned some of the feed costs. Even though starting a new small farm—particularly a small dairy farm—goes against the dominant woe-is-me pandering prattle of mainstream agriculture, most specialists seem to truly get a kick out of helping.

There are exceptions. A few years ago when some of the local Amish church districts started to allow milking machines, several farms almost immediately expanded from 15 or 16 cows all the way up to 25 or even 30. Seeing a real educational opportunity, I placed a call to our state specialist who works with farmers wanting to expand cow numbers and asked for help in developing expansion, or new start-up budgets, for 30-cow herds. The state specialist—I'll call him Norman because that's his name—failed to share my enthusiasm. Rather impatiently he explained that there was no way to make a go of it with 30 cows. I politely pointed out that many of our local farms were doing just fine with 30 cows or fewer and asked again about developing educational materials that might meet the needs of these smaller farms. Still more impatiently, he explained that we needed to be looking at herds with a minimum of 600 and preferably over 1,000 cows. I've not called Norman again. At this point in my career, I try to avoid instigating conversations that are likely to turn grotesquely stupid.

No expansion materials for the 30-cow herd were ever developed. That's a shame because I could've used them this morning. Instead, generic agricultural economics materials for larger herds needed to be modified down to the place where they make sense for Eli and Katie. The numbers are all there, and with some explanations and back-and-forth questioning, I think the meeting will go fine. Good thing, because their driveway is the next one on the left.

I park the car, walk up the path, pat the dog, bang on the side door, and say, "Good morning" to Eli. The kitchen table is completely cleared off. If there are any children around, they must be playing quietly in another part of the house or they may be visiting grandma today. Katie looks up and greets me warmly from the corner of the kitchen where she is chopping some vegetables. Eli offers the same chair I sat in last time and asks again if the table would be alright. "It's just fine." The faint aroma of coffee that is not quite ready lingers in the room. And there is tension.

Katie and Eli are friendly, courteous, polite, . . . and anxious. We make small talk for several minutes, catching up on mutual friends, community auctions, and local farm activities. Katie stays busy with her kitchen chores and is mainly quiet. After an uncomfortably long pause in our conversation, I look directly at Eli and ask him if he's ready to get started. He simply says yes and Katie nods, even though the question was not specifically pointed in her direction. They've been waiting for this morning's meeting for two long weeks. Should they become a farm family? With any luck in an hour or so, they'll have a pretty good idea.

"Well, then, let me start with kind of a standard disclaimer. You do understand that the numbers here are at very best a guess?"

Eli shifts slightly in his chair and quietly utters, "Yes, we've talked about that. We know there's always a risk that things might not work out like we hope."

"Yeah, that's true. Any number of things will ultimately affect what actually happens, should you decide to go ahead and start a farm. The price of milk is always volatile. It can go way up and then turn around and go way down. Same with the price of feed and other supplies. Then there is always the risk of some problem with the health of the herd, and as you know that can cripple milk production."

Eli is listening intently without saying a word. I don't want to sound too negative; it's just not necessary. A lot of this caution is based on my own insecurities. I would just hate to give someone the wrong advice. In an effort to set a slightly more positive tone I mention that "I did talk with our state specialists to get their best predictions on the price of milk and feed, at least in the short run. So the numbers are based on the best advice we can get." Eli still doesn't say a word.

"Okay, then, here's the big picture. In general terms, the numbers say that the farm can work. However, it is going to be really tight for the first four years. You may need to plan to do some part-time work off the farm for the first four years. After that, things should loosen up a bit." I slide a thin folder across the table to Eli and open an identical manila folder in front of me. "Let's actually work through the numbers, so you understand where they come from."

He opens his folder and starts to leaf through the few pages in front of him, then stops, looks up, and asks, "What's so important about four years? I think I know; but what are you saying? I mean, how are you looking at it?"

"Well, I don't want to jump too far ahead, but the four-year shift is because that's when you told me you would be able to pay off the original farm mortgage. Is that still correct?"

"Yes, we should have it paid off in four years if everything works out like we have planned." Eli isn't smiling, but he's not frowning either.

"Okay, that's real good. You'll see in a few minutes here how paying off the mortgage will pretty dramatically improve cash flow in the plan. Let's take a look at the first sheet there in front of you marked 'Dairy Cow and Replacement Budget—Large Breed.'" The muscles in my shoulders are way more tense than they should be. I take a few deep breaths and try to relax. It doesn't work, so I push ahead and explain. "Take everything in this budget with a grain of salt, and try not to get too tied up with the details quite yet. This budget is actually designed for a large Yankee herd. So what we're going to do is try to modify the budget to fit your farm."

Eli is staring intently at the page. There are a lot of numbers. I hate to start off with this complicated budget, but unfortunately it's the best thing

I have to work with. I give him a few minutes to study and then say, "Why don't we go ahead and start working down the page, if that's okay with you?"

"Sure, let's go ahead." Eli looks up from the jumble of the numbers on the page and with a very faint smile says, "I hope you're going to explain what all this means."

"Well, I'm going to try. If you look down the page, you can see places where I have changed the numbers, and I really want to talk about those to be sure you agree. The first thing you'll notice is that I changed the milk price to $12 per hundredweight. Are you still okay with that?"

"Yeah, that's what we talked about, so I guess it's alright."

"Well, Eli, I should tell you that our state specialist in Columbus says that number is probably too low, at least for the coming year. He's saying the price should average at least $14 per hundredweight. By keeping it at $12 we are probably being overly conservative. But, on the other hand by being very conservative with the milk price, we will reduce the chances of you having really ugly surprises for the first year. So are you still okay with keeping it at $12?"

"Yes," he pauses, looks very seriously down at the sheet, and then looks back at me and says, "let's keep it that way for now, anyhow."

This is just way too tense. Katie isn't even pretending to work anymore. She's simply standing with her hands resting on the kitchen counter and listening. I need to find a way to lighten the mood a little, but I have no idea how. "Okay, Eli, if you look at those first few lines on the page you'll see 'Total Receipts.' That number is the amount of money one cow should generate each year."

"Yep, I see it." He still isn't smiling, which is unlike him.

No choice but to push on with the budget. "Now you can see that the total receipts per cow is made up mainly of milk sales, with a little bit in there for the sale of bull calves, heifers, and finally cull cows. There is a formula for how each of these is calculated on the back of the budget. You can look at these later, and if you have any questions, let me know."

"Well, my first question is, why is there a number in there for heifer sales? I thought we talked about me raising my own heifers."

"That's right, we did. Notice they only have calculated in $27 for the heifer." Eli nods. "It's a very small number, and it simply accounts for the occasional heifer that isn't good enough for the herd. If you look at the explanation on the back, it will say that once in a while even *you* will have the heifer that just doesn't make the grade and has to go to be sold." Eli chuckles quietly at this. It's not a hearty, boisterous laugh, but it does lighten the mood.

Katie is still listening closely, but she has resumed some kitchen chores as we go on with the budget discussion. It's going much more smoothly now. I show Eli how I adjusted feed cost up slightly because he will need to buy more feed due to the limited number of acres on the farm. We work through several of the other changes with very few questions, and fairly quickly we find ourselves at the proverbial bottom line.

The coffee must be done because Katie pours two cups and brings them over to the table—one with cream and one without. I'm flattered that she remembers I take mine black. The aroma coming from the cup absolutely demands a pause in our discussions. "Thank you, Katie, the coffee is great."

"So if we did this right, your total receipts for each cow should be around $2,400 per year, maybe a little less, or quite a bit more if the price of milk is at $14 per hundredweight, rather than $12. We subtract from that a little more than $1,500 for feed, vet bills, and other supplies, and you get in the neighborhood of $850 to $900 left per cow. Do you see where that all came from?"

"Yeah, it's pretty clear." Eli seems calm, very interested, and a little less tense. Katie is now standing behind Eli looking over his shoulder at the numbers. Eli looks up at Katie and she nods ever so slightly, showing that she is also comfortable with the numbers so far.

"Now you can see I multiplied the receipts per cow by 30 cows and came up with approximately $26,000 a year in gross receipts, plus $3,000 from the oil and gas well, for a total of about $29,000 a year." Time for another sip of coffee. I lean back in my chair and make eye contact with each of them before nervously proceeding. "Now for the bad news. Well, I shouldn't say 'bad.' It's not really bad. That's the wrong word. Really, these are just the rest of the numbers you need to look at."

I take another sip of coffee in an effort to calm down and start once again. "A 20-year bank loan to buy the cows and finish the barn is going to cost about $6,000 a year. Add that to your current mortgage, and you end up with loan payments of around $13,000 a year. Subtract that from the $29,000, and the grand total is approximately $16,000 a year for family living expenses. But, remember that's based on a $12 per hundredweight milk price."

They are both staring intently at the papers in front of them, and neither one of them says a word. I have no idea what they're thinking. Finally, I shake my head and just start talking again. "Now if you look at the next line, you'll see I use the same income numbers to show what will happen after you pay off your current mortgage. So in year five you should have at least $23,000 or $24,000 for living expenses." I take a deep breath and lean back a little in my chair. "That's kind of all I have. Remember there's a lot of guesswork here." Lacking the courage needed to look up and meet their collective gaze, my eyes stay riveted to the table as I hear myself mutter, "Do you have any questions? What do you think?"

They are silent. Finally my eyes pull away from the table and light on Katie's face. She's smiling—she's smiling for goodness sake! So is Eli! What am I missing here? Eli clears his throat and says, "You are right. The first four years are going to be tight. I don't mind working out part-time though. There's plenty of carpentry work, and I can pretty much pick the days I want. Particularly when it's slow around the farm here."

He's already calling it a farm. Katie pipes up. "We can cut back a little on our expenses too, as far as that goes." I'm sitting in a house without a TV, radio, computer, refrigerator, electricity, or car, and she is confident they can find ways to cut back on expenses. Amazing.

I speak up to point out, "You know, even after the first four years are over, your income probably won't be that high, relative to the average family income in the country."

"That's probably true," Eli agrees, "but we generally don't spend as much as your average Yankee family."

There is undeniable truth in his words. Most Amish families do spend less than their Yankee neighbors. Yet this family is not poor, by any stretch of the imagination. The children are well, if plainly, dressed, fed, and educated. The house is spacious, clean, and comfortable. There's hot and cold running water in the bathrooms and kitchen, along with books to read, pets to pamper, and games to play. It may well be a simpler lifestyle, but it is by no means impoverished. They do not have car payments, monthly electric bills, or insurance. Between the chickens, the garden, and an occasional hog, they grow a lot of their own food, and Eli hunts. He mentioned during our opening small talk that he got a nice buck last season. Katie cans meat, fruits, and vegetables and supplements whatever else is needed, once every week or two, from the grocery store in Middlefield. The family "fashion" budget stays small because it pretty much stops at blue. In Katie and Eli's case, since they are on a farm, even the house payments are simply part of the larger farm business mortgage and do not come directly out of a paycheck. They enjoy a slightly different lifestyle than most of Main Street America, but they are not poor. Indeed, they are rich in family, friends, and the emotional support of a close Amish community.

Suddenly anxious to leave, I hear myself say to Katie and Eli, "That's really all I have, so I'm going to take off and let you folks look this stuff over."

"No need to rush off, there's more hot coffee if you want."

"Thank you, Katie, but I really should be getting back to the office." As I push the chair back and stand, I remind them one more time to give me a call if they have any questions. "After you've had time to think about it, I would be interested in knowing whether or not you decide to go ahead with the farm idea."

"Oh, I think we'll probably do it." Eli casually announces. He's smiling now, and so is Katie. He is holding my crude summary page in his right hand. "We'll talk about it a little more, but we were afraid this might be a whole lot worse. So I think we'll probably go ahead."

I'm a little stunned and a little shaken. I had fully expected them to say they would look over the numbers and get back to me. They've had two weeks to talk about how this meeting might turn out and go over options and all of the possible what-ifs. Still, I'd be more comfortable if they took a little more time. It's their decision, not mine, and I'm sure they've been thinking about this moment for years. I pray that I have made no mistakes in this work, and that I have not been too optimistic with the numbers. I know that I've done the best I could, and I guess that will have to do.

Standing with my hand on the doorknob, I caution them one more time. "Remember there's a lot of guesswork here. A lot of things could change the final outcome." They are standing close to each other across the room by the kitchen table and smiling at me and at each other. What more is there to say? I wish them luck, ask them to keep me posted, to call with any questions they might have, and to let me know if there's anything I can do to help.

The morning is bright and sunny as I step outside, walk down the path, pat the dog, and get in the car. Just for a moment, with the keys in the ignition, my hand pauses and leaves the engine silent as I marvel once again that someone actually pays me to do this stuff. Looks like it could be a good day.

WHOLE FARM BUDGET

SUMMARY PAGE.

ELI AND KATIE GINGERICH
APPROXIMATE VALUES.

Total Receipts/Cow	$2,400	
Total Feed & Variable Costs/Cow	$1,530	
Return Above Costs/Cow	$870	
Return Above Costs/30 Cows	$26,000	
Oil and Gas Well	$3,000	
Total Farm Receipts	$29,000	
20-Year Loan Payment/Year	$6,000	
4-Year Mortgage Payment/Year	$7,000	
TOTAL NET SURPLUS/YEAR	$16,000	(First 4 Years)
TOTAL NET SURPLUS/YEAR	$23,000	(Starting Year 5)

5

Get Bigger and Specialize

In the days following our meeting, it is impossible for me to get Eli and Katie and the small farm they are about to establish out of my mind. Actually, I don't even try to stop thinking about them. This is, hands down, the most rewarding and interesting part of my job. While my colleagues at the university wrestle with big questions about thousands of acres, thousands of cows, thousands of pigs, or millions of chickens, I have very slowly over the years become completely immersed in the critical, everyday questions of these smallest of farms.

The mantra of agriculture has long been: get bigger and specialize—or get out. Way back in my early college days, I remember so clearly the professors drumming into our heads that in order to be a successful farmer you had to grow bigger every year, and you had to specialize. So if you have chickens and pigs and cows, get rid of the chickens and pigs and concentrate on cows. If you have 50 dairy cows this year, have 60 next year, and aim your sights at 600 five years hence. In this country, we take almost as an axiom that bigger farms—or any business for that matter—are more efficient, profitable, and successful, so the professors' message was readily accepted by all of us, with little to no reservation.

At the beginning of my career as a young county agent, I frequently told Amish farmers in the settlement they needed to find some way to get bigger and specialize. Fortunately, they steadfastly ignored me and everyone else at the university. For the first few years, I secretly reasoned they would simply fade away as time went on, slowly selling failed farms one after the other. After all, they refused to follow the prescribed business model. Besides that, they farmed with horses for goodness sake. The rest of agriculture gave up on horses more than a generation ago. How could these people possibly believe they could continue to farm this way and stay in business?

It was years later when it became clear that Amish farms were decidedly not going away. In fact, they seemed to be thriving. That I began to timidly question agriculture's sacred mantra of "get bigger and specialize." Almost immediately, I learned that questioning a core belief is not one of the ways to be popular with colleagues in the College of Agriculture.

The bias toward large farms is an ongoing problem, but perhaps one of the most insidious and least understood threats to the long-term survivability of any new farm is the constant barrage of doom-and-gloom messages that the U.S. agricultural complex spoon-feeds to reporters, government officials, and the general public. No matter what the current conditions down on the farm actually are, it is devilishly easy for a reporter to find a farmer or an agricultural academic who will moan into the microphone on cue. Of course, we have paid these folks well to develop one of the worst cases of persistent adult diaper rash in history. After all, would we as a country support $20 billion of agricultural welfare payments year after year if the farm industry told us things were pretty good right now? Or, heaven forbid, what if the farm industry carefully explained to the public that the average farm family annual income is consistently higher than the average non-farm family income? Therefore, by definition, all agricultural subsidies are transfers of wealth from the relatively poor to the relatively rich.

So why does all of the doom-and-gloom, sky-is-falling rhetoric of the agricultural industry have any impact on a potential new farm? Well, to begin with, young families who rarely, if ever, hear about successful small farms are unlikely to investigate the economic possibilities of starting a new farm. Farmers in the United States have always faced real challenges, but there are real success stories as well. Withholding small farm success stories at a time when the general economy is humming along nicely is a travesty. Withholding these success stories during a recession or depression is unconscionable. Further, businesses, local government, and the public make real decisions on zoning, taxes, store locations, power line rights-of-way, and a plethora of other things based on the carefully honed misconception that agriculture is in serious trouble and probably won't be around very long anyway.

Fortunately, Eli and his family want to start a farm within the Geauga Amish settlement. In years past, the farmers in this settlement were perfectly capable of moaning with the best of them. Then a few years ago an astonishing and remarkable thing happened. A small group of Amish elders looked at the negative, down-in-the-mouth attitude of the local farm community and decided it just wasn't good enough. While no young family would ever be forced to farm, they wanted to be certain that young families would at least have an honest opportunity to explore the possibilities of starting farms.

The Amish quietly set about the task of challenging and changing the entire community's attitude about farming. The results were dramatic. It turns out most people really don't want to moan all day about their carefully and thoughtfully chosen occupation, but in farming it had kind of gotten to be a habit—a bad habit. Now, the entire community is supporting Eli and Katie in their decision to start a new farm; that would not have happened just 10 years ago. In a wonderful turn of events, this new Amish attitude about farming has spread right out into the surrounding non-Amish community, and the local growth rate of both Amish and Yankee new farms has accelerated. In a very real sense, all of Geauga County will be the Gingeriches' personal cheering squad. GO GINGERICHES!

As I said, people hereabouts weren't always so positive about farming— not even close. It was back in 2002 when I stopped out to see a longtime Amish friend, and I still remember the meeting like it was yesterday. Stroking a gray beard, Andy Byler had just ruptured my placid morning wide open with, "Several of us were sitting around the table the other night, talking about how much it would cost for a young Amish man to start up a new farm. By the time we were done, we figured it would be $100,000, or more, just for the equipment."

My blood pressure spiked somewhere in the range of 1,000 over infinity, as I struggled to keep my rage under control. How in the world were we ever going to get young Amish families to take an objective look at the possibility of starting new farms if Andy and his elder Amish buddies spent most of the day trying to come up with innovative ways to throw cold water on the idea? I knew he was wrong about the equipment price, but I also knew I had no data to prove it.

For way too many years I had been asking the agricultural economists on the main campus of the university for *some* information on the economics of small farms. It didn't have to be Amish farms; any small farm would do. But concentrating on small, diverse farms simply did not jibe with the thundering, dominant, almost religious academic chant that "to be successful, farms must get big and specialize." So for way too many years we county agents out in the field got tons of educational, economic information to help the large farms—which didn't need much help in the first place—and almost nothing that would be the least bit useful for economic planning with a small, diverse farm.

Nodding stupidly at Andy—for I had not the first shred of university-generated economic data to refute him—something snapped inside. At the risk of being even more of a reprobate in the academic community, I decided to research some of the economic mysteries of the very small, very diverse, and very successful farms in the Geauga Amish settlement. I would study Andy's farm and others like it.

In a meeting the next morning, my assistant, Les, learned all about his role in this exciting new research project. Les was delighted to discover (well, maybe not delighted, but mildly enthusiastic—well, maybe not enthusiastic, but he had no choice) that our first task was to challenge agricultural academia in its entirety by freshly examining the economic realities of using real draft-horse power on real farms in the first decade of the twenty-first century. Some trepidation and hesitancy on Les's part was understandable. After all, U.S. agriculture had abandoned draft horses more than a generation ago, and no one could seriously think they had any place on a "real" farm; still, I had decided this was important research, and we were going to do it.

Over the next few days we developed a list of over 20 major pieces of field equipment that a typical Amish farm in the Geauga settlement was likely to have. We listed everything from corn binders to threshing machines. Most of what to include on our list was straightforward, consisting of machinery that almost all of the Amish farms had, things like corn planters, hay wagons, manure spreaders, plows, silage choppers, grain drills, and the like. But we had to make a judgment call on some things. Most of the church districts allow hay balers, but some don't. A few of the church districts allow horse-drawn corn pickers, but most don't. So hay balers were in and corn pickers were out.

Once the list was complete, I took it around to a few farmers and asked them to look it over. They seemed satisfied that we had caught about everything, so we were almost ready to start gathering data. The primary reason for all of this bother was to use the results right here in the settlement;

hopefully, we could use this information to help young families like Eli and Katie's get a better idea of what it might really cost to start farming.

However, in the off chance that someone else in academia might be interested in a current economic analysis of farming practices that were largely abandoned in the United States shortly after World War II, the research needed to be conducted under the strict rules of academic rigor. In order to eventually publish the results in some stodgy academic journal, we first needed a "methodology." I selected a "modified focus group process," which basically means we were going to go out and talk to some guys. But "modified focus group process" just sounds so much more erudite. Actually, we wanted to talk to three small groups of farmers, with a total of about 25 people in all.

List in hand, I set about the job of finding three farmers to host meetings in their homes (commonly know as "kitchen meetings"). I figured it shouldn't be too hard. It was early winter, the crops were in, the snow was flying, and most farmers would be happy to spare an hour or two to sit with their neighbors in a warm kitchen and talk about farming.

My first stop is Raymond Yoder over on Bundysburg Road. It's about 10 o'clock in the morning and I find him out in his barn with a five-tanged pitchfork, loading manure out of the trough behind the dairy cows and into an old wooden-sided manure spreader. Two coal-black Percheron horses are hitched to the spreader in the center aisle. The horses are looking at me, but Raymond is facing the other way as he methodically jabs at the manure and bedding. Then he swings another forkful over the wooden box, turning the pitchfork upside down as he goes to deposit yet another cake of wet straw and brown dung on the steaming pile growing up in the center of the spreader.

The wind is blowing outside, and I suspect Raymond did not hear my car pull in the driveway. I stop short of the horses and interrupt his work. "Hello, Raymond, looks like you're having quite a bit of fun there."

The light in the barn is not overly good, and it takes Raymond a few moments to recognize me. A friendly look of recognition slowly spreads across his long, thin face. "Why, hello, Randy. No, I wouldn't say this is a lot of fun, but I have another pitchfork if you want to give it a try."

"Not today, Raymond. Thanks for the tempting offer, though. Maybe some other time. Actually, I'm out here to see if you might be willing to host a kitchen meeting for me."

"What kind of meeting?"

Handing him a copy of the list, I explain. "Just a little meeting in your kitchen for six or eight of your neighbors. We're trying to get a handle on what it costs to buy the equipment for an Amish farm, so we can use that when we're working with new farms."

As he intently studies the list, I notice for the first time a few strands of gray creeping into his otherwise red beard. He must be a few years younger than me, maybe 45 or so. Finally looking up he straightens his back and says, "Well, that could be interesting. Who would do the inviting to this meeting?"

"You would, Raymond, just a few of your neighbors. We'd like at the least six and no more than 10. The meeting shouldn't take more than an hour or so, and this time of year we can probably do it midmorning. I think it should be kind of fun."

"Yeah, it just might be. Okay, I think we can probably have a meeting here. When do you want to do it?"

"Some time in the next two or three weeks if we can."

"I'll have to check with my wife and see if there's anything planned. I don't think we have anything up, but I'll need to check."

"Is she here now?"

"Oh yeah, she's in the house."

"Why don't you go ahead in and talk with her now. I'll wait out here."

"Well, you can come in, you know."

"That's okay. This'll give me a chance to look over the herd."

Raymond nods, leans the pitchfork against the manure spreader, and heads off for the house. A little brown and white dog comes out from behind the spreader and timidly walks over to sniff my shoes. I have to reach down below my knee to pat his head, and, as I do, his tail wags even faster.

It's quiet now, and I'm enjoying spending a few minutes alone with the 25 or so cows in two rows of stanchions, one on each side of the barn. Walking up and down the center aisle, I see a few of the more curious ones turn their head around to look at me, but most quietly chew their cud or nibble on some hay. The barn is peaceful and I'm reminded once again that cows really are some of my favorite people.

Raymond strides back in the barn. The meeting is on, and we set a date for two weeks from today. Back on the road I plot a course toward my next potential kitchen meeting host. By four o'clock, two more farmers have agreed to invite six to 10 of their neighbors over for coffee, homemade sweet rolls, and a lively discussion on what it costs to equip an Amish farm.

The meetings are scheduled almost back to back during the same week. Raymond is first on Tuesday, the next one is Wednesday, and the last one is on Friday. I would have liked to schedule the last one on Thursday, but Thursday is "wedding day" in the settlement. Pretty much everybody gets married on a Thursday. So you're bound to run into last-minute scheduling conflicts, and a wedding undoubtedly trumps a kitchen meeting on farm equipment. Even though a farmer might be really interested in the kitchen meeting, he'll end up going to the wedding—just ask his wife.

6

Four Big Questions

With the three meetings coming up fast, Les and I continue to refine our list of equipment and decide what questions we will ask the farmers about each piece. We finally come up with four questions.

1. Purchase Price. How much should you expect to pay for this piece of equipment at auction?
2. Useful Life. How long might you use this piece of equipment until it is worn out and you have to get a new one or completely rebuild the old one? We capped this at 30 years. If it's well cared for, some equipment will last much longer, but most farmers won't. After 30 years, they'll likely be looking to pass the farm on to the next generation or sell it. So 30 years seemed about right.
3. Salvage Value. When you are all done with it, after it served its entire useful life, what would this piece of equipment be worth if you dragged it back to the auction and sold it again?
4. Annual Maintenance Costs. How much do you need to put into this piece of equipment each year to keep it working?

There's one major complication: most of the equipment used on Amish farms is no longer manufactured. Farmers have to buy it used—sometimes very used. So we decide to ask our kitchen meeting crowds to come up with numbers based on good, serviceable used equipment that a full-time farmer might buy. However, some things like the harrow, hay wagons, forecart, hay tedder, and field sprayer are usually bought new, so we'll ask the farmers about new equipment in these cases. Then a few things, like manure spreaders, are a real mixed bag. Some farmers buy new, and others buy used. For these, we'll get both prices.

The plan is to get the farmers in each of the three kitchen meetings to talk about each piece of equipment and agree on answers for our four questions. It sounds like a tall order, and I am somewhat dubious about its success. But if it really does work, we will end up with some fairly powerful data in an oddly current and extremely useful area of agricultural economics that has not been looked at in a long, long time.

The four questions are written across the top of the page, and the equipment is listed along the left-hand margin. The total list takes about a page and a half. Using a blue ballpoint pen and a wooden ruler, we run vertical lines down the pages between each question and horizontal lines to divide each piece of equipment. The result is rows and rows of neat little blue boxes. During the meeting, all Les needs to do is write the farmers' agreed-upon number in the corresponding box.

For our purposes, calling this grid of machinery names and questions the "Equipment List" will work just fine. The farmers will understand what it is, and we won't get confused either. However, should the gathered data ever be written up for an academic journal, the simple little boxes of our "Equipment List" will elegantly morph into a very exact and correct "Set Interview Guide," or a bit more ominously into the "Survey Instrument."

Item	Purchase Price/$	Useful Life/Years	Salvage Value/$	Annual Maintenance/$
Corn Binder				
Corn Planter				
Disc				
Drag				
Feed Grinder				
Fertilizer Spreader				
Field Sprayer				
Forecart				
Grain Binder				
Grain Drill				
Hay Elevator				
Harness (1 set)				
Harrow				
Hay Baler				
Hay Loader				
Hay Tedder				
Hay Wagon				
Manure Spreader				
Plow				
Rake				
Sickle Bar Mower				
Silage Chopper				
Threshing Machine				
Tractor				
TOTAL				

Finally, two weeks have passed and this is the morning of Raymond's kitchen meeting. Les and I drive out over the hills through Burton and then Middlefield on our way to the farm. We go over our roles again in the car. I will lead the meeting and ask the questions. Les's job is to write down the figures for each item, and each question, after the farmers have agreed on a specific amount of money or time, depending on the question. He has a clipboard, two pencils with erasers, and three copies of the equipment list and questions.

It's about 25°F outside and a little windy. There was a dusting of snow last night. Maybe four or five inches of new snow, but there was very little on the ground before, so this shouldn't slow anybody down. We here in Geauga know how to drive in this stuff. Hopefully, enough farmers will show up to conduct this meeting, but you never know for sure until you get there.

As we pull off the gravel road and my wheels crunch onto the ice in the driveway, three black buggies randomly parked beside the barn come into view. The pointed ends of the empty front shaves hang down and disappear into the snow. The three chestnut-colored Standardbred horses that pulled these buggies here a few minutes ago are already unhitched and standing in the barn visiting with Raymond's horses over a few nibbles of timothy hay and some cool water.

This is a real good sign. It means that at the very least three farmers are here and probably several more. Hitching a horse and buggy in the morning to make a trip takes a great deal more effort than rotating a key in a car and turning on the heater. Therefore, anyone who lived within a mile or so would have walked here this morning. The three buggy drivers also probably picked up at least one neighbor along the way. Kind of like carpooling with a horse, or maybe Amish buggypooling.

Les and I make our way up the freshly shoveled cement walk to the backdoor of the mudroom. He knocks, and within five seconds the main backdoor of the house opens. Ten feet across the cold room and three steps up in front of us, a bearded face pops out and we hear Raymond's scratchy voice say, "Come on in. It's cold out there."

I pull the door open with a loud, prolonged creak and step onto the cement floor of the mudroom to begin the *ritual of the shoes*. Bending down to loosen the laces, I hear Raymond's voice announced through a puff of cold condensing breath, "Oh, don't worry about your shoes."

"That's okay. I think I'll go ahead and take them off."

Remember the old song "These Boots Are Made for Walking"? Well, my boots are made for slogging through mud, manure, and three-day old slimy bovine afterbirth—in just the past week. I disinfect them, scrub them, and try to wear disposable plastic boots when the going gets truly yucky, but in the end they still emit foul vapors. Surely by now Raymond has had time to examine my badly stained work shoes. But, manners must be maintained, and he tries one more time, albeit with far less conviction than before. "No, really, it's okay. You don't need to take them off."

Without a word I pull the second one off and put it in line with the other shoes already on the floor. With them now safely stowed in this odor-controlling chamber, I'm ready to go inside. Padding up the three steps in woolen socks, I step into the room and find eight Amish men sitting around the table and Raymond standing by the stove, for a total of nine. More than enough to make this meeting a success, and if our plan works, gather all of the numbers we need this fine morning.

I find a chair near the middle of the table, and Les sits down near the end. As we are shuffling through papers and pens to get ready, I start the process of greeting each farmer. Levi and his brother Enos are directly to my left. They each own separate farms about two miles from here. Then there's John, Eli, Crist, Ervin, another Eli, and finally Noah sitting here on my right. Most of these guys are in their mid-50s to mid-60s, with the exceptions of Crist, who is about 45, and Ervin, who is probably in his late 60s or very early 70s. There are two Yoders, three Millers, a Schrock, a Kempf, and two Detweilers. The two Elis are not closely related, but they do have the same last name, so the taller one is Eli L., and Eli J. G. is the one wearing glasses. It's not surprising that three of these guys are Millers. About 30 percent of all of the people in the settlement share the last name Miller. The important thing for our meeting is that nine separate farms are represented around the table this morning, which will give us a more powerful set of data than if fewer farms were represented.

Raymond brings the tall, insulated plastic carafe of steaming black coffee that his wife, Barbara, made earlier, over to the table, along with some cups, cream, and sugar. While we pass the coffee around, he returns to the counter to fetch a large platter of cold, cubed meats, cheeses, and crackers. On his final trip back from the counter, he brings two plates of fresh-baked sweet rolls slathered with maple syrup icing. Like many of the farms in the settlement, this one has a woods full of maple trees, and Raymond and the family make maple syrup every winter. They keep enough for family use on pancakes and to frost some sweet rolls for guests. The rest they put in barrels and sell to a local wholesale buyer.

As Raymond settles into a chair across the table from me, I say, "Please thank Barbara for getting all these refreshments ready for us. They look mighty good."

He chuckles quietly and says, "Well, I don't know how this meeting will go, but it looks like we'll eat pretty well."

With that, it's time for me to call the meeting to order and see if our research plans actually work. "Thanks again guys for coming out this morning," I say to the men at the table. "I suppose Raymond filled you all in on what we are trying to do. Basically, we would like to get a better handle on what it would cost to fully equip a new Amish farm. We want to use this information when we are helping new farm families set up a business plan and budget."

Eli J. G. tilts his head forward to look over his glasses. "He told us what we're going to try to do, but not how we're going to get it done."

"Okay, well, here's the plan. We have a list of over 20 major pieces of equipment that most Amish farms have. I'm going to ask the group four questions about each piece of equipment. Hopefully, you guys will talk about each question and come to a general agreement. Then Les will write down your answers."

Over his glasses again, Eli interrupts to ask, "What are these four questions?"

"I was just coming to that, Eli. We want to know what each piece of equipment should cost to buy, how long it will last until it's worn out, what is it worth when it's worn out, and how much money do you have to put into it each year to keep it running. Again, you'll all talk about each question and agree on an answer, and then Les will write it down."

Once more peering over his horn-rims, Eli asks, "Are we talking about new equipment or used equipment?"

"For most of it we are talking about good, serviceable used equipment that a full-time farmer might buy at auction. In a few cases, we'll talk about new equipment because that's what most people buy. Finally, for a few things we'll look at both new and used."

"Are there any other questions before we get started?" I look around the table and am generally greeted with accepting nods and shrugs. The body language is good. They seem interested and ready to start. "Okay, let's give this a try. Are you ready, Les?"

"Yep."

7

Binders, Planters, and Other Such Stuff

The first piece of equipment on my list is a corn binder. This should be easy enough. A corn binder is a fairly simple contraption made of wood and metal and held together by bolts. It's used for making corn silage, and they all look about the same. It's pulled through standing corn, one row at a time, by a team of horses. A set of knives in front cuts each corn plant off about six inches above the ground. Metal fingers and the forward motion of the machine pull the cut stocks upright into a holding bin near the back of the binder. When enough stocks are gathered into the holding bin, the binder automatically slings a single strand of binder twine around the stocks, ties it, and flips the bundle out onto the ground. Other members of the farm team follow behind picking up the bundles by hand and throwing them on the wagon to be hauled to the barn and cut into silage.

I clear my throat and say to the group assembled around the table, "Okay, let's start with the corn binder." There are general nods around the table seeming to indicate that these guys are ready. "Obviously, we're talking about a used corn binder. So, how much might a full-time farmer expect to pay for a good serviceable binder, at auction?"

Both Eli L. and Enos start talking immediately and at the same time. After a few seconds of the stereo conversation, Enos looks at Eli and says, "You go ahead." I am delighted. My great fear was getting these guys to talk might be a good deal like pulling teeth. I had practiced leading questions and other techniques to coach them into the discussion, but it looks like that won't be needed.

Eli nods to Enos and picks up with, "What I was starting to say is my son bought a corn binder at the equipment auction right down the road here last spring. He had to replace the seat, but other than that it was in good shape. I'm pretty sure he ended up paying about $850 for it. He used it this fall and it worked real well."

Eli seems to be done so I look over at Enos, and he starts talking with no hesitation. "What I was about to say is my nephew bought one last summer at an estate auction. The man had quit farming back in the '60s. He was a bachelor, and when he stopped he just cleaned up the equipment and stored it under tarps in his barn for all those years. When he died the heirs found it all out there in the barn in mint condition."

To find horse-drawn farm equipment in an almost new condition is a rarity, and everyone around the table is impressed. Crist interrupts Enos and asks in a slightly puzzled tone, "Was this an Amish man or a Yankee?"

"He was a Yankee."

"Was he from around here?" John asks.

"Yeah, he was right over in Trumbull County."

Noah chimes in. "What did your nephew end up giving for it?"

That was supposed to be my question to help get the discussion going, but these guys are off and running, so I keep quiet and sit back to watch the show.

"Well, there were several guys bidding, and he ended up paying almost $1,300. I think it was $1,270 or $1,280. But remember, this thing looked almost new."

At least four more farmers tell abbreviated tales of recent corn binder sales, followed by a few questions from the others to help determine each binder's relative condition. After a few minutes the conversation seems to be winding down, and I asked the group to come to a consensus on a reasonable purchase price.

Crist throws out to the table, "How about somewhere around $1,100?"

"That seems like maybe it's a little high to me," Ervin quietly says.

Several more numbers ranging anywhere from around $900 to $1,100 are very briefly discussed. Finally, Noah says, "Sounds like we're all pretty close to $1,000. How would it be if we use that?"

"Yes, $1,000 sounds about right," Raymond says and looks around the table at the others. Heads nod all around and nothing more is said.

I am truly excited. This is really going to work. In under five minutes we have our first number, our first piece of research data! I look over to Les and say, "Write down $1,000."

He calmly picks up a pencil, scratches $1,000 into a box on the paper in front of him and says simply, "Okay."

The farmers around the table seem ready to keep going so I only briefly pause to say, "That worked great, guys. Let's go on to the next question. How long would you normally expect a corn binder to last, before it's completely worn out or needs major rebuilding? Now, we set an upper limit on this of 30 years. Some equipment may last a lot longer, but we figured most of the time the farmer won't, so the limit is 30 years."

This time Raymond draws in a long breath, looks around the room, and finally says, "Well, there's really not a whole lot that can go wrong with a corn binder. You might have to fix one of the chains or something once in a long while, but not too much generally goes wrong."

"All right, so what do you think its life expectancy might be? How many years do you expect it might last?"

"Well, I'd say maybe 25 years." Raymond looks around the table for confirmation from the other farmers.

Ervin slowly shakes his head and says, "Actually, I was thinking more like 45 or 50 years, but I guess we're limited to 30, so I'd say at least 30."

"I wouldn't argue with that at all," Raymond says, as he leans back in his chair and looks around the table. The rest of the farmers are quietly nodding their heads in agreement.

No one else comments, so I break in. "Okay, is everybody comfortable with 30 years?" Heads nod all around, "Write down 30 years, Les." He picks up his pencil and scratches 30 in the appropriate box. "Alright then, two questions down and two to go for the corn binder. So let's move on to the salvage value. If you dragged this corn binder back to the auction, after using it for 30 years, what do you think it would sell for?"

It takes the group only about a minute to settle on $100.

I'm amazed at how well this is going and move directly on to the last question for this piece of equipment. "What do you guys think it costs each year to maintain a corn binder?"

Crist starts out with, "You're probably going to need to replace the seat at least once. I just bought one last year and it cost $45."

"Yeah, that's true," Noah says. "But you have to divide that by 30 years, so it's only about a dollar and a half each year."

The group talks about drive-chain links, grease, sprockets, and a replacement wooden tongue, then quickly settles in on a total figure of $10 to maintain a corn binder each year.

I take just a minute to go over the numbers generated by the group. "Hey, guys that went quicker and better than I could have possibly dreamed. Let me go over the numbers with you. For the corn binder you said the purchase price is $1,000, its useful life is 30 years, the salvage value is $100, and the annual maintenance cost is $10. Any questions?"

With the corn binder neatly dispatched, it is time to move on to the next piece of equipment on our list, which happens to be a corn planter. The corn planters used on Amish farms are about the same as the planters used on small Yankee farms, except they are pulled by horses instead of tractors. The machine's job is to open up a small furrow in the dirt, drop uniformly spaced corn seeds in the furrow, and then cover them over with dirt, using heavy press wheels. All of the planter's functions are ground driven, meaning that it gets its power through the movement of its two large metal wheels as it is pulled through the field by either a tractor or a horse.

It takes the farmers assembled in Raymond's kitchen this morning only a few minutes to settle on the economic statistics for a horse-drawn corn planter. The purchase price is $450, useful life is 20 years, salvage value is $110, and the annual maintenance cost to keep this machine running is about $5.

With little prompting, the group methodically marches down each piece of equipment on our list. Les and I mainly stay out of the way and let these farmers take over the whole discussion. The group talks about each item at some length, but in a little over an hour they are done, and Les now has numbers filling in all the previously blank spaces on our equipment list.

The next two meetings go off like clockwork, and in a little under six hours of total face-to-face interview time, we have all the information we need. The next Monday morning back at the office, we average the results from the three meetings, do a few more calculations, and suddenly there on the desk an elegantly simple research project has congealed into a page and a half of precious results. Results we can use right now to help new farms, like the one Katie and Eli are thinking about, get a better handle on what their start-up equipment costs are likely to be.

Item	Purchase Price/$	Useful Life/Years	Salvage Value/$	Annual Maintenance/$
Corn Binder	1,000	28	70	7
Corn Planter	436	22	105	7
Disc	450	27	33	0
Drag	37	17	0	0
Feed Grinder	1,500	27	167	6
Fertilizer Spreader	850	25	30	1
Field Sprayer	800	30	0	2
Forecart	342	27	200	4
Grain Binder	700	28	100	10
Grain Drill	467	22	90	10
Hay Elevator	700	27	230	7
Harness (1 set)	200	10	0	10
Harrow	800	27	200	0
Hay Baler	1,767	22	430	50
Hay Loader	575	30	300	4
Hay Tedder	1,066	30	600	2
Hay Wagon	1,000	27	230	17
Manure Spreader	1,300	10	30	90
Plow	530	30	67	43
Rake	1,500	30	670	4
Sickle Bar Mower	830	30	217	33
Silage Chopper	1,230	30	167	4
Threshing Machine	2,170	30	1,330	28
Tractor	2,130	30	666	50
TOTAL	23,457	NA	7,432	983

Even I am shocked at how small the average total equipment costs turn out to be. Why, $23,457 won't even buy the first pickup truck on the Yankee farm, where just the combine alone is likely to run near $150,000, and total equipment costs are routinely several hundred thousand dollars. But the research method was good, and all the big pieces of equipment are accounted for.

Taking a few more moments to quietly admire our work, I still can't shake an uneasy feeling that something is missing. All of the machinery seems to be there, all of the blanks are full. But something is missing . . . the horse! We forgot the horse! None of this machinery does anything without horses! We have to figure out how much it costs to own and operate a draft horse before this great stuff on machinery makes any sense. That will be tomorrow's first project.

The very next day I drive back out to see Andy one more time. After the normal pleasantries and talk about farm prices, and the weather, and then more talk about farm prices, and the weather, I finally get around to the point of the visit. "Andy, we are doing a little work to try to find out just what it costs to own and maintain a draft horse and are trying to get a handle on what a farmer might pay for an average horse."

The broad, black brim of his felt hat bobs up and down a few times as he says, "Well, now, that could be real interesting."

A big-boned, blond Belgian mare is standing out in the pasture, over near the corn crib, with her hindquarters pointed in our direction. "Take that animal over there by the corn crib, Andy. Tell me a little bit about her."

"What'd you want to know?"

"Well, how old is she?"

"She's a four-year-old." Andy pauses and then goes on, "I bought her about two years ago."

"Where'd you buy her?"

"I got her from Abner Mullet, over on Mumford Road."

Abner Mullet isn't ringing any bells, and what I really need to know is whether he is a horse dealer or a horse breeder. Andy immediately sees the lack of recognition in my face and says, "You know him—Lester's Abner."

I'm still relatively clueless as to who Abner is. But I do now know that he is Lester's son, and he must be somewhat younger than me, because Lester is at most 10 years my senior. I also know that Abner's middle initial is "L." So if I end up having to look him up in the Amish Directory later, I'll know

I'm looking for Abner L., and not Abner E., Abner S., Abner J., or Abner F. Mullet. Hopefully, there will be only one Abner L.; otherwise, I'll likely find some combination of Abner E. L., Abner S. L., or Abner J. L. However, right now I just need to know how it is that Abner came into possession of the horse he finally sold to Andy. Is he a horse dealer, a horse breeder, or a farmer who breeds a few horses on the side?

"I'm still not sure I can place him, Andy. Is he there on the southwest on the corner of Hoover and Mumford Road?"

"No, he's two or three houses north of Hoover, on the east side of the road. Has a small dairy herd and breeds a few mares each year. Usually only one, sometimes as many as three."

I still can't place Abner, but it doesn't matter. He is a small farmer who breeds a few run-of-the-mill horses on the side to sell to other farmers. That's precisely the horse price I'm looking for. "So you bought her as a two-year-old mare. Was she broke to harness?"

"Yeah," Andy scratches the side of his face, thoughtfully gathers the unruly, long hairs of his beard into his left hand and pulls them down into a wiry, gray point, swaying gently like a stone mason's plumb bob, six inches under his chin. "She was pretty well broke in for most farm equipment."

"What did you have to give for her?"

"I don't remember exactly, but right around $1,100."

That's the number I've been looking for. It took a while, but Andy finally came through. We'll need to verify that number with a whole bunch of other people to be sure that Andy didn't get some really good, or bad, deal. I'm running behind today, and I really do have to go. "By the way, Andy, what's her name?"

"Oh, we call her Dolly."

Over the next few weeks, Les and I visit local livestock auctions, talk to horse breeders, auctioneers, and farmers. It turns out that Andy was right in the ballpark with what he paid for Dolly. Person after person confirmed that a two-year-old mare, or gelding draft horse, broke to harness, usually costs somewhere in the neighborhood of $1,100 at auction. That's not a meat animal, and that's not a show animal. It's an average run-of-the-mill workaday draft horse. The actual price range varies from a few hundred dollars for meat animals, who have any variety of deficiencies that make them unsuitable for fieldwork and are probably destined for human consumption in some other part of the world, to many thousands of dollars for show animals, who are normally bought by draft horse breeders and bred to other show animals to produce highly marketable foals. So, like Dolly, the draft horse that a farmer is likely to buy normally costs around $1,100.

Most draft horses have a productive working life of approximately 12 years. That means they are bought as two-year-olds and worked along with other horses in normal fieldwork around the farm until they're about 14, and they start slowing down. Old horses have very little value in the meat horse market; they are too tough. Besides, after working with these animals every day for years on end, many farmers are reluctant to ship them off to market. Very often they are either kept on the farm doing light chores, sold to a semiretired farmer who only has a little light farm work to do, or put out to pasture, where they spend the rest of their days wandering around the meadow, munching on only the best grass until they die or become sick and have to be put down and buried.

Since a lot of these older horses are buried and not sold, there is no "salvage" value at the end of their lives. Therefore, real depreciation on a draft horse like Dolly is fairly easy to calculate. Simply take her $1,100 purchase price and divide it by the 12 productive work years. So $1,100 ÷ 12 years = $91.67 per year, or about $.25 a day. This is not how the IRS calculates horse depreciation, but only a complete fool would look for logic, fairness, or reason in the U.S. tax code.

But Andy still needs to feed Dolly and the other horses. It should cost him around $675 per year to feed a horse. That's valuing the oats at $1.50 a bushel and hay at $90 a ton, and it includes a little money for a horse mineral supplement. If we put in an additional $25 a year for vaccines and health care, the grand total hovers around $700 a year.

Like most working draft horses, Dolly is not shod, so there are no farrier expenses. Andy takes care of the small amount of trimming and hoof care she needs, at little or no cost. Like all horses, Dolly rarely lays down. She sleeps standing up in the stall, so bedding is almost an afterthought and largely unnecessary. As a result, bedding costs are trivial. In these small, highly diversified farms, draft horses are generally commingled with all the other livestock, both in the barn and in the pasture. Since Dolly is primarily on the farm to help grow the feed for and haul the manure of the other livestock, it is reasonable to charge the cost of the pasture and barn to the other livestock.

Winding this all up, the annual cost for Andy Byler to own and maintain Dolly, here in the Geauga Amish settlement, is about $92 for depreciation, plus $700 for feed and healthcare, for a total of $792 a year, or about $2.20 a day. However, a harness is absolutely necessary to utilize Dolly's power, and it needs to be included in her total cost. The cost to buy one new set of leather harness for one horse is about $200. A harness should last about 10 years, and with repairs and other costs it boils down to about $36 a year, or $.10 a day, to own and maintain a harness for one horse. Add that to the costs for the horse itself, and the total daily cost of the draft horse, including harness, is about $2.30 per day.

Dolly's Dollar Demands Deciphered

Depreciation per year	92.00
Salvage Value	0.00
Feed	675.00
Vaccines and medicine	25.00
Pasture andhousing	0.00
Leather harnesses	36.00
TOTAL Annual Cost	792.00
TOTAL Daily Cost	2.30

With today's fuel prices, you can barely start a John Deere for $2.30. First puff of smoke as it turns over, and you're done. . . . Dolly won.

The very next year we did yet another study, again interviewing three groups of Amish farmers, in order to get a handle on the hours of horse—and human—labor involved in producing various farm crops. Then we put a value on the time, so we could calculate the total cost of production. We shook all those numbers around in calculators and computers for a little while, and here is what they spit out. The "Return to Labor and Management" per acre—or what the farmer actually puts in his pocket—was consistently higher on Amish farms! According to the calculations, an Amish farmer could pocket about $126 for each acre of small grain, like oats, wheat, or speltz that he grew, while his Yankee neighbor would get approximately $28. ("Speltz" is an obscure variety of wheat that produces high-quality straw. Other areas often use the word "spelt," but in this settlement folks generally keep the "z.") For alfalfa, the Amish guys could get $233, and the Yankees maybe $124. When it came to field corn, Amish farmers could only expect somewhere in the neighborhood of $65 per acre, but that's a lot better than their modern farm neighbors who would most likely lose about $9 an acre.

How in the world could they afford to grow corn and lose $9 on each acre? Ever hear of government farm subsidies?

A few months later I was able to find a peer-reviewed agricultural academic journal that was actually willing to publish this stuff. The article clearly documented that in the right circumstances, on an acre-to-acre basis, horses could be more profitable than tractors. The very same article cemented my position on the radical fringe and further alienated me from a substantial portion of the mainstream Agricultural Academy . . . oh well.

8

Why Cows Need Names

A little over five months have passed since I last drove down the Ginger-iches' driveway to go over a possible new farm plan. Thick snow covered the gravel then. Now summer is on the wane. It's already September. Where in the world did the summer of 2005 go? I've talked to Eli on the phone a couple of times and know he's been working on the barn, but I really don't know if this young couple decided to go through with their plan to actually start a dairy farm. If they did, this is the month when they should be thinking about getting some cows. Once again, the family dog—I think they call him Chip—is the first to see me pull in and is already standing at the car door wagging his tail. It's odd that I remember his name; I usually don't, but I like this dog. He's a mutt, white with some random splotches of rust-red hair gathered principally toward the anterior. The coat's medium length with gray undertones, especially around the muzzle, which dulls the overall sheen. He's a slightly older dog with long legs and a slender body. The total package looks to be about 30 pounds.

Even though Chip's slender with a long nose, the squared off, angu-lar features of the face and head mark him unmistakably as a male. It's surprising how many people—including loving, devoted pet owners—are oblivious to the obvious secondary sex characteristics of other animals. We all do okay with people; it's rare to see the face and shoulders of an adult man or woman and not know what we're looking at. But most of the time with animals, we just don't seem to notice.

So what? Who cares if we mistake a she dog for a he dog? For most of us, it really doesn't matter, but on a farm it's important to know what you're up against. Mistaking the massive head and shoulders of an old bull Holstein for the delicate features of a cow can be fatal. Likewise, knowing at a glance the pig loose in the barn aisle in front of you is probably a docile boar and not a sow, who may be protecting shoats (baby pigs), can save your life. Most often, boars ignore people, but a 600-pound sow with shoats just might run you down and tear off hunks of flesh with her massive teeth and jowls until your lifeless body stops twitching. So what?

As the car door swings open, Chip backs up a few steps, never barks, hangs his head low, and furiously wags a long hairy tail. He's afraid but desperately wants to say hi. He's naturally timid, with a personality molded in young puppyhood by his status as "the runt of the litter," a true "underdog." No wonder I like him. Crouching down so we're much nearer eye level, he waggles up to my outstretched hand, and suddenly the two of us are friends once again.

From what seems like miles away, Eli's volcanic voice rumbles across the darkened kitchen, through the screen door, into the sun-drenched yard. "Well, hello Randy, I just did call you. Didn't expect you'd be here this fast."

"Well, I've got to be honest, I didn't know you called. I was south of here over at John Detweiler's and thought I'd stop by on my way back to the office. But since I'm here, what did you need?"

Eli's round face and steady smile break through the screen door into the light. He's got a hacksaw in one hand and a pipe wrench in the other. "I called to see if you'd stop over and go through the barn with me. I don't know if you heard, but I'm milking now."

"No, I knew you were getting ready, but I didn't think you had the cows yet."

"Yeah, I got 20 cows at auction two weeks ago now, and I've been milking since that day. If you've got time, I'd like to show you the barn."

"Are you kidding? Of course I've got time. By the way, Eli, what's the hacksaw and pipe wrench for?"

"Oh, the milk inspector made me change the air filter on my water pump. It took almost two weeks to get it shipped from a supply house down near Minerva; then it was the wrong one. Had to send it back and wait about a week for the right one to get here. It's on now though, and hopefully the inspector will be happy the next time he's out."

I just smile and shake my head knowing this has to be one of a thousand start-up frustrations Eli's been wading through. As we walk off toward the barn, the screen door flies open again and Eli's towheaded son, Daniel, runs up and falls in beside his dad. Without thinking or breaking stride, Eli reaches down and pats him gently on the head, letting him know that it's fine for him to tag along.

Daniel's lanky, and maybe a little tall for his age, which I'm guessing to be about four or five years old. He's barefoot and shy but seems anxious to make contact. Eli only speaks to him in Dutch, so I'm guessing he's not in school yet. I look down, hold my hand up, and wave as I would to any small child. He holds his hand up and waves back. It's all that's needed.

For a moment I consider trying to talk to Daniel and then decide against it. At home and on the farm, Amish families speak "Dutch"—actually, "Pennsylvania Dutch"—which is a German-based dialect that's been changing and adapting to local circumstances since the Amish first started moving into this country, almost 300 years ago. Little children, like Daniel, don't learn English until they start school.

Eli's long strides charge the air around him. There's so much to do, and the entire family is caught up in the excitement. Walking briskly beside him toward the barn, I stop before we enter to take time to admire the new addition, including the new milk house, before we move on. The milk house, or milk room, is a completely separate room attached to the front of the barn. It's used to clean and store all the milking equipment. There are stainless steel sinks, equipment racks, and hangers, and the whole place is covered with a fresh coat of white paint. The center of the room is dominated by a large, refrigerated, stainless-steel vat, where the milk is cooled and stored until it is pumped out and hauled away by a tanker truck. Because this is an Amish farm, the power needed to operate the refrigeration unit is supplied by a diesel motor, quietly humming away in a compartment resembling a doghouse immediately outside of the east wall. Government health regulations require that the entire milk room be separated from the rest of the barn by tight-fitting screen doors and that the windows be screened to keep out flies.

We haven't gone inside yet, but I can see that the new cow living area has large open window spaces. These are four-by-eight-foot openings all along the walls. Eventually, the openings will be covered with translucent, insulated curtains. These aren't house curtains but rather specialized agricultural curtains designed to enhance cow comfort. Each window space will have a curtain that can be lowered from the top or raised from the bottom. When fully closed, they act as an insulated wall to conserve heat in the winter. In the summer they can be pulled to the top to maximize cross-ventilation and light and keep the cows cool. In fact, when all of the curtains are open, the cow living room has somewhat the feel of a picnic pavilion in a park. In spring and fall, the curtains can be adjusted to allow just the proper amount of ventilation to maintain comfortable conditions.

In terms of animal comfort, these agricultural curtains are one of the best things to come down the pike in a long time. They're not cheap, but they make the barn immeasurably more pleasant. It's hard to add them to old barns but relatively easy in new construction. I'm delighted Eli plans to use them in this barn and question him as to when they'll be installed.

"They were supposed to be put in last week," Eli says, "but you know how that goes. It's a busy time of year. I called and they promised me they'll be out the first of next week. I guess we'll see."

"It's really not important this time of year, Eli, and I'm sure they'll get them up in plenty of time for winter."

He agrees and then adds with a good-natured chuckle, "I know, but it seems like just one more detail I don't need to handle right now."

We enter the main floor through a door opening into the oldest part of the barn. This area is clean and whitewashed like the rest of the barn, but it seems cramped. Two or three small windows cut out of solid stone walls let in light onto the cement floors. The ceiling is lower, only about seven or eight feet tall. Some feed storage and several horse stalls take up the area. The cement aisle we are on slopes down past some more spacious stalls and a slightly higher ceiling, finally leveling off onto the floor of Eli's new bright addition. The ceilings here are at least 10 feet high and there's a totally different "airy" feeling.

Eli begins to tell me again the story of how his grandfather and father both milked cows in this barn. I've heard the story before, and I'm surprisingly glad to listen again. "That top part there's where my grandfather milked cows," Eli says. "He just had a few."

"How many?"

"Oh, five or so, never more than 10. My dad added on the middle part of this barn when he took over from his dad."

"How many did he milk?"

"Usually about 15, sometimes a few more or less. I think the most he ever milked was maybe about 20." Eli turns and spreads his arms wide, looking at the new addition, and says, "And now here I am adding on to what I'm taking over from my dad."

Daniel has stopped petting the dog and is focused intently on Eli's face as he recounts the story of his great grandfather's farm . . . and then his grandfather's farm . . . and finally his father's farm. Eli's hand falls to rest on the young boy's shoulder for just a second before we all turn and walk on into the new part of the barn.

The new addition looks great. Eli used his considerable carpentry skills, first to build and rebuild it in his mind, then to put hammer and nail to wood. It's all clean, new construction, lots of light and ventilation, clean-swept cement aisles, and a thick coat of whitewash covering the walls and ceiling. And now there are cows filling most of the stalls. This barn is once again alive.

Eli explains that he bought 20 cows in Clymer, New York. There's a fairly large Amish settlement in Clymer. In fact, I think it's a daughter settlement of the Geauga settlement. A "daughter" settlement just means that most of the original Amish people who moved to the Clymer area were from here in Geauga County. Likewise, the Geauga settlement is considered a "daughter" of the Holmes County settlement, because the first settler, Samuel Weaver, moved here from Holmes County, Ohio. It's still considered a daughter settlement even though Samuel moved here well over 100 years ago in the 1880s.

I suspect Eli may have had a contact in the Clymer settlement and was able to buy these cows from an Amish farmer. But not knowing for sure I ask, "Did you get them from an Amish farm?"

"No, they're off a 1,000-cow Yankee dairy just south of the Amish settlement up there."

"Do you know why they sold out?"

"Well, according to the folks up there, the owners just couldn't get along. So they decided to sell out, split the money, and go their separate ways."

Eli and I are walking up and down the aisle, giving me a chance to stop and study each cow. Each is a fine, large black-and-white Holstein, weighing anywhere from about 1,200 to 1,500 pounds. They're young, probably all first lactation. In other words, each has had her first calf, and this is her first milking cycle. Nowadays, we usually call any animal that has "freshened," or had a calf, a "cow." Before she freshens, she's a "heifer." However, I can remember when we typically called cows in their first lactation "first-calf heifers." They only became "cows" after they had their second calf.

Being a first-calf heifer was kind of like being on probation. She was part of the herd, but just barely. During the first lactation she was expected to produce somewhere around 70 percent of her later lactations. Based on this percentage, her later lactations could be estimated. If the estimate was at or above the herd average, she became a welcome member of the barn family. If her estimated future milk production was low, her travel ticket read something like departure location: farm . . . departure time: now . . . destination: butcher . . . return: cut, wrapped, and frozen.

The genetics, record keeping, size, and management of the dairy farm industry has changed a lot, and the term "first-calf heifer" is somewhat obsolete and seldom used. Usually now, "heifers" have never had a calf, and "cows" have had at least one. However, the likely final destination of any cow, regardless of age, that produces substantially less milk than the rest of the herd has not changed.

Eli continues to talk about the sale and shipping of the cows, but I'm having trouble focusing on his story. In my mind, I'm quietly ticking off the strengths and weaknesses of each animal. One's stance is too narrow; the next just right. She has strong ankles and shanks; that might keep her in the herd longer. I don't like the way the udder is attached on the cow across the aisle; it's too low and loose. Better to be pulled up tighter, more like the one to the right. The one on the right also has the proper wedge confirmation, formed by an almost perfectly straight top line and a clean, tight bottom angle sloping gently from between her front legs back to the udder. The next one is a little swaybacked, but she has a feminine dairy-type face. The one up front has good prominent milk veins along her udder and a broad, flat rump. These are pretty good cows.

My first lessons in judging dairy cows happened way back in high school. I worked summers, and sometimes after school, at a small dairy farm on the other side of the township. Curt Cooper was the owner, and he was as much a "cattle jockey" as a dairy farmer. A jockey is always on the lookout for any animal that's being sold for less than what it's worth. If he's at the auction and sees an animal going cheap, he'll buy it and then drive out into the countryside looking for some farmer who needs, and will pay for, this animal. Sometimes Curt would own a particular cow, heifer, steer, bull, mare, gelding, colt, or stallion for only a few hours. Other times he may milk a skinny cow for months, feeding her right so she could put weight back on her frame, and then sell her again at auction for a handsome profit. Between the regular herd, and animals that were being rehabilitated, Curt's barn generally had somewhere around 30 or 40 milking cows. Watching him buy and sell, I learned an awful lot about the quality and defects of individual cows.

One time after school, while I was helping Curt's son with chores and getting ready to milk, Curt showed up, unloaded a smallish black-and-white Holstein cow from his truck, and led her into a stall. He told us he got her real cheap at the auction because she had torn up the barn and put her previous owner in the hospital. No one was bidding on her in the dairy ring and she was about to be sold as beef and slaughtered, so he bought her . . . right!

I had a great deal of respect for Curt's judgment and knowledge of animals. Yet as he turned to adjust this cow's halter, I remember so clearly thinking, what kind of lunatic are you? No one else was bidding. This cow practically killed someone! The sooner this Holstein is the bottom half of a quarter-pounder with cheese, the safer mankind will be. All of the other buyers understood. But no, not you . . . she was a deal. Why not bring her home and see if two half-grown teenage boys could figure out how to milk her—and stay alive. Fortunately, my habitual deference to age, coupled with my tenuous status as an employee, came together in such a way that I was able to hold my withering, murderous tongue. As he turned back around to face us, I was afraid and angry, but thankfully silent.

Maybe he sensed my unease, or just saw our quivering terror. In any case, he did offer an explanation as to why he was moved to buy this cancer on four hooves. He said as he watched her walk around the sale ring, he noticed she jumped when anyone approached from her right side. There it was, what no one else saw: she was blind in her right eye. He told us to milk her from the left side, and she'd be just fine. And, as long as we stayed on her left, she was.

Later, in a college animal science course, Professor Wilson patiently refined our dairy cow judging skills, pointing out not only desirable features in cow conformation but also why they were desirable. A wide chest means there's good heart and lung capacity. Forelegs need to be short and straight. In order to be a "good feeder" she needs strong jaws and a large muzzle. Cattle judging was not only an art, it was an important component of the science of animal husbandry.

Judging dairy cow conformation like this is largely considered a quaint throwback to old times by our modern dairy industry. The general manager of a huge dairy production facility, trying to buy another 500 or 1,000 cows, has little interest in actually looking at them. Production records and genetic potential are summarized on the computer printout, looking at each animal unit is a pointless waste of time.

But Eli and his family only needed 20 cows out of the 1,000 at the auction in Clymer. Each cow there had a number that corresponded to a brief production history and genetic potential summary on the computerized sales sheet each potential buyer was given. The sales sheet was very helpful, but since he only needed 20, Eli did have time to look over each one, to quietly tick off in his mind the strengths and weaknesses of each animal, before he ever raised his hand to bid. I'd say he did a pretty good job. These few precious cows are the foundation stock of this farm. Their ability to produce milk and quality of their offspring will in a large measure determine the radiant success or dismal failure of this fledgling family farm.

As we walk down and back through the barn, Eli does not rush my inspection of each animal. After the last cow, I turn and say, "Looks like a fine herd, Eli. How many are you actually milking now?"

"Just 16, three were dry when I bought them, and I dried off one more towards the end of last week."

A "dry cow" is simply one that's not producing milk. Cows are usually bred two to three months after they've had their last calf. As the new calf develops in her body, the cow's daily milk production slowly tapers off. Then around two months before the new calf is born the farmer "dries her off" (stops milking her) so all of her energy can go into her fast-developing new calf. So the cow Eli just dried off should have a new calf in a couple of months, which will kick her into milk production again and start her next lactation.

"How are they producing?"

"Good, I'd say. The herd average is a little over 60 pounds (or about five gallons of milk per cow per day). Which I'm well pleased with, considering the move and new feed and new barn and everything."

"Sixty pounds is very respectable considering all they've been through."

These girls have been on a steep learning curve ever since they got here. They've spent their whole life in confinement. As young heifers they were grouped together with dozens of other heifers and raised in large barns with cement floors. Later, after they freshened, they were moved to the huge cow barns where they milled around, again on cement floors, with hundreds of other cows competing for space at the feed bunks, water troughs, and for a stall to lie down. Modern confinement dairy barns are usually built with about 15 percent fewer stalls than there are cows to fill them. So a cow who is ready to lie down wanders around the barn waiting for some other cow to decide it's time to get up to eat or drink. Then, like a frazzled shopper in the Wal-Mart parking lot on December 24th, she wheels into the vacant stall for a much-needed rest.

This is a tie-stall barn, so for the first time, each of these girls has her own place. When she's not outside on the pasture, she's loosely tied in her own individual stall. After the first couple times in and out of the barn, each member of the herd finds her own spot in the lineup. Eli doesn't assign cows to stalls; the cows do. When it's time to come in for milking and feed, each cow invariably returns to the same stall. It really does become her own little efficiency apartment.

In reality, the stalls are all the same. Each one's about twice as wide, and a little longer, than a cow. The stalls are made of two-inch metal pipe. There's a pipe in the front, where the cow's head is loosely tethered when she's in the barn, and a single bent pipe on each side of her, separating her from the cows in neighboring stalls. There are no walls between the cows, just the pipes. The tie-stall arrangement allows each cow to stand or lie down, and stay comfortably in contact with rest of the herd, as she naturally would outside. Yet she does not have to compete for water or feed. Her grain and hay are placed on the clean cement floor in front of the stall, and she only needs to turn her head to access the watering cup at the edge of the stall.

There's a cement curb at the front of the stall to keep the feed and hay in front of her face, and not under her feet. Cows naturally pull their head down and back as they are eating; without the curb they would continually spread the hay and grain under their feet and belly. That's frustrating for the cow and wasteful for the farmer. Ergo, the curb.

The floor of the stall is covered with a thick rubber mat for cow comfort. A little straw bedding is put near the back to catch any manure and urine that doesn't fall into the manure trough that runs behind all of the stalls. A couple of times a day, Eli or one of the children walk through the barn and use a hoe or pitchfork to pull any of this wayward dung into the trough.

Until they got here, these cows had never so much as seen a pasture. Eli says, "The first time we let them out, they just went crazy and kept running around in great big circles. It took the better part of an hour for them to calm down and look at the green stuff they were walking on. After a while one by one they started to nibble, and then before long they figured it out and really started grazing."

Very much like us, these cows had to *learn* where their food came from. They grew up understanding that food was brought in twice a day, by one of the servants, in a nice, freshly painted green or red wagon. How could they possibly imagine this stuff grew in fields? They had no idea what a field or a pasture was. Such a thing was just completely outside their frame of reference. Until a couple of weeks ago, these were urbane *barn cows,* unaccustomed to and uninterested in these quaint rural ways.

Sound familiar? Ask most first-graders where their food comes from and they will tell you without hesitation—the grocery store. A former colleague of mine in home economics once told me about a Dairy Council project to educate city children about the nutritional value of milk. As part of the project, they brought a live cow to the schools. After a short classroom presentation, each child was invited to come outside and touch the docile animal. As the first little girl laid her hand on the cow's side, her eyes opened wide with astonishment and she exclaimed in bewildered confusion, "It's warm." How could this thing be warm, when the milk at her grocery store was always very cold?

Just now, Eli's pointing his finger at a thick white string above his head. I notice it is strung around and between all of the posts and beams in this part of the barn. It snakes near the ceiling above each of the cows. On closer inspection, I see numerous black motes, which turn out to be flies, stuck to the string. Eli asks, "You ever seen one of those?"

"No, I can't say that I have."

"It's a new kind of a fly string. It's sticky, like flypaper, and has some kind of bait that attracts them to it. It only costs $26 per 1,000 feet, and I think it's doing a pretty good job. I told Katie this afternoon maybe we could get by without spray."

Unless it's midwinter, flies are an ever-present problem, or potential problem, in almost all livestock barns. Thanks to modern spray programs, insecticide-treated lumber, frequent whitewashing, and things like Eli's sticky string, flies can be pretty well controlled in dairy barns. However, it's pretty nigh impossible to completely control flies out in the pasture. The most effective fly-fighting device a cow has is her long tail with its bushy clump of coarse hair on the end. Cows out on pasture nonchalantly swish their tails over their backs, keeping the flies largely at bay.

Unfortunately, Eli's cows don't have tails. Well, to be precise, each one has about half of a tail. All of these girls had the bottom half of their tails "docked," cut off, when they were just a few days old. When they were baby calves, the plan was that they would spend their entire life in confinement barns and never so much as look at a pasture. Since, at least in theory, flies in confinement barns are controlled principally by pesticide spray programs, they would not need to swish flies. Therefore, their tails were unnecessary appendages.

In fact, in large confinement barns, cow tails are an absolute nuisance. When a cow lies down in a stall, her tail usually flops out behind her. In Eli's barn, that means her tail (if she had one) would most likely land in the manure gutter behind the stall. Obviously, it can get a little dirty. But, usually the end of the tail ends up resting on some straw bedding and stays relatively clean.

On the other hand, when a cow lies down in a modern free-stall confinement barn, her tail unerringly winds up in the cow aisle behind her. These barns have no manure gutter, and straw bedding is seldom used. So her tail flops out into a sloppy mess of soupy manure, accented with urine and stirred by the endlessly wandering hooves of her herd mates. To be fair, the factory farm managers do try to keep the cow aisles clean by scraping them with a tractor or flushing them one or more times a day. However, if these methods really did keep the aisles clean, I wouldn't be staring at 20 docked tails right now.

So why would any farmer care if a cow has a dirty tail? What could be worth the time, bother, and expense needed to dock tails? The answer's simple. All cows are milked two or three times a day. In large confinement operations, the cows are slowly herded through the milking parlor. Most parlors have two rows of cement platforms where the cows stand. The farm workers stand in a cement pit directly behind the cows. As each cow is brought in, one of the workers leans in close and reaches under the cow's udder to attach the four cups of the milking machine to her teats. When she's milked out, the human worker again leans in very close and reaches under her to take off the teat cups.

In Eli's barn the procedure is pretty much the same, except there is no milking parlor. Eli, Katie, or one of the children kneels beside each cow, leans in close, and attaches or removes the milking machine teat cups.

It's the "leaning in close" that has put cows' tails in jeopardy. Any time you get your face that close to the rear end or the side of a cow, you are in imminent danger of being swished. Being swished in the face at 5 o'clock in the morning by a coarse, dry cow tail is a distinctly unpleasant experience. Being swished by a dry, slightly dirty tail is much worse, and being smacked in the face by the sodden mop of a dripping tail, freshly soaked in warm manure and steaming urine, is a gagging, painful, and degrading ordeal. Multiply this experience by the thousand or so cows going through the parlor each morning, and suddenly the time, bother, and expense of cutting off cow tails is completely rationalized.

While I accept that tail docking is an expedient solution for the problem of the thousands of manure-soaked tails in huge confinement facilities, I've never really liked the practice. With all of our marvelous, modern, expensive agricultural technology, does it seem too much to ask that we find a more humane way to keep the end of a cow's tail reasonably dry and clean? The very personal result, for Eli's 20 cows, is that they will spend many long summer days grazing on lush pasture, while hopelessly swishing their deformed stubs at biting and buzzing flies. Fortunately, their offspring will be allowed to keep their tails. The few handfuls of very low-tech straw, which the Gingerich family spreads behind the cows each day, will keep their tails clean enough. So watch out all you flies, this younger generation will be ready to swish you good.

It's about time for me to go. I know that Eli has a lot to do and I don't want to hold him up, but he seems in no hurry when I say, "Well, I guess it's about time for me to get on back to the office."

"If you've got just another minute, I want to show you my new water heater." Eli leads the way over to the other side of the barn, right outside of the room where the milking equipment is stored. He jerks the cover off a new in-line water heater and starts to extol its advantages. Like most farmers, he loves new gadgets.

"See, it doesn't have a pilot or a hot water tank, so the salesman says it will really save energy. I guess we'll see."

I'd like to know if the heater runs on natural gas or propane. I start to ask and then check myself because using natural gas is sometimes a church issue. Some of the church districts in this settlement are allowed to use natural gas and others aren't. I know this farm, like many others in the area, has a gas well on it. The well, which is over 4,000 feet deep, is owned and operated by the gas company. The landowner, in this case Eli, gets a royalty based on the amount of gas or oil sold.

These aren't Texas-size wells. Most of the time landowners will get a small monthly check, although with some wells the check can be several hundred dollars or more each month. There's usually also a "free gas" clause in the lease, which allows the landowner to use a certain amount of gas without charge each month. In any case it would make a lot of sense for Eli to use the natural gas from his well for this water heater. That is, of course, unless the *Ordnung* of this church district doesn't allow it. Then it's simply not an option.

I'm really not sure why some of the Amish church districts shy away from natural gas. My hunch is that it has something to do with the pipeline. The gas pipe is a tangible, physical—and once a house is hooked up, almost inseparable—direct connection to the outside world, which goes against the Amish desire to stay as separate as possible from the larger world. But again, that's only a guess.

It really is time for me to go, but I can't help walking back to take one more look at Eli's new herd. At the far end of the barn, there are two much larger stalls, each about 10-by-10-foot square, with wood plank fences for walls. A cow, who is obviously about to freshen, paces nervously through deep clean straw bedding in the first stall. A baby heifer, not more than three days old, runs and trips through the straw to get to the front of the second stall, where she stares at us through her huge dark eyes. Looking back into her timid face, with my years of hard scientific training, economic calculations, and mountains of agricultural facts, I find myself wondering, as I always do, what in the world is she thinking?

The cow that is about to freshen in the first stall is fine here in the barn. She has plenty of room to move around, and if there's any problem with the birth, Eli will be here to help or call the vet. The heifer calf is a different story. She really should not be in the barn. She'd be much better off in a calf hutch outside. A calf hutch is just a little building about the size of a large doghouse, big enough to hold one calf.

Until about 15 or 20 years ago, everyone kept calves in a warm barn with the cows. Unfortunately, many of them died. Even on very clean, well-run farms, it wasn't unusual to lose half of the calves each year. The young calves were simply unable to fend off the normal bugs and germs of the cow herd. Finally, some researchers began to question why calves were kept in the barn at all. It was probably just custom or habit. We'd always known calves really don't need the warmth. Beef cows freshen on the open range out West, where the temperatures can plunge well below zero, and the calves do just fine. So calf hutches were designed and built for the newborn calves. Nowadays on most farms in this area, calves only a few hours old, sometimes still wet from birth, are taken outside and put in a hutch, regardless of the weather. The results have been dramatic. Calf mortality is a fraction of what it used to be, and calves are healthier too.

I make a mental note to talk with Eli about calf hutches on my next visit. For right now this calf looks to be fine, and Eli has quite enough on his plate. I turn and stare back down the barn for a moment and simply say, "That's a fine-looking group of cows, Eli."

"Yeah, I'm well pleased." I can see in his face and his whole demeanor that he truly is.

As we've been talking, we've slowly wandered around to the little aisle in front of the cows. Each of their heads is bent down low as they munch on fresh alfalfa hay spread out in front of them. Some are daintily nibbling, while others are attacking the stems like a football player on steroids. The one just down the row is not only wolfing down her feed but stealing a little from her neighbor every few bites. None shows the slightest interest in us. Looks like alfalfa trumps humans once again. I'm not offended.

The cow directly in front of me has a mostly white head and jet-black ears. Her left ear has a yellow plastic tag in it. Bending down, I can make out the number 962 and immediately understand this was her identification number when she was part of the 1,000-cow herd up in Clymer, New York. Suddenly it strikes me that with all the new things these cows have had to get used to there's probably still one more . . . a name.

Pointing down at her white face I look at Eli and ask, "Do you have a name for this cow here, or you are you still using the number in her ear?"

He looks a little puzzled as to why I might ask, but then says, "Oh no, we call her Judy."

"What about this bigger cow here on her right? Let's see here. Number 418, I think it is."

"Well, the children decided we should call her Molly." Eli is laughing out loud now and shaking his head, amused at my curiosity. "Don't ask me why, because I really don't know, but that's her name."

"And the one beside her, #728?"

"Now, that's one of the few in the barn we haven't gotten around to naming yet. It's kind of a slow process, but the children are having fun with it."

Making our way toward the door, I learn that the biggest cow in the barn used to be #327, but lately she's been sporting the name Betty. The last, rather smallish, animal in the row doesn't appear to have an ear tag, and I can't help asking one more time. "What about her? Does she have a name?"

"Oh yeah, that's one of the heifers we raised here ourselves, so she's had a name ever since we got her."

"Well, what is it?"

"Sally. Well, actually Stubborn Sally. She has always been the hardest animal to get into the barn, and then the hardest animal to drive back out. That's why she got the name."

So animal unit #962 has morphed into Judy, #327 is Betty, Stubborn Sally is still Stubborn Sally, and #418 now goes by Molly because the children thought that would be a good name for her. The arduous task of naming all the animals in the barn routinely falls to the children on a small family farm like this. And they love it.

A new calf, still wet from being born, will be watched and studied for physical marks or personality traits that might hint at her proper name. The children will select, reject, and debate several names until they settle on just the right one. It's important work. After all, she'll have this new name for the rest of her life. What's more, the whole family, even Mom and Dad, will use it forever. Assigning an individual name somehow also gives an animal moral authority and provides a powerful deterrent to wanton cruelty—a deterrence that is absent on enormous dairy farms with thousands of completely anonymous, sequentially numbered animal units.

9

Silage 101

Finally outside, I'm drawn toward the shiny new piece of equipment sitting on six-by-six wooden blocks, over next to the corncrib. I think I know what it is. I think it's a silage loader. I've heard about these, but never really seen one up close. Better be sure. "Eli, is this one of those new silage loaders?"

"Yep, it was just delivered the end of this week past."

"Who makes these?"

"Well, this one came from Schrock Brothers Manufacturing. They're an Amish equipment maker over in Lancaster County."

It's funny, but over the years even with all of my training in modern agricultural technology, I've become more than a little skeptical about "new" equipment. One of the real secrets that allows Amish farms to compete—and even outcompete modern corporate farms—is their extremely low equipment costs. "How much did this cost, Eli?"

Without hesitation, he says, "Oh, a little over $1,000. But it's well worth it."

Now I'm really skeptical. This was not in the original budget. A thousand dollars for a piece of harvesting equipment on the Yankee farm is trivial. But without running the numbers, my guess is this piece of equipment may have almost doubled Eli's silage harvesting equipment costs. Sometime in the next few days I'll try to find the time to push a pencil and figure out how much this one piece of equipment increases his total harvest cost per acre. Right now I just nod and say, "Well, I hope it's worth it. How's it work?"

"It mounts right on the side of the corn binder. Then this shaft hooks onto the end of the drive shaft and runs the loader. I haven't had a chance to mount it yet, so for the time being I'm going to use the neighbor's."

"Which neighbor?"

"Jonas Burkholder," Eli is pointing off vaguely toward the northeast, "around the corner. David Kempf and Jonas and me are working together this year to get all of our silage in."

Jonas is Freeman Burkholder's son. I can't say I know him well, but I've met him. He used to farm on shares with a Yankee owner over on State Route 168, but I understand he's running his dad's farm now. Freeman quit milking several years ago because the milk price at the Amish cheese factory was so low. Then a few years ago, his church district allowed farmers to use bulk milk refrigeration tanks run by diesel engines. Just recently the bishop also allowed some farmers to start using milking machines. By this time, Freeman was semiretired so he worked out an arrangement with Jonas, and I think Jonas has been milking on the home farm for about a year.

If I've ever met David, I don't remember it. He's one of Albert Kempf's younger sons, so I'm sure I've seen him. Albert is one of the first people I met when I came to Geauga County and one of my oldest friends in the settlement. He has always been willing to take the time to help me understand the community and the unique Amish farming methods. David's older brother, Lester, is running the home farm now, and Albert and his wife live in the *daadihaus* next door. Albert still helps on the farm sometimes and works part-time at his nephew's cabinetmaker shop.

It's getting late and I do want to get back to the office and return phone calls before the end of the day. Still, I am intrigued by the silage loader and mention to Eli that someday I'd like to see it running.

"Well, we'll be making silage tomorrow morning if you really want to help. We can always use an extra hand." Eli's laughing as he says it because he knows silage making is hard work, and his invitation to help is also somewhat of a challenge.

Unable to resist, I find myself rising to that challenge. "Are all three of you working together tomorrow?"

"Actually, five of us—Jonas, David, my Dad, Katie, and me."

I'm hooked. I just can't pass up the chance to work with three new dairy farmers. Plus, I don't think I've ever met Eli's father. I must've run into him over the years, but I cannot picture his face. "Okay, Eli, let me get back to the office and see if I can clear my calendar for tomorrow. No guarantees, but if I can move a few things around, I'll be here."

At about 8:40 the next morning, I turn south onto the road that leads to Eli's farm. He said they would start around 8:30 and I could easily have been here by then, but I didn't want to be early. I wanted to get here and meet the others just as we were ready to start working. That way I would have time get to know each of them, slowly, over the course of the entire workday.

Just south of the house and farm buildings, my little Toyota bounces onto the rough gravel driveway beside the cornfield where we'll be cutting silage today. About 150 yards away, near the middle of the field, there is a large pod of wagons, draft horses, machinery, and three members of the human crew. Eli and Katie have just pulled out of the barnyard on a flatbed hay wagon pulled by a team of two draft horses and are on the road coming our way. I decide to wait for Eli rather than approach the group in the field. In about five minutes, he and Katie swing in behind my car. Eli stops the horses, waves good morning, and suggests that I should pull my car farther up the driveway so it will be out of the way of the wagons.

"If you think it would be better, Eli, I'd be happy to take it back and park it in the barnyard."

"Well, that might be best, if you don't mind."

"No, that's fine, I'll be right back."

Eli pulls the team and wagon into the field so I can back my car onto the road. The barnyard's only a couple of hundred yards away. I park under the shade of a large tree and start to walk on the side of the road back to the field. Traffic's not a problem; not a single car has passed by in the 15 or so minutes since I've been here. On the way to the field, I meet Katie walking back toward the house and ask if they sent her back because I came. She nods yes. "It's a poor trade," I tell her. Without a word, she smiles, laughs a little, and walks on toward the house. She's far too polite to say it, but I'm left with the uneasy feeling that she agrees with my assessment of our relative value and is delighted to return to the important work of running the household.

Turning into the field, I walk up to where Eli is standing and ask him what I should do.

"Well, I thought we'd have you drive the teams, if that's okay. You know how to drive horses, don't you?"

"Yes, not as good as you, but I can drive them." The truth is I'd rather not drive the horses. I've only driven draft horse teams a handful of times in my life, and I'm always keenly aware of what a novice I really am. It's doubly intimidating when I'm surrounded by the real experts—Amish farmers. These guys use horses every day; they understand them and are completely at ease around them. In a timid attempt to get out of driving, I suggest to Eli that maybe I should load corn instead.

Eli smiles and shakes his head. "Sure, you can if you like, but I think maybe driving would be better . . . at least to start."

All right, I get the drift. There's real work to do, and I'm too old to do the loading. "Okay, I'll drive."

It's time to meet the rest of the crew. Standing next to the first wagon is a man in his late 20s or early 30s who is loosely holding the reins of the two horses hitched in front. He's slightly shorter than me, about five foot eight, medium build, with dark, thick, reddish-black hair sticking out from under his broad-brimmed straw hat. He's wearing a short-sleeved dark blue work shirt with an odd, thickly padded, long cotton sleeve pinned to the bottom of his short right sleeve. Like everyone else except me, he's wearing coarse blue jeans that button in the front and are held up with two thin black leather suspenders. I'm certain I've not met him, but it is obvious who he is. The resemblance to the rest of his family is striking. As we shake hands, I confidently announce, "You're David aren't you."

Surprised, he asks how I could possibly know. "I hate to be the one to break this to you, but the sad truth is, you look an awful lot like your brother, Lester."

David laughs out loud and whatever little bit of tension there might have been evaporates into the morning mist.

Levi Gingerich, Eli's dad, strides over to where we are standing, smiling broadly and obviously interested in making my acquaintance. He looks vaguely familiar. I'm sure I've seen him in meetings but I can't say that I really know him. He reaches out and shakes my hand with the two large, slow pumps, typically used by Amish farmers of his generation. I always find this slow, deliberate, slightly exaggerated handshake strangely comforting. When I first came to the settlement, everyone used it—if they shook hands at all. Contact with the outside world was less frequent then, and the universally tepid palm vibrations that pass for handshakes in our modern world had not yet been adopted.

Levi is 63 years old. At six foot one, he's slightly taller than the rest of us, with a full head of white hair, and a long white beard highlighting his slender face. I am delighted that he is so welcoming; his acceptance is important. This day is looking like it just might be a lot of fun.

Chip, the family dog, is beside himself with excitement. He's dancing around the field, running headlong toward one team, annoying the horses, and then turning sharply to surprise one or another of us. Then he jumps high in the air, landing with hind legs pointing south, front paws to the west, and slobbering tongue headed due north. Just now he's snuck up behind me and put his wet mouth on my hand, begging for attention. It always gives me pause when a dog, however playful, tickles my hand with his teeth. I reach down and cuff him behind the ear—if dogs could smile, this one would.

Jonas Burkholder, the last of our crew, is standing 10 feet away in front of two Belgian draft horses. He's probably in his late 30s, a little quiet, but friendly. His black bushy eyebrows almost grow together above a prominent nose. He's wearing a straw hat and a tan long-sleeved shirt, with extra padding pinned on the right arm. Jonas is pleased to find out that I remember him from our past meetings. I make a mental note to ask him about his father. However, right now Eli's looking a little impatient. It's time to get started.

I crawl up on the wagon with Eli. He's the most heavyset of our group and is wearing a green short-sleeved shirt, again with a padded cotton sleeve pinned to the right arm. I can't help asking, "What's the sleeve for?"

"Oh, it helps protect your arm when you're catching the bundles of corn. You'll see."

We are all lined up and ready to go. Eli hands me the reins and explains that the loader chute needs to stay in front of the person loading. The loader chute delivers bundles of cornstalks from the binder up to the deck of the wagon. Actually, the bottom of the chute is about chest high as we stand on the wagon. Eli will stand with his back to me, looking toward the back of the wagon. As the corn bundles come off, he will stack them on their side, against the six-foot-tall back standard (wooden rack) of the wagon. My job is to pace the horses so that the binder and loading chute, driven by Eli's dad, stay within the three- or four-foot space between Eli and the back standard. I will also need to keep my horses close to the team driven by Eli's dad so the end of the chute stays over the wagon, not the field. If I go too fast, the chute will hit the rigid back standard of the wagon and be ruined. Too slow, and it will smash into Eli. This all looks well-nigh impossible. I am fundamentally unsure of my ability to drive horses with this precision. I am apprehensive. . . . I am nervous.

Eli's father will be driving the binder today, which is poised now to cut a single row of corn. He's perched on a spring-loaded metal seat, slung so close to the ground that he's about eye level with the knees of the three massive Belgian draft horses hitched to pull the machine he's on. He's concentrating on the horses, but looks relaxed, and is holding the reins in each hand looped over the index finger with the ends passing under the ring finger and hanging loosely in front of his little finger.

With absolutely no fanfare, he suddenly says "get up" and the horses and binder lurch forward.

A split-second later, I hear Eli, standing behind me on the wagon, calmly say "get up" and the two-horse team at the end of the reins I'm holding springs to life. Ten seconds later Eli says, "Come on, Judy," urging the lead horse to pick up the pace. For me, the world has become unnervingly chaotic and filled to the brim with noise, awkward motions, and dust. Gaining some composure, I pull on the right reins, nudging my team closer to the three horses pulling the binder. It is an awesome sight: five huge, golden Belgian draft horses pulling together. Looking down over the broad rumps of Judy and Mae, I shake the reins above the two mares to make them walk faster. They need to walk out ahead of the three horses pulling the binder so the wagon will move forward and the chute on the binder will move toward the back of the wagon where Eli can unload the bundles.

A few more yards down the field, Eli's deep voice rumbles over my shoulder again, "Come on, Judy." He wants her to speed up so the chute will move back a little, making it easier for him to unload the bundles. She and Mae respond, but almost immediately I have to pull back on the reins to keep the chute from crashing into the back standard of the wagon. Eli is trying to direct the team I'm driving, and it's not helpful. This is like two people driving a car at the same time. The poor horses have one person telling them to speed up and another holding them back. Fortunately, as I gain confidence, Eli gradually curtails his backseat directions and lets me drive the team.

A never-ending stream of 40-pound corn bundles methodically drops from the chute into Eli's waiting arms. As fast as he can toss one bundle onto the stack another is ready to fall. He is sweating profusely and working at a pace I know I could not—oh yeah, I remember that's why I'm driving the horses. As the load fills, I need to gradually hold back my team, so that the team pulling the binder catches up and slowly moves the loading chute toward the front of the wagon. The trick is to keep the chute between Eli and the ever-growing stack of corn bundles. Halfway down the field I'm getting better, but it's a real challenge.

The row of corn we are cutting and loading looks to be about 300 yards long, but I'm not sure. The wagon is about half full now. With Herculean effort, Eli mechanically throws the heavy bundles higher and higher until they're stacked at least eight feet deep on the wagon.

Three-quarters of the way down the field, I finally have the opportunity to look down at Levi. The binding machine he's riding is probably 50 or so years old. It has a wooden tongue stretching from between the horses all the way back under his seat. There are two small metal wheels, 12 inches in diameter, in front of his feet and two large metal drive wheels, about 30 or 35 inches in diameter, behind his shoulders. As the drive wheels turn, the binder moves forward and the cornstalks are pulled into the machine by three-inch-long metal fingers on each side of the row. The fingers are attached to a square-linked drive chain and driven by sprockets attached to the axle. The fingers pull the cornstalks back into a cutter knife about six inches off the ground. The stalks are cut off and pulled back another foot or so into the machine, where a group of them is gathered into a bundle and tied with coarse twine by an ingenious mechanical knotter.

It's at this point—just past the knotter—where things have really changed. In years past, or even today in more conservative church districts, the tied bundle of corn would fall off of the binding machine onto the field. Then some time later the farmer would come by with a wagon and team, pick the bundles up off the ground, and throw them onto the wagon. But with the new Schrock Brothers Loader from Lancaster, these bundles fall onto a rubberized canvas belt with rows of metal teeth about every 18 inches that pull the corn bundles up to the top of the metal chute and into Eli's waiting arms.

I'm still troubled by the extravagant cost of $1,000, but I can't help marveling at the machine's relentless, maddening pace, and at how quickly it has been able to train Eli to keep up. Clearly, this new machine is in charge. It gives the orders, sets the pace, and will not tolerate a slacker.

We are near the very end of the row and the task has gotten infinitely harder. The machine has obviously just ordered Eli to bury me in cornstalks. The bundles are halfway up my back, pressing my stomach and chest against the wooden boards of the wagon standard in front of me. I can't really see the end of the chute; it's too close and Eli is in the way. Focused like a man possessed, he throws the bundles ever higher in an effort to complete my cornstalk grave. I'm on the verge of panic. Perhaps sensing my distress, Eli is able to shift my attention away from the cornstalks at my neck by using the heel of his work boot to stomp down hard on my right-foot toes.

Completely buried and in excruciating pain, I magically finish the row and we break into the edge of the adjoining hayfield. The mechanical chute suddenly stops vomiting cornstalks and settles into kind of a metallic dry-heave rumble. Levi quietly says "whoa" and all five horses come to rest. The cornstalks of my photosynthetic crypt are heavy, and the sharp edges of the leaves scratch at any patch of exposed skin. Clawing my way up and over the front standard of the wagon, I jump down and hand the reins to Eli, who's now standing on the ground behind the team. With completely feigned jauntiness, I hear my voice casually ask, "What d'ya want me to do next?"

"Well, I thought we'd just keep you driving the wagons, if that's okay with you."

"Oh, sure, that's fine." I'm lying. I'm lying. I'm lying. Please don't make me drive another wagon. But my Welsh heritage commands me to be stoic and not show my mounting distress.

Eli raises a rigid arm, like the gray, stern Ghost of Christmas Yet to Come directing Mr. Scrooge, and points across the hayfield to where Jonas and his wagon await.

It takes far too few minutes to walk across the field. I crawl onto the wagon and a smiling Jonas hands me the dreaded reins. Then he lightly slaps the rear end of the gelding on the right to get him to step up even with the other horse in the harness. Then Jonas turns to me and explains, "Mack has learned that if he hangs back, Mike will do most of the pulling. So try to keep him up where he belongs."

Levi pulls the binding machine and loader into place, straddling the row of corn to the right of Jonas's wagon. Almost immediately, he commands "get up" and the machine lurches forward.

I spontaneously shake the reins in my hands and utter a weak "get up" that sounds embarrassingly more like a plea then a command. Thankfully, the harness snaps to attention as my team steps out, jerking the wagon forward. Now all five horses are in motion again. Mack immediately falls half a step behind Mike. Mike doesn't seem to notice, and I'm far too busy trying to keep the end of the chute from bashing into Jonas, the wagon, or both. I'll deal with Mack's laziness later, when things settle down a bit.

Actually, things are going pretty good with this load. For some reason, this team is much easier to drive and I'm having almost no trouble keeping the chute where it belongs. The two animals are moving smoothly together, and the wagon is filling up nicely. Mack is still not pulling his weight and I have a little time to consider modifying his unacceptably shiftless behavior. I do know what's called for here. I am to take the loose ends of the reins dangling from my hands and slap them across Mack's rump, thus signifying that he should take half a step forward to more equally distribute the load between himself and Mike.

Unfortunately for Mike, I simply lack the requisite courage needed to startle 2,000 pounds of Belgian horseflesh into action. It would be nice, not to mention much fairer to Mike, if Mack would take that half step forward and pull his weight. So, I'll slap him with the straps—but, on the other hand, the downside risk is pretty big. Old Mack here isn't doing much work, so likely he's plodding down the field half asleep, daydreaming about that bag of oats back at the barn. Now the plan is, when I hit him with the straps, he'll be just startled enough to take that half step forward, yet not so startled that he might, for instance, rear straight up in the air, lurch ahead, and jerk both of my reins-holding arms out of my shoulder sockets. Nope, no possible way. Sorry, Mike, looks like you're in for one long hard day.

We're already at the end of the field, the wagon's loaded, and all of the horses are stopped. I'm a little embarrassed for letting Mack get away with not pulling his weight, but overall I think this load went really well. Before I get down off the wagon, Levi calls up to Jonas, "Randy drove those horses like he's been doing it all his life." I chuckle a little inside because I know from his vantage point Levi could not have seen Mack's errant ways or my timid horsemanship. Nonetheless, his compliment is sincere, and it means an awful lot to me. Striding back across the hayfield toward David and his waiting wagon, this simple remark has given me the confidence that I so sorely lacked just a few moments ago.

David's standing on the wagon, holding the reins of the last team I'll need to get to know today. Little Daniel, Eli's son, is standing on the wagon bed with David. Arriving at the side of the wagon, I lift my left foot high and slide that side of my body onto the bed and then awkwardly struggle to pull my right side on. Before I'm properly standing, David hands me the reins. "These horses aren't like Ben and Lucy—they're more in the reins." I look at him completely puzzled. I haven't driven a "Ben and Lucy" today.

"You know, the horses in the book." David laughs.

Suddenly, I realize he's talking about some of the horses in my first book, *Why Cows Learn Dutch: And Other Secrets of Amish Farms.* "Did you know who I was talking about in that chapter, David?"

"Yeah, I had a pretty good idea while I was reading it. Then I got to the part where you talked about the horses, and I knew for sure."

In my first book, I had very carefully changed the names of all the farmers, their family members, the locations of the farms, and some other details in order to protect the identity of each farmer. What I had obviously failed to do was change the names of the horses. I'm sure David and many other Amish farmers were able to figure out exactly who some of the people were because they knew the names, breeds, and personalities of the horses. Feeling more than a little foolish, I can't help joining David in a protracted, hearty laugh at my expense.

Levi pulls up and straddles the next row of corn. With a short "get up," we're off again. I'm starting to get the hang of this horse-driving thing, and this team is responding pretty well. The work is fast and hard, but David honestly seems to be having fun. He smiles the whole time as he furiously flings bundles higher and higher onto the wagon. Young Daniel stays out of the way by moving closer and closer to the front of the wagon as the stack grows from the back. We finish the row with Daniel and me both pinned against the front standard and the wagon completely full. Daniel obviously likes David, and he stays on his wagon all morning long. At times, when it's safe, David will even hand the reins to Daniel and let him drive a little.

I jump off while David and Daniel immediately head for the barn to unload. Back across the field, Eli and his team are waiting with an empty wagon. In the time it has taken to load Jonas's and then David's wagons, Eli has gone back to the barn, unloaded his wagon into the silo, and returned.

The rhythm of the work is consistent, and it goes on unabated for the entire morning, except for a few short breaks to rest the horses, squeezed in between the loads. Mercifully, Katie has stashed a large blue-and-white, plastic insulated jug full of ice-cold water and a couple dozen chocolate brownies beside a rock at the end of the field. In just over three hours, we manage to put 18 wagonloads—which I later calculate to be almost 40 tons of corn—into the silo. By the end of the morning, both the horses and us people are more than ready for a midday break.

Jonas's wagon is the last load of the morning. As we come to the end of the row, both Levi and I rein our teams to a stop. I push my back into the bundles of corn stacked against me, wiggle to the side of the wagon, and hand the reins back to Jonas. I'll let him drive down the road, into the barnyard, and over to the silo. Levi's already busy unhitching his three-horse team from the binder. He'll leave the binder in the field, pick up the reins, and walk behind the team, carrying nothing but their harness back to the barn for some water, feed, and a much-deserved rest.

On Jonas's command, the team steps out, the harness tightens, and the wagon lurches forward. Top-heavy, it rolls back and forth like an over-loaded rowboat, and cornstalks shift across our backs with each undulation of the field. The dominant noise is the rustling, grinding, and squeaking of the ever-moving stalks. As the wagon's steel wheels pull onto the level road, the stalks stop shifting. The air is now filled with the muted rolling crunch of steel on asphalt and the rhythmic clopping of eight massive hooves.

From the side, Jonas looks a little like his father, Freeman. I don't think I've seen Freeman more than once or twice since he sold the cows and stopped milking several years ago. The place sat pretty much idle until Jonas bought some cows and brought it back to life last year. He could be renting, but I suspect he's in the process of buying the farm from his parents. I know there's a small *daadihaus* on the place, and quite probably Freeman and his wife have moved in there.

Freeman is one of the wittiest and most gregarious men I know. He's always ready with a joke, a smile, and a high-pitched, infectious laugh. In contrast, his son, Jonas, is a quiet man, not at all standoffish, just quiet. He manages the team with practiced confidence, first pulling the reins to the left to keep the horses from wandering into the ditch and then gently right to keep them in our lane, all the while sporting a relaxed half grin. I'm content to take the five- or 10-minute journey back to the barn in silence, taking time to gather in and savor the sights, sounds, smells, and feeling of this warm September day.

As we pull through the yard around the barn and back to the silo, the pulsating rattle and roar of a faded green, old John Deere 70 tractor over-powers the area. David's just finishing unloading his wagon, and Jonas pulls his team to a stop three feet behind. Less than five minutes later, David drives his now empty wagon out of the way. Jonas pulls forward and stops the wagon beside an old silage blower that's so rusted I can make out neither the make nor model. The blower/grinder is an odd and slightly ominous-looking thing. There's a chute four or five feet long and about 18 inches wide sticking out toward our wagon. A jagged metal conveyor belt rotates endlessly in the bottom of the chute, waiting to pull cornstalks into the mouth and guts of the machine.

One bound bundle at a time, Jonas begins unloading the corn onto the chute. Once there, each bundle—corn ears, stalks, and binding twine—is pulled relentlessly into a grinding metal mouth, where the whole mass is chewed into one-inch or so lengths. The chewed mass then falls back into the main body of the machine, which is essentially a large, round fan shrouded in rusty sheet metal. The fan blows the chopped corn through a hole in the top of the shroud, and on through 50 feet of connected stovepipe, to the top of the silo. Once there, it's forced by the air pressure from the fan below through a curved pipe and directed down, falling onto the growing mass of corn in the bottom of the silo.

This whole unit gets its power from the old John Deere 70 tractor, parked about 30 feet away. A wide, rubberized belt connects a large wooden pulley sticking out of the side of the tractor to a similar pulley on the back of the blower. The tractor is used as a stationary engine to supply power for this and other machines around the barnyard. In this Amish settlement, tractors are not allowed in the fields to pull plows or other fieldwork, and they all have steel wheels (even though rubber wheels are available), so they can't be driven on the roads.

Suddenly the machine jams and rocks loudly back and forth as it tries to force another corn bundle down the throat of the gagging metal chopper. Jonas jumps off the wagon and steps over to a lever near the back of the chopper that disengages the unit. The machine settles into a jerky idle and slowly pushes the jammed stalks backward. Jonas pushes the lever forward and reengages the machine. It immediately slams the stalks back into the throat of the chopper. This time it works. With one loud, long groan, the entire bundle is chewed into small pieces and blown up the pipe into the silo. Jonas crawls back on the wagon and resumes his unloading.

When he's got just over a quarter of the wagon done, I shout up to him, "Why don't you let me spell you, so you can unhitch the horses?"

With a quick nod, he jumps off the wagon, walks up between the horses, and starts to unhitch them. He'll take them in the barn for feed, water, and rest, while I unload the wagon. We can leave the wagon here, and after the noon break, we'll rehitch the team and be ready to go.

Unloading the wagon is heavy work, but nothing like loading it. After a few minutes, I notice that Jonas and the team are disappearing into the barn. The machine jams two more times while I'm unloading. Each time I disengage the chopper the same way Jonas did. I'm glad that I was here when it jammed for him because I would have never figured this out by myself.

Just as I finish unloading, Jonas reappears, climbs up on the John Deere, and turns it off. With the dying of the engine, absolute silence settles in. It's a blessing.

10

Lunch, Talk, and Silage 102

Eli steps around the corner of the barn, his round face almost cut in half by a huge, infectious grin. He's pleased with the morning's work and orders everyone to come inside for "lunch." I'm a little surprised, usually on the farm the noon meal is called "dinner." It's normally the biggest meal of the day and at night you have "supper." There is no "lunch." Yet today both Eli and David have talked about "lunch."

Then it dawns on me: both of these men are new farmers. David started milking in May and Eli just two weeks ago in September. Before that, Eli had his own carpentry crew, and David was a carpenter on his uncle's house framing crew. As contractors working out in the world, they got used to pulling sandwiches out of their lunch buckets during the crew's lunch break. Somehow, "lunch" just lacks grandeur, and it doesn't sound as special as a big farm dinner. So while these guys are going in for "lunch," I think I'll follow just a step behind and get my taste buds ready for the "dinner" Katie's been working on for most of the morning.

My legs and arms feel unnaturally heavy as we follow a gently curving path to the back screen door of Eli and Katie's large white farmhouse. In the mudroom, Eli shows us a double sink with hot water, coarse soap, and a thick cotton towel hanging on a ring next to the sink. A whole row of children's shoes and boots are lined up neatly on the cement floor beside the three white-painted wooden steps leading up into the main floor of the house.

Wooden pegs on the wall above the shoes support a row of broad-brimmed straw hats. These are everyday farm hats and range in size from

85

toddler (which is a little bent up) to Dad's (which is a little dirty). I hang my sweat-stained baseball cap on the farthest peg; its short, green bill stands out on the wall, and is clearly not in complete fellowship with the other straw headpieces. However, at least for now, they seem to be getting along well enough.

Just as we finish cleaning up, a car pulls into the driveway, and Eli goes out to talk to whoever it is. He turns his head as he pushes through the screen door, and tells us to go in. But none of us is anxious to barge into the kitchen, so we nervously mill around the mudroom until Katie opens the door and comes to our rescue with an insistent, "Well, come on in."

Obediently, we file up the steps and through the door. I ask Katie where she wants me to sit. "Oh, anywhere," she says but then pulls a chair out about halfway down the right side of the table. There is a bowl for a child in the place setting to my right.

Katie speaks in Dutch and tells Daniel to come sit down next to me. He quietly shakes his head and points to the chair beside David. "Oh, I see, you want to sit near David." Katie opens her eyes wide, smiles down at Daniel, and laughs—the whole table laughs. The place setting is changed so Daniel can sit beside David, and Levi sits down at the plate now to my right. To his right is the head of the table, reserved for Eli. Katie says that Eli wanted us to go ahead because he might be a little while talking to the visitor.

When everyone is settled, Levi looks at me and says, "Well, let's have a silent grace." I realize he's not sure if I know the Amish custom of a moment of silent prayer both before and after each meal, but of course I do. It has been my great joy to have the privilege of breaking bread with many Amish families over the years. But I appreciate his thoughtfulness. Everyone at the table, including the children, bows their head. After a few moments of silence, Levi clears his throat and grace is over.

Katie is at the other end of the table, directly across from where Eli soon will be. Barbara, their adorable blond baby girl, is in the high chair on her mother's left. Her older brother, who's on a booster seat and looks to be about three, is next in line. His grandmother, Laura, Levi's wife, is in the chair next to him, so she can help with his plate if he needs it.

Laura has a delightful presence about her. I liked her immediately the very first time we met, a few months ago. She's tall and slender, with gray-blond hair pulled back and tucked neatly under her white cotton organdy cap. Her fine features and lively eyes are frequently overcome by a smile that spreads until it simply dominates her entire face. She laughs often and uses her soft voice to animate and invigorate the various mealtime conversations.

"Go ahead and dig in," Katie announces to the table. "It's nothing fancy, but it's hot."

She passes around a basket of fresh-from-the-oven homemade baking powder biscuits, just as her husband Eli comes in and takes his place across the table from her. David picks up a large crockery bowl filled with chunks of chicken and vegetables in thickened broth and sends it around for each person to ladle over the biscuits. Katie and Laura help the children with the ladle. Butter is on the table, and a bowl of applesauce completes the main course. There is a pitcher of water to drink.

I look down on a steaming full plate of chicken and biscuits, drink in the comfort-food aroma, and am struck with the realization that it doesn't get much better than this. Katie canned the vegetables from her garden late this summer, and chances are this chicken was scratching for bugs, grubs, grass, and bits of grain in the barnyard yesterday. The ritual of the mealtime grace and thanksgiving takes on new meaning over a meal like this. Something strangely spiritual is gained when we truly know the food we eat—something is lost when we don't.

Talk around the table is lively, and mainly about mutual friends. Who's traveling where, who's sick, who got better, and news of the 20 or so families who moved up to the new Amish settlement in Richfield Springs, New York. Of course, since this is a farm table there's also a lot of talk about the weather, the crops, the livestock, and the ever-important price of milk.

Eli brings up Andy Byler's name. Andy is one of my oldest and closest Amish friends. Eli says he saw him at a benefit auction about a month ago. A benefit auction is where people in the community donate quilts, sometimes a pig, or anything else of value to "benefit" some local need. Usually the proceeds go to an Amish school or a family with medical bills or any other worthy cause. The auctions are fun and attended by Yankees and Amish alike.

Eli says, "As soon as Andy saw me, he came over and said, 'Pretty soon you won't be doing this kind of thing anymore.'" Andy was teasing him, suggesting that now that he was a farmer he wouldn't have time for auctions.

Eli says he looked at him and said, "Oh, I think I can ask my dad to milk once in a while."

Andy countered, "I don't know. He's getting older."

Eli had him. "That's true, but the difference is over in our neighborhood we have older people who actually work." Eli said Andy was "speechless."

Andy is not often speechless, and our whole dinner table explodes into laughter over Eli's story.

Andy is about 30 years older than Eli and, even though she's laughing, Katie doesn't want me to think Eli would normally be disrespectful. She stammers to soften the story a little, "You see, Andy is my uncle. That's why Eli might've talked to him that way."

"Oh, don't worry about it, Katie. I tease Andy all the time. He just seems to have a target on him, you know."

I couldn't be more comfortable with this meal, this family, and these friends.

The chicken and biscuits are passed around again, and I am flatly unable to prevent my hand from grabbing the ladle and scooping out just a bit more. A moment later, a platter of homemade chocolate brownies appears as Katie gets up and pulls a carton of store-bought Breyer's ice cream out of the icebox. The brownies, ice cream, and a piping hot pot of black coffee circumnavigate the table. A few minutes later, stuffed to the gills, we bow our heads for a short silent grace and the meal is over.

Before we get up from the table, Laura mentions that last week she and Levi went to a local Methodist church in Middlefield to hear David Klein, an Amish man from the Holmes County settlement, give a talk. Laura says it was good and was sorry that more people weren't there to hear it. Levi nods his head in agreement. They're both surprised to learn that I've met David several times at various conferences and field days.

David Klein is a dairy farmer. He's also an author and the editor of *Farming* magazine. This quarterly publication is basically a trade magazine for Amish and other small farms. But it's more than that. It includes the usual advertisements from farm equipment dealers, banks, seed and fertilizer companies, and the like. It also has a wide variety of articles on various farming practices and news releases for upcoming meetings and events. There's a market report that usually gives the price of Holstein heifers, dairy bulls, and some other livestock. To me, one of the things that make this magazine special is that it isn't all about the "business" of farming. Many articles deal with family life on the farm, even the philosophy of why certain farming methods might be better than others. It's not strictly organic, but there's a strong bent in that direction. There are editorials, book reviews, and a poetry section. It seems that, unlike many trade magazines, David and the staff who put together *Farming* get it. They understand the expansive value of the intertwining links among the farm animals, crops, and families, linkages that are purposely developed and nurtured on small farms and that are so starkly absent on the factory farms where so many of the calories we consume each day are manufactured.

David is also a real proponent of a rotational grazing or, perhaps more correctly, "management intensive grazing." When they think about it at all, most people assume that dairy cows get most of what they eat by grazing pastures. But they don't. Dairy cows on huge farms across the United States are normally kept in "confinement." That means they spend all day aimlessly milling around huge "loafing sheds" with hundreds or even thousands of sister cows. Most of these sheds are little more than a roof held up by a series of treated lumber timbers. For these cows, there is no access to pasture. After all, pastures are darn inconvenient; it would be very difficult to round up 2,000, 3,000, or 4,000 cows that were outside munching pasture before each milking.

In rotational grazing systems, David and many others advocate that relatively small herds of cows get most of their nutritional needs through grazing. Not all day in one big pasture, but in a carefully managed segment of the pasture. In the most intensively managed systems, temporary electric fences are moved once or twice a day so the cows are always getting fresh new growth. The trick is to have the cows munch down the grass quickly, but only munch each plant once. Ideally, the herd completely harvests the area of pasture they are given in a day or so. After that, the fences are moved and the cows harvest the next area. After grazing, each area is allowed to rest and regrow. Done properly, this system of grazing allows the plants to build up energy (starches and sugars) in their roots and, ultimately, produce many more tons of high-quality forage than a single, continuously grazed pasture.

In the past 25 years, I've worked with many farmers in the settlement to help set up rotational grazing systems. In fact, Eli and I discussed a possible grazing system for his pastures just a month or two ago. It's always a bit more of a challenge on an Amish farm. None of our 90 or so Amish church districts allow farmers to use electricity from the road to charge fences. Some districts are okay with solar-powered fence chargers, and many will allow the use of standard car batteries to charge fences. Of course, there's always the problem of recharging the batteries. Finally, there are a few districts that frown on electric fences altogether. Often, the most workable default position in the Geauga settlement is to set up the grazing system using permanent, small paddocks divided by standard, nonelectric barbed wire. These pasture systems are harder to put in, less flexible than movable electric fences, and probably produce a little less forage. They are, however, vastly better than a single large pasture. Perhaps most importantly, this minor concession to barbed wire avoids "discord" within the church community, and at the end of the day, lack of discord completely trumps a few tons of grass.

It is so very tempting to believe that managed pastures and careful rotational grazing is a return to the traditional farming methods of our grandfathers. After all, until very recently, cows were always on pasture. But in fact, all of our grandfathers were pretty clueless when it came to grazing. They might occasionally rotate cows off of one pasture and onto another once or twice a summer, but even that was rare. On most farms, cows spent the entire year trampling back and forth over the same worn-out pasture. It wasn't until the 1980s that a group of researchers and farmers in New Zealand worked out the principles and practices of intensive rotational grazing. Shortly thereafter, researchers and extension personnel at land grant universities across the United States began working with farmers to adapt and perfect the systems here.

After a few more minutes of table talk, Eli pushes his chair back. "Well, I guess we'd better get at it again."

Obediently, we stand up and start to file out into the mudroom. Katie and Laura start to clear the table with some help from Katie's older daughter. I pick up my baseball cap and leather work shoes, step outside, and sit down on the cement stoop to pull on the shoes. Eli's little daughter is standing on the stoop beside me. She seems to enjoy the fact that we are now almost eye to eye. I'd like to talk to her, but I can't. At this age, she only knows the Pennsylvania Dutch that the family always speaks at home. Finally, I simply wave, with an exaggerated hand motion, as you would to any baby. She beams and waves back. It's good enough; we've made contact.

With profound effort, I pull my body off the stoop and start walking toward the barn. Silently categorizing various aches and pains and evaluating whether it is my legs, shoulders, back, feet, arms, hands, or neck that is the most fatigued and unresponsive. What I can't believe is that I'm actually, and voluntarily, going back out into that field. Every one of my muscles seems to be screaming at the control center behind my eyes, "You're supposed to work behind a desk—fool! What in the world are you doing here?" Ignoring the angry protestations of both my muscular and nervous systems, I dumbly decide to stay the course. Stepping into the barn, I'm committed.

Two of the draft horses are loose and standing in the middle of the aisle, not trying to go anywhere or get away, just standing. All of the others are loosely tethered in their stalls, drinking water and nibbling on oats and hay. The other men go about the business of rehitching the horses. I pretty much stay out of the way. In about 10 minutes, all the horses are hitched, and we are ready to head back to the field. I hop on the wagon with Eli, and we are on our way.

The afternoon work is a mirror image of the morning, except a little hotter. I'm much more comfortable driving the teams, and the horses, people, and machinery fall into a steady, hurried rhythm. Between wagonloads, there's usually a few minutes to talk, and we take several short breaks around the water jug at the end of the field.

Just after 4:30 in afternoon, word comes to the field that the silo is almost full. I ride in on the last load, 14th of the afternoon, 32nd of the day, but who's counting. We pull this load into place behind the silo, and Eli and I take turns unloading it. About halfway through, the old tractor runs out of gas and sputters to a stop. The silo is completely full. It will settle some during the night and there will be enough room for Eli to put the rest of this load in tomorrow.

David turns and waves as he pulls his wagon and team out onto the road, heading home for evening chores. Jonas is right behind, the steel wheels of his wagon clattering over the gravel driveway. Both of these men will get home just about in time to start milking. Twice a day, every day, the cycle of milking goes on, but they don't seem to mind.

The barnyard is quiet now. Eli steps out of the barn with a big pitcher of homemade mint tea in one hand, a stack of glasses in the other, and an immense smile on his face. He pours a glass of tea for me and his dad and then one for himself. Takes a gulp of tea and says, "I'd say that was a pretty good day's work. How about you?"

Levi and I nod our agreement. The tea is truly delicious and welcome. Eli heads back to the barn to get ready for evening milking. He is obviously pleased with the day's work, and he should be. This day's crew of horses, humans, and equipment managed to harvest and store around 70 tons of green corn silage. Each wagon was filled and refilled 10 or 11 times. The silo is full but there's still some corn left standing out in the field. That's no problem. Eli will leave the stalks standing in the field to dry. Then some time in late fall or early winter, he'll hitch a team of horses and a wagon and go back to the field to handpick and husk the dry ears. The stalks will be left in the field to be plowed down next spring, and the ears will be put in the corn crib and ground into feed for the livestock this winter.

It has taken three full days to fill Eli's silo. I only helped on this last day, and I'm exhausted. This was the third straight day for the rest of these guys and horses, and they also have silos to fill for both David and Jonas. Eli's silo is 14 feet wide and 50 feet tall. It holds a little over 200 tons of silage that will be one of the principal components in the herd's ration this entire winter. A fairly typical dairy cow diet is made up mostly of equal parts of dry hay and succulent corn silage, with several pounds of dry grain concentrate mix rounding out the meal and filling the major nutritional needs of a cow in winter.

The silo will be left undisturbed for at least a few weeks now, giving the chopped up corn time to cure. It will start to ferment and form the alcohol and acids that ultimately preserve the corn. The airtight sides of the silo exclude air, which would cause the mixture to dry out and mold. In the end, if the system works—and it usually does—the finished corn silage comes out very moist with an odor that is somewhat similar to sauerkraut. The best thing is cows really seem to love eating it.

In the late afternoon sun, Levi and I draw up two lawn chairs and sit down to enjoy the tea and talk.

"Well, Levi, now that you've run it for a while, what do you think about this new silage loader?"

"Oh, I'm pretty impressed. It really speeds up the work. We could never fill a silo this fast back when I was farming."

"Yeah, it's fast all right. I really don't think I could keep up with it, but these young guys seem to be doing fine. And it is good to fill a silo faster."

The faster a silo can be filled, the less likely there will be any spoilage in the finished silage because the outside air is excluded more quickly. Still, I'm not totally convinced this silage loader is really a good thing, so I press Levi a little more. "It's pretty expensive. I think it's going to add quite a bit to the overall harvest cost."

Levi concedes that, "Yeah, it is expensive." Then he goes on, in an off-the-cuff manner, to offer a perspective on farm economics that is uniquely Amish. "You see, what I like about it is that it creates another time in the year when these guys need to work together."

I mutter something like, "Oh, uh, yeah, I suppose that's true." It takes a few moments before the profundity of Levi's simple statement begins to settle in.

No factory farm, or other Yankee business for that matter, would assign value to the act of working together with your neighbors. It makes no economic sense. Silage loaders help each farm fill the silo a little quicker. But more wagons, horses and people are needed to keep up with the pace of the loaders, so now each farmer is committed to helping fill three times as many silos, two-thirds of which he has no economic stake in filling. If there is any net gain for each farm, it is negligible. In fact, since each of the farms spent $1,000 to buy a new loader, there is very likely to be a net economic loss due to the higher machinery costs.

Every big-business or big-farm innovation that I can think of over the last 50 years has been expressly designed to promote less, not more, interdependence on our nearby community, our neighbors. Gone are the days when groups of farmers would get together and help each other during particularly busy seasons. The threshing circle (still used by Amish farmers), in which several farms jointly own one threshing machine and work together at harvest time, has been replaced by a massive, lonely, single-operator grain combine. Sitting in the incredibly expensive, air-conditioned cab of his combine, listening to his favorite music, the modern farmer really has little need for his farm neighbors. Actually, he is in direct competition with them. Each farmer, sitting in his own "combine palace," is constantly on the lookout for more acres of grain to keep this beast fed. If a neighbor loses his farm, there's that much more land available to buy or rent.

The same basic principles hold true for nonfarm businesses and for nonfarm communities. Precious little effort is expended on innovations that might actually strengthen our local community. Take, for example, the cell phone. It allows for instant communication. But does the way we use it actually bring us together with our neighbors? At the grocery store, 10 years ago, when I accidentally banged my cart into another, there would by necessity be some interaction—"Excuse me" . . . "I'm sorry I bruised your grapes" . . . "Let me pick that up for you." There's no need to say anything now. Invariably, my fellow shopper has an idiot box stapled to the side of his or her face, and it is there specifically to exclude any interaction with bothersome, cart-pushing neighbors.

Driving home, I'm still grappling with the economics of the silage loader and with what Levi said. What business principle am I missing? What can't I understand that Levi so clearly does? Is it possible he is hinting that Eli's farm might be as important to this community as the next Super Wal-Mart, or that the business school principles and ethics that brought us Enron and bank failures may be obsolete? Nah, couldn't be that.

11

Milking—A Family Affair

It's late Wednesday afternoon and the weather is a little cloudy but warm and dry, as I leave the office and head over once again to visit Eli and Katie, this time to be there while they milk the cows. This isn't something I routinely do, but it's sometimes helpful when a new farm is still getting started. The Gingeriches have been milking for about six months now, and I'd like to see how the barn and milking system are working. Besides, it's always fun to be in a dairy barn at chore time. I stopped out two days ago to ask Eli if it would be all right any day this week. Of course it was fine, but he did not pass up the opportunity to pull my chain just a little. Without hesitation he asked, "Do you want to help with morning chores, or just evening? Morning might be better."

I know where this is leading but see no reason to interrupt his sport. "Alright, Eli, what time do you normally start morning chores?"

"Oh, if you get here somewhere around 4:30 it should be fine."

"No."

"Well, if you want, you can sleep in and show up at about a quarter to five."

"No, Eli. What time do you start evening chores?"

With a huge grin of satisfaction on his face, he condescendingly shrugged. "If you really would rather do evening chores then, we start milking at five but are generally in the barn by a little after four."

"The evening milking will be fine. I'll see you on Wednesday."

Not much more than a mile from the office, the red flashing lights of a stopped school bus appear up ahead in front of an Amish home. Getting closer now I can see it is a special needs school bus. An old man with a cane is slowly making his way across the yard as the hydraulic lift lowers a wheelchair with a severely disabled person down to road level. The girl in the chair seems unable even to move her head. The old man exchanges a short greeting with the bus driver, rests his cane over the wheelchair, pushes her 10 feet into the driveway, and stops. A thin woman with silver hair showing at her bonnet edges comes out of the house and ties a rope around the arms of the wheelchair. She pulls, he pushes. The chair rolls up the ramp onto the porch, and all three disappear into the house.

Suddenly, I realized that the bus has long since pulled away while my car is aimlessly idling in the middle of the road. There's no traffic; there seldom is. I'm not sure what box to file this scene in. Maybe it's family love, or courage, or strength, maybe it is simply grace, but it is the type of scene that makes up the fabric of this community, and describes what it's like to be here in the settlement, every day. Once again, I am humbled. It is only the presence of the white barn towering above the driveway on the left that brings me back to the Gingeriches and today's dairy farm mission.

The dog greets me first, of course. Then Eli, holding the receiver, steps half out of the little white wooden phone booth perched in the yard over by the barn. "I'll be right with you, Randy." I move over to the heavy wooden door, pull it open, and step inside the barn to wait. Several minutes later, Eli comes in, "Sorry, I was on the phone with my cousin over in Pennsylvania."

"Where's your cousin live in Pennsylvania?"

"Guys Mills."

There are many Amish settlements in Pennsylvania, but I'm not surprised that his cousin is in Guys Mills. It's a daughter settlement of Geauga, and most of the folks who live there came from here at one time or another. "Is this the cousin you said was a dairy farmer?"

"Yeah, he called because he's having trouble with his butterfat. I had the same problem a few months ago. I finally changed feed companies, and things got a lot better. He is still using the same company I used to use, and things are not good."

A problem with butterfat always means the same thing on a dairy farm: less money. Farmers are paid a premium for butterfat content. Therefore, if the butterfat is low, the farmer gets less money for each gallon of milk shipped.

"Just how low is the butterfat in your cousin's herd?"

"It's only 3.1 percent."

"Well, yeah, that's a little low but really not too terrible for a Holstein herd. He is milking Holsteins, right?" Eli nods his head in the affirmative. "What about you? Where's your butterfat running?"

"Right now it's around 3.9."

"That's real good for Holsteins. Don't change anything."

"The kicker is he's paying a whole lot more for his feed than I am."

We talk for a few more minutes about dairy rations and butterfat. We talk in generalities because formulating dairy rations is simply outside my area of expertise. Butterfat content in the milk is strongly influenced by what the cows eat. Not only the chemical composition, but even the size of the individual pieces of silage or other ground feeds can impact butterfat content. Individual farmers rely on their feed salesmen to help them properly balance the diet and optimize butterfat content. There are genetic differences between breeds of cows that also impact butterfat. In general, Holstein milk tends to have lower butterfat content than smaller breeds like Jerseys, Ayrshires, and Guernseys. Even within a particular breed, there are some genetic differences between individuals that can impact butterfat. But when two small Amish Holstein dairy herds, in similar conditions, are nearly a full percentage point apart in butterfat, it should raise red flags.

Formulating dairy rations is a real science. There are specialists at the university who are experts in this field. However, on a day-to-day basis it's really up to the farmer—working with a feed company representative—to come up with the best ration for that herd. Many of these "feed salesmen" are also true experts in formulating dairy rations. But some are better than others, and Eli and his cousin are right on target in questioning the abilities of this particular feed salesman and the feed company. My hunch is the cousin's feed salesman will have a lot of explaining to do the next time he visits the farm, and if he is not very careful it may well be the last time he visits that farm.

It's getting close to five o'clock milking time, and Eli excuses himself to go get started. While we have been talking, Katie slipped into the milk house and is cleaning equipment for tonight's milking. I open the screen door and step into the room with her. "Did Eli tell you I was going to be around for milking tonight?"

"Oh yes, he said you didn't want to be here for morning chores though."

"That's not quite true, Katie. Morning chores are fine; I just didn't want to drag myself out of bed at four o'clock in the morning. So I'm here to thoroughly enjoy evening chores."

We both laugh and I follow her into the main area of the barn with two stainless-steel buckets. Setting the buckets down near the cows, I turn and almost run over a darling little girl holding a gray kitten. I'm sure she is too young to know English, so I slowly wave my hand in her direction. After a few moments of looking at each other, she holds the kitten out so I can scratch its neck, which I do. The kitten doesn't seem particularly interested but purrs anyway as if purring is simply part of a kitten's job. Over the course of the next hour or so, each of the children in turn brings the same gray kitten around for me to scratch. I'm glad there are no more children or this poor thing would soon have no hair about its neck.

There's a dull thud behind me as Eli starts to throw bale after bale of hay out of the storage loft one floor above the cows. Katie is busily getting all the equipment ready for milking, and I concentrate hard on staying out of the way. The oldest daughter is at the other end of the barn so I walk down to see what she's up to. She looks to be maybe 10. I'm not very good at judging children's ages, but she must be in school, probably I'm guessing around third, fourth or maybe even fifth grade. In any case, she's been in school long enough to know English, so I'll try to talk to her a bit. Obviously, like most children, and particularly most Amish children, she is uncomfortable and shy but willing to answer direct questions.

"Hello, what's your name?"

"Regina."

"Hi, Regina. I'm Randy. What's your job while the cows are being milked?"

She seems to perk up a little at the question. "I feed the heifers."

"Oh, do you feed them milk replacer?"

"Yes, but I mix it with water first."

Unable to suppress a quiet laugh I say, "Well, that's very good."

She seems puzzled at my amusement. After all, she didn't say anything funny. She told me exactly what she does to feed the heifers. Putting on a straight face I encourage her to "keep up the good work." Then I tell her that I'm going to wander on down to the other end of the barn to see what her mother is up to.

She smiles brightly and says, "Okay."

The joke Regina did not get is that milk replacer comes as a dry powder and must always be mixed with water in order to get it into a liquid form that the calves can drink. The calves simply can't use it dry. Milk replacer is used on almost all dairy farms for calf raising. I've never really looked at the economics, but apparently it is cheaper than feeding whole milk from the cows. In any case, it is used a lot and the calves seem to do just fine.

On my way back to the other end of the barn, a small boy riding a scooter zooms past making loud crashing noises. There's no danger, but it is funny. Just the kind of thing you expect a little boy to do. As he beeps and dashes off to the other end of the barn, I am struck that this particular little boy could be quite a handful.

Eli has left the hay loft and returned to ground floor with the cows. Right now he's busy opening the bales, one by one, and spreading the fresh hay out in front of the two long rows of cows. It must be good; certainly the cows seem to be enjoying it. Katie is totally engaged in the process of milking the cows. A few of the church districts in the settlement still require hand milking, but, fortunately for Katie, this district allows milking machines. The milking machine is basically a closed-top stainless-steel bucket that hangs loosely suspended under the belly of the cow on a leather belt draped over the middle of the cow's back. Dangling on rubber hoses at the top of the machine are four stainless-steel teat cups—one for each teat. Each teat cup is lined with soft rubber so it is comfortable when attached to the cow.

The milking machine is totally pneumatic and is powered through a rubber hose that is attached to a PVC vacuum line running above and in front of each row of cows all the way through the entire barn. The actual vacuum is supplied by a pump, powered by a stationary diesel motor outside of the barn. The flexible rubber hose is attached to a small control box on top of the milking machine, commonly called a pulsater. This ingenious mechanism's job is to convert the constant vacuum in the PVC pipe into a gently pulsating vacuum in the teat cups, in order to emulate the sucking of a calf. After each cow is milked, the machine is taken off, and the top of the milking machine opens so the milk can be poured into a large bucket parked in the middle of the aisle behind the cows. When the milking machine is empty it's moved on down the line to the next cow.

Katie appears to be doing almost all of the milking, and Eli is busy carrying the 65-pound full milk buckets out of the barn and into the milk house. This all happens at a pretty good clip, and there's not a lot of time to spare between when Eli gets back with an empty bucket, and it's time to haul another full one back to the milk house. If he does have a few minutes between hauls, he will jump in and help Katie with the milking, bring more warm water, or do some other small chore, but there is no standing around waiting.

Katie never stops. While one cow is milking out, she swings around on the little stool she sits on and starts to prep the next cow. First she thoroughly washes and dries the cow's udder to remove any debris that might get into the milk. She takes her time with the washing and drying, because massaging the udder helps the cow relax and let down her milk once the machine is attached. Next, she carefully places each teat, one by one, into a bottle of "teat dip" and dries the teat end with a paper towel. Teat dip is a diluted solution of iodine or bleach that helps to partially sterilize the teat end so the milk finally getting into the milking machine is as clean and germfree as possible.

After the milking machine is removed, she post-dips each teat once again in the solution and carefully dries the small opening of the teat end with another paper towel. The post-dip really is about cow health, not milk quality. In the few minutes right after a cow is milked, she is particularly vulnerable to germs that can enter the end of the teat and cause mastitis, a painful inflammation of her entire udder. The post-dip helps ward off these nasty germs. Katie, completely focused on the milking procedures, is relaxed and moves smoothly from cow to cow, and from what I can see, she's a real pro.

On his next round of milk bucket hauling, I decide to follow behind Eli and watch him do this part of the milking chores. I have to hurry to keep up. At the other end of the barn, the little girl holding the kitten slides a pink plastic dish out in front of her with her toe and quietly says something to Eli in Pennsylvania Dutch. Eli's shoulders relax as he stops, pours a splash of warm milk into the dish, pats his daughter on the head, and then hurries off to the milk house.

As Eli strides away, Chip pounces out of nowhere and shoves his muzzle into the milk. Still holding the kitten in one arm, the little girl pulls on Chip's collar with all her might and sternly commands "no." But it's no use. Chip laps up the last of the milk, just as Eli disappears into the milk house. Defeated, she lets go of the dog's collar and stares mournfully at the little ball of warm gray fur in her tiny arms. Her features slowly harden into a stone sculpture of painful resignation. From my old-man vantage point, I'm certain Eli will happily splash more milk into the dish on his next go-round. But in the dejected eyes of this little girl, there's little hope.

A few steps later, I'm standing next to Eli watching him pour the milk in the bucket through a filter and into the large, stainless-steel bulk refrigeration tank. He's standing on two wooden steps to get high enough to tip the warm milk into a large metal bowl, with a paper filter fastened in the bottom. This bowl, with the filter, sits on top of a circular opening in the top of the bulk tank. I stand aside and watch as the milk slowly swirls around and drops into the tank. He is done with this bucket and starts to back down two steps. "You might want to put a little more milk in that cat's dish next time you go by."

"How come?"

"Well, the dog got to it before the cat could, and I think your daughter might be a little upset."

It takes a few seconds for the words to sink in. Eli's face relaxes and he laughs quietly, shaking his head. "Chip can be a nuisance."

On his next trip Eli pours a little more milk into the dish. But this time he shoos the dog away first and waits long enough for the little girl to position the kitten in front of the bowl. He then turns to stand guard against the greedy canine. Problem solved, and once again all is right with the world.

For the next half hour or so, I follow Eli as he carries milk back and forth across the barn floor. In order to pour the milk into the tank, he needs to climb up two steps and then hold the bucket about chest high as he pours. "That looks like work, Eli."

"Yeah, when my dad helps he complains that the tank is too high."

"You could add another step."

"Oh, I suppose I could, but I'm used to it now."

"Give it a few years, Eli. I'm betting you'll build another step."

"Well, yeah, I suppose I probably will."

A few minutes later, I'm back at the tank watching Eli once again pour the milk, but this time something is wrong. The milk in the bowl on top of the tank is barely trickling through. Eli stops pouring and waits for the milk to go through. After a little while he shakes the big bowl and the milk goes down a little faster, but nowhere near fast enough. He looks in my direction, and I just shrug. We both know what the probable culprit is. When the last of the milk finally disappears into the tank, Eli removes the paper filter, and our suspicions are confirmed. The surface is clogged with viscous globs of clotted milk. The diagnosis is complete: one of the last few cows milked has mastitis.

He replaces the filter with a new one, pours the last of the milk in the bucket through, and walks back into the milking barn to talk with Katie. He tells her about the mastitis and then, pointing to the last three or four cows milked, asks, "Did any of these cows seem jumpy or tender?"

"No, I didn't notice anything, but it probably just started flaring up, or we would've seen it this morning or yesterday."

Cows with mastitis get nervous and jumpy during milking because it hurts. The infected udder becomes swollen, tender, and sore. However, often for the first day or two of the infection the cow isn't bothered enough to make it noticeable for the person doing the milking. That's undoubtedly what has happened here.

Eli says, "Okay, let me see if I can find out which one it is." Katie goes back to prepping the next cow, and Eli begins methodically going down the line of the last four cows milked. He kneels down beside each cow, and using his right hand pulls a few squirts of milk onto his other hand. Then he looks for clots as the milk drips off onto the floor. He does this with all four teats on each cow because mastitis is often confined—at least in the beginning—to just one of the four quarters of the udder. This whole process takes some time and slows down the milking routine. Katie is dumping the full milking machine into the bucket in the aisle by herself, while Eli continues to look for the sick cow. When the aisle bucket is finally full and needs to be taken to the bulk tank, she simply stops milking and waits for Eli to finish.

Not surprisingly, he didn't find any clots. When the infection is just getting started, most of the clots come out in the first few squirts and the rest of the milk is clear. So the clots came out when Katie first started milking, and it only became apparent that something was wrong when the filter paper got clogged. Tomorrow morning she'll repeat Eli's examination of each teat of these four cows by squirting out a little bit of the first milk and looking for clots. It may take them a couple of milkings to isolate the sick cow, but they'll find her and treat her as soon as possible.

Eli looks back over the suspect cows and says to Katie, "We'll just have to watch them." She nods, but by then Eli, with bucket in hand, is already hurrying toward the milk house. Again watching him pour the milk into the tank, I'm curious to know how this farm handles a cow with mastitis. "When you do find that cow, what are you going to do with her, Eli?"

He has a number of choices when she is identified. Some farms immediately remove the cow and send her to slaughter. The mastitis doesn't hurt the meat, the farm recoups the beef price of the cow, and she is no longer in the barn to potentially infect other cows. Other farms will treat the infected udder with antibiotics. This option usually works; however, all of the milk must be thrown away while she is being medicated, and there's a good chance her overall production will go down a little. Antibiotics are expensive and there's also growing concern that the use of antibiotics in agriculture is diminishing their effectiveness in people, so some farmers are trying to cut back their use. Still other farms isolate the sick cow and try to nurse her through the infection without antibiotics. I really have no idea what Eli will do.

"Well, recently, we've been having some pretty good luck with just putting her in a separate stall, and cutting back on her feed. Usually they get over it right away, and we can put them back in the milking string after several days. We try not to treat any of them with antibiotics, but once in a while it's the only choice."

His response seems like a reasonable approach to me, and I make no further comment. Actually couldn't if I wanted to because he's already back in the milking barn catching up on chores. Following him back into the barn, I stop at the heifer pen where Regina is finishing up with the milk replacer. Two young heifers have locked muzzles and are trying to suck the milk out of each other, one's mouth cupped over the other's nose, and the other sucking with all her might on a bottom jaw. Regina slaps both of them on the top of the head at the same time, and they break up. No harm done, just another charming, funny moment.

Things are slowing down and Katie is finishing up the last few cows. Another 20 minutes and the milking is done. The pace settles. The equipment needs to be cleaned and put away; that won't take long, and there's no hurry. Katie gives a few simple instructions to the children, and then both she and Eli come back to the center aisle, where we can all talk.

Katie gets the conversation going. "Well, what do you think? Are we doing everything right?"

"How should I know, Katie? You folks are the experts here. But everything I saw looked fine. Everything is very clean, and the whole process moved along smoothly. I don't know what more you could ask for."

"All in all, we are pleased." Eli says with some confidence, and Katie's head moves in agreement.

"One thing I noticed is the herd seems very calm. There didn't seem to be any kicking. Are you doing anything special? I mean usually at least the new heifers will be kicking."

"We've been working on that," Eli says, "and I think we're starting to get ahead of it."

"Well, what are you doing?"

"About a week or so before a new heifer's going to freshen, we bring her in with the rest of the herd every day, and just let her be there in line while the other cows are being milked. Then Katie and I make it a point to stand beside her, and pat her, so she gets used to being around people. Seems to be working."

"Yeah, it does. Like I say, the herd seemed really calm, and that's a good thing."

It's getting late. We've been in the barn now for about two hours, and they still need to clean the equipment, so as a group we start working our way slowly toward the door at the other end of the barn. I am still interested in knowing a little bit more about how the herd is doing in general. As we shuffle along, I pose the question to both of them. "Other than the little mastitis, which every herd has, how is the overall health of the cows?"

Katie answers first. "Pretty good, I would say. We have an occasional cow get sick with one thing or another, but overall the herd is fairly healthy."

"Yeah, that's right, although this week we've got some problems." Eli takes several steps back toward the herd, points to a particular cow, and says, "This cow right here is probably going to go to the sale on Friday. She's been losing weight and eats very slowly, if at all." He walks over and pats her flank. She doesn't react. "Both the vet and I thought she had a twisted stomach. He operated on her, but that wasn't the problem."

Moving around to the side of the cow, the shaved area of fur and stitched up incision are plainly visible. "Did the vet find anything that might be the problem?"

"Yes, in the end, he did. He had his arm in her side for over an hour, feeling around. He finally found a blockage in her intestines. Said it was real hard and tried to crush it between his finger and thumb," Eli holds out his hand emulating the crushing motion, "but he wasn't optimistic. And she hasn't gotten any better. So, like I say, she'll probably go to the sale on Friday."

The sale he is talking about is the weekly livestock auction over in Bloomfield. Eli will call a livestock truck driver on Thursday to haul her over on Friday morning. She'll be put in the beef pen with the other cull dairy cows and sold for hamburger later in the day.

"Did the vet say he thought it was hardware disease?"

"Probably, but he wasn't sure. She's a good cow. I hate to lose her."

Both Eli and Katie are obviously troubled about this cow. All I can say is "that's a shame" and leave it at that. It really is a shame to see a cow sent to slaughter over hardware disease. It's one of those conditions that is very often preventable. It's caused when the cow eats a piece of metal "hardware." It's not that cows go around looking for a chance to eat metal, but if a wayward nail, a piece of wire, or a bolt happens to find its way into their feed trough . . . well, cows aren't very discriminating.

Now there are at least two ways to prevent hardware disease. The first is to keep metal out of the cow trough. But with hay balers, silage choppers, grain elevators, wagon beds, truck beds, feed grinders, and all the other machinery that comes into direct contact with cow feed, some metal inevitably gets into the system. Unfortunately, even a small piece of sharp metal can potentially wreak havoc on a cow's digestive system.

The second prevention technique is a simple little magnet, about the size of a human thumb. This takes a little planning and forethought, but not much. When a young heifer looks good enough that she might make the grade and join the milking herd, it's time to intervene with the magnet. This generally takes two people—one to hold the heifer's head up high and the other to slide the magnet down her throat with the help of a pill gun. The pill gun is just a long semiflexible shaft with a cup on the end to hold a pill—or in this case the magnet—and a plunger to push the magnet out when it is far enough down her throat that she has no choice but to swallow. It sounds traumatic, but it's over very quickly when done right, and the heifer wanders away as if nothing happened.

Once inside the cow, the magnet settles in one of her four stomachs and stays there for the rest of her life. From then on, any stray metal that she might happen to eat gets caught by the magnet, and is held harmlessly in the bottom of the stomach and out of the rest of the digestive system. Magnets are a beautifully simple solution to a common problem on dairy farms. They are even recyclable. When the old cow is eventually sent to market, the magnet will be retrieved in the slaughterhouse, cleaned, and sold again to be fed to the next heifer in line. Feeding magnets to heifers was common practice in small dairy herds for many years. As herds have gotten larger, it's not as common, and that's a shame. There is no way to know if the cows Eli and Katie bought several months ago to get this herd started had been fed magnets or not. Sadly, it looks like at least this cow was not, and as a result she will die early.

"Are you feeding magnets to the new heifers when they come into the herd?"

Pulling the dull yellow straw hat from his head with his left hand, he brushes a thick shock of black hair off his forehead with his right. "We are now."

Katie and I turn back in the direction of the door, but Eli is walking toward the opposite end of the barn, talking as he goes. We obediently shift directions and follow him to a cow about halfway down the barn. "This cow right here has Johne's and we'll be shipping her to the sale on Friday too."

Looking at her, she's typical of a cow with Johne's [pronounced yo-neez] disease. Ribs ghoulishly outlined by the black-and-white shadows of her loose hanging pelt. Johne's is a sad disease to watch play out. These girls have constant diarrhea and lose weight rapidly. They eat well and have a very good appetite, but because of the disease they are starving. There is no vaccine or medication that seems to help. Farmers do all they can to prevent the disease, but it's spread throughout the dairy industry. It's in the environment and the manure, and it's just plain hard to keep the herd completely Johne's free, particularly when a farm is buying cows and heifers, like the Gingeriches had to do to get this farm started. Fortunately, I guess, this is one of those diseases that strike sporadically. One cow might get it and wither down to nothing, while the cow beside her goes along unfazed for her entire life.

"She just never had enough will." Katie seems to be quietly talking as much to herself as to me. Then she turns to face me head-on and tries to explain. "Even when she was a little heifer and it was feeding time. All of the other heifers would be at the gate waiting, but she would still be back in the field munching grass."

"What's her name?"

"Oh, we've always called her Faul Coo."

Katie must be able to tell by the look on my face that I have no idea what she said, so she explains, "Faul Coo just means Lazy Cow in our language. But she's not lazy exactly, she's just not as pushy as most of the other cows. She won't push her way in for feed or anything. Like I say she just seems to lack will."

"Well, I guess it's time for her to retire." The typical lighthearted banter is gone from Eli's voice. He sounds drawn, maybe even solemn. "She was the best cow in the barn. Wouldn't have taken $3,000 for her. Look at the poor, scrawny thing now."

"I'd say that's about right, Eli. You'd better get this cow off to the market soon, before you end up having to bury her here on the farm."

Again, Katie and I turn in the general direction of the door. But again, Eli has other plans. He takes three or four steps farther down the barn and points to another cow way down on the end. "She has Johne's too, look at her. She freshened and then had ketosis. I treated her like the vet said, but her veins are gone and she's not getting any better. I would've sent her to the sale last week, but because she had antibiotics, she can't go till this Friday."

The cow does look bad. Ketosis is a metabolic imbalance that sometimes happens to cows right after they freshen, and for some reason it often hits the highest-producing cows in the herd. One of the most common treatments that farmers or veterinarians use is a pop-bottle-sized dose of a special solution put directly into the sick cow's neck veins. The results are often dramatic. A few minutes after the treatment the cow is up and eating, as if nothing were ever wrong. Unfortunately, in this case it didn't work, maybe because she also had Johne's disease. In any case, she'll be hamburger by next week.

This time Eli joins us as we turn and slowly walk in the direction of the door. "You folks haven't had the best week here, have you? I mean, three cows going to the sale on the same week can't be good."

Eli's mood seems to lighten and, with a chuckle in his voice, he says, "I just hope we don't lose any more."

Katie agrees and adds, "This really is unusual. Normally the herd is pretty healthy. For some reason things caught up to us this week, but by and large, we've been blessed."

Standing now with one hand on the car door and the other patting Chip's head, I ask, "Do you have any heifers coming up to replace those three cows that are going to market?"

"Yeah, we have several coming along." Eli says.

Katie adds a little clarification. "Actually, we have two heifers that should freshen next week or at latest the week after that. And then there are a couple more that will freshen in the next month or so."

Crawling into the car, I thank them for allowing me to interrupt their milking today. They both wave as the engine starts, and Eli's husky voice drifts through the open window. "Come on back any time."

The sun is low in the sky as I turn north and start the journey back into my Yankee world. I'm struck with how little all of this has changed since I last milked cows, probably 35 or 40 years ago. This coming Friday the Gingerich farm will lose three milking cows out of about 30, or roughly 10 percent of their production capacity. The milk check will take a substantial hit. Fortunately—and this is another secret of Amish farm success—the heifers with babies about to come into the world will soon fill the milking herd void, so the Gingeriches will not have to buy replacement cows. Neither hardware nor Johne's disease prevents a carcass from entering the human consumption market, so the farm will also get a check for the meat of the three soon-to-be slaughtered cows.

In a subtle way, the personality of the barn will change a little bit on Friday morning. The cow with hardware disease and the one on the end with Johne's will slip from the herd with little notice. My sense is, however, Faul Coo, the one in the middle with Johne's disease, the one who lacks "will," is going to be missed, at least for a time. All three will eventually be replaced by new heifers, and life in the barn will go on. Sending cull cows to the slaughterhouse is an economic reality. It is a normal and natural process that the herd must go through to stay healthy. Intellectually, it simply makes sense, but that does not mean it is easy.

In the end, what the Gingeriches went through this week was rough on a number of levels, but they'll get by just fine. There is silage in the silo, grain in the bins, hay in the loft, and healthy young heifers on pasture. More importantly they own the type of business flexibility, creativity, and staying power, which seem to grow best on small family farms. They will be fine.

Around about halfway home a voice from the Economic Analysis Department of my brain squeaks forward to ask, "Could a modern dairy farm do this? Could a firm milking, say, 4,000 cows stay afloat with a 10 percent loss of production? Could they send 400 animal units to the beef market in one week and get by?" There would be financial and logistic turmoil. Just finding 400 new heifers and then locating somewhere near $800,000 in loans to finance them would be a nightmare. Feeding, milking, and shipping schedules would all need radical adjustment. Trimming employee payroll would naturally be a top priority. Once again the voice asks, "Could a 4,000-cow dairy production unit survive this?"

Right then as I pull into my home driveway, a clear, condescending, new voice from way down in the Department of Ethical Reasoning answers, "Could a 4,000-cow dairy make it? . . . Who cares?"

12

The Comfort of Friends

It's simply doesn't seem possible that an entire year has gone by, and Eli and Katie Gingerich are filling the silo for a second winter's cow sustenance. I'm also surprised by how much I'm looking forward to helping again this year. Tonight I will be totally exhausted, and yet I can think of nothing I'd rather do with this day.

There's Eli's farm just ahead on the left. I need to park my car somewhere out of the way, so if the tank truck comes by to pick up milk it won't have to maneuver around my car. Under that big maple tree next to the shop should be just fine. It's 8:30 A.M. as I step out into a warm, sunny morning with a thick blanket of fog in the low spots and some lingering haze on the hills. Noise coming from the barn tells me that Eli is hitching horses and getting ready for the day's work. I round the corner into the open barn door and almost smash my face into the spongy nose of a startled, half-harnessed Belgian mare. Our eyes lock in a moment of mutual surprise and fear. As my heart finally slows down and stops thumping on the walls of my chest, I'm left with a distinctly uncomfortable feeling that the mare, who is now looking around the barn with benign disinterest, recovered from the encounter so very much faster than I did. I can't be certain, but my feeling is this exchange may not bode well for the time when, a few short minutes from now, I'll be expected to pick up her reins and act as if I'm completely in control.

Eli is clipping the harness together on the Belgian's far side and thankfully missed the entire embarrassing episode. "Good morning, Eli."

"Hello, Randy. You ready for another long day?"

"Sure, I can stand it if you can." This is purely feigned bravado on my part. A very large part of my psyche is actually consumed with the fear that some time during this day, I will screw up—big-time. I am hoping against hope that none of the horses temporarily under my control run off and smash some equipment or one of the farmers or me. Mainly, I'm hoping that I'll have the physical stamina to make it through the day, thereby avoiding the embarrassment of admitting that I just can't do it anymore. I decide it's best to temper the bravado by adding, "Well, maybe not. We'll see. What would you like me to do right now?"

Eli laughs, "Actually there's not much to do until we get these horses hitched."

I suppose I should offer to help with the hitching, but I've never really figured out how to properly hitch horses, at least not with confidence. I'd have to ask Eli what to do at each step in the process. Like as not, I'd just be in the way. To me it's always a jumble of singletrees, traces, doubletrees, padded horse collars, levelers, clips, whiffletrees, and reins. Besides, Eli gave me an out by saying there really wasn't much to do now. Gracefully, I dodge the whole hitching conundrum by saying, "Okay, guess I'll just look around the barn for a few minutes."

Chip has already found me. I'm a sucker for most dogs, and cats, for that matter, but I particularly like this dog, and he seems to know it. I pet his head and pat him on the side and try to make my way into the cow barn. He wags his tail and dances around in front of me, so close that I can barely move. I try to ignore him, but this dog is not to be ignored. Finally, he takes his paw and lays it firmly on my foot. I give up, and bend down to give this good dog all the attention he seems to need. After a few minutes, he's finally sated and ready to run off into this morning's next adventure.

The cows are out in the pasture munching grass right now, so the barn is pretty much empty. There are a few young Holstein heifers in a box stall at one end of the barn and at least two black-and-white barn cats that I can see. Jonas Burkholder steps out of the haze and through the backdoor of the barn, wearing his typical smile and the same padded cotton sleeve pinned over his right arm. He looks exactly the same as he did last year at this time. With Eli and Jonas accounted for, the only other farmer missing from this three-farm working circle is David Kempf.

I raise my voice to carry the length of the barn and say, "Morning Jonas."

"Why, good morning, Randy."

"Looks like a fine day for silage making, don't you think?"

"Yeah, I'd say so."

Jonas tends to be a little quiet, always friendly, but quiet, so I let the conversation drop. We'll have plenty of time to talk throughout the day. The metallic click of horseshoes on cement coming from the next room signals that Eli has finished with the harness, and it's time to get started.

Back outside I walk around the team of Belgians and ask Eli what he wants me to do. Before he can answer, we hear a rumble of hooves and the fast crunching of steel wagon wheels out on the asphalt road, as David flies by and waves through the thinning morning fog. He is on his way straight to the cornfield, ready to get this day started, and has no time to stop in the barnyard for idle talk. Eli shakes his head and grins at David's ever-present and irrepressible enthusiasm for farm work. Then, still chuckling, he turns back my way and asks me to ride down to the field on Jonas's wagon. Forty yards away, Jonas is already standing on his wagon, reins in hand, ready to start for the field.

"Hold on a minute, Jonas, I'm going to ride over with you."

He waits patiently as I walk over, crawl up onto the wagon bed, and walk up next to him so I can hold onto the front standard. With a relaxed shake of the reins and a quiet "get up," two tons of horseflesh steps out, and the wagon lurches forward. Even though I've braced myself and I'm holding onto the standard, I still almost lose my footing and go down. A few seconds later, I've regained my balance as the wagon slowly rocks back and forth over the uneven gravel driveway.

Jonas pulls the horses to a stop at the end of the driveway, and we both listen and look down the road as far as we can see. There are headlights coming way off to the south. If we were in a car, we'd pull out, but with the horses Jonas decides to wait. The headlights disappear into a dip in the road and seem to never come out. Finally, after about 30 seconds, I turn to Jonas and ask, "Where'd it go?"

"I don't know."

"Do you think it pulled into a driveway or something?"

"Just don't know, but we better wait to be sure."

Finally the headlights crawl up over the hill down by the cornfield. Now we can tell it's a small blue car going no more than 20 miles an hour. As the car gets closer, the older gentleman driving it waves, and we wave back. If I were in a car right now I'm sure I'd be impatient, maybe even a tad bit irritated, but standing here on the wagon waiting with the horses, it's all okay. It seems as if there's just a little more time in the day and I don't have to rush. I'm not bothered in the least by this trivial delay in the schedule. There is something strangely calming in being transported by real draft horsepower—that is, unless I'm the one holding the reins, in which case I'm generally terrified.

Jonas pulls the team onto the road and turns south. The sounds of the horse hooves and steel wheels change a little as we pull out of the gravel and onto the asphalt. There's still a general rumble, only it's a little less crunchy. After about five minutes, Jonas reins the team into the cornfield and the sounds change again. The steps of the horses turn into dull thuds and the wheels roll quietly over the soft dirt.

Levi is already here. He drove his team of three horses in harness to the field a few minutes before Jonas and I left the barnyard. Now he's hitching the team to the corn binder that was left in the field last night. David is standing nearby talking to him. His wagon and team are waiting unattended about 20 or so yards away. Chip is running back and forth between David, Levi's team, and David's team. Neither David nor any of the horses are paying the first bit of attention to Chip, but that doesn't seem to slow him down at all.

The whole crew—except me—worked in this field yesterday, so about two-thirds of the corn has already been harvested. The center third of the field is still standing. These rows of 12-foot-tall cornstalks are surrounded by rows and rows of six-inch-tall cornstalk stumps. This field is about five acres. There's a slightly smaller field, probably about four acres, directly behind this one. All but a few rows on the outside edges of the back field are still waiting to be harvested.

The few outside rows were cut yesterday to "open" the field and get it ready to be harvested today. Each new field has to be "opened" with a corn binder that does not have the new loader attachment mounted on it. The loader drops the corn about eight feet away from the binder, and at the edge of the field the bundles of cornstalks would likely end up in the ditch, the woods, or the adjacent pasture. Using the binder without a loader, the bundles fall in the row and are picked up by hand later, which allows room for the loader to be used on the inner rows.

These three farms have substantially changed their line of equipment and costs from last year. Before last year's season, each farmer bought a new $1,000 silage loader. In round numbers the loaders roughly doubled each farm's silage harvesting equipment costs. The loader does speed up harvesting, but it doesn't increase yield or number of corn silage acres grown. The acreage is set by available land and silo space. The result is that the addition of the loader increases cost with no corresponding increase in production. So, cost per ton of silage produced goes up, and overall farm profitability goes down.

Fortunately, things happened so fast during last year's silage season that two of the new loaders were never mounted onto binders. They ended up sharing one loader for all three farms. Sharing one binder with the loader worked just fine. At the end of the season in a conversation that was the rough Pennsylvania Dutch equivalent to, "Well, duh—why weren't we smart enough to think of this earlier?" the three men promptly decided to sell the other two brand-new loaders and own the remaining one on "shares," which reduced each farm's cost of ownership for a loader by two-thirds.

Looks like it's time to get started. Levi's three horses are hitched to the binder and lined up on the inside row of standing stalks. Jonas is ready at the back of the wagon. I'm in position, holding the reins of two tensing draft horses. Everyone else seems calm enough, but for me the air is charged with anticipation that would rival the starting line at a NASCAR track. An imaginary flag drops. Dual "getups" sound, and we're off. Levi holds his team straight down the row and the binder spits bundles onto the loader and up to Jonas's position. I look down over the backs of this magnificent pulling team and realize that . . . Oh no, the one on the right is "lazy Mack" from last year, and he is already half a step behind Mike, who is now doing most of the pulling. So much for the races. Reality has set in.

Same as last year, I do know what is needed. I'm to take the ends of the reins and slap them sharply across to Mack's rump. Same as last year, I lack the requisite courage needed to startle old Mack with that slap on the rump. Same as last year, poor Mike will be doing most of the work all day. At least I'm at peace with it. I know from the very beginning that I'm not going to slap Mack. I offer a silent apology to Mike, and shake the reins to speed him up a bit.

Levi's team sets the pace, and it's fast. Bundles of corn fly up the loader into Jonas's waiting arms. He barely has time to throw one bundle on the stack before the next one is ready to fall. My job is to keep the loader chute between Jonas and the corn stacked on the wagon. That means as the wagon is loaded, the chute needs to move slowly forward toward the front of the wagon. My team starts out a few paces ahead of the team pulling the binder, but by the time we get to the end of the field and the wagon is full, they will need to be behind the other team. To do that, I need to almost constantly pull back on the reins, to slow the team down—or in this case, to slow Mike down, since Mack is only along for the ride.

In what seems like less than 10 minutes, we are coming to the end of the field, and I am completely entombed in an eight-foot-tall mass of cornstalks, pressing me hard against the front standard of the wagon. Jonas is still throwing more bundles on top. We reach the end of the field, and I hear Levi mercifully call out, "Whoa." I do the same, and the wagon rocks forward and settles to a stop.

Clawing my way out of this cramped chlorophyll crypt, I slide off the side onto the ground and start walking toward David's waiting wagon. Levi's team passes on my right going at a pretty good clip. I break into a trot and jump onto David's wagon, just as Levi pulls into position. David hands me the reins as Levi says, "Get up." With a shake of the reins, the team in front of me moves out. I remember these two Percheron horses from last year. Mare on the left, gelding on the right, a beautiful team, and at least for me they're by far the easiest to handle. Before I really get my bearings, we're already half loaded.

At the end of the row, I jump down and immediately start out in a half-trot toward Eli's wagon. Levi still beats me over and starts cutting as I jump on Eli's moving wagon. He throws me the reins as the horses run into position. Eli barely makes it to the back of the wagon in time to catch the first bundle. The whole operation is a flawless maneuver with no room for error.

After each wagon is loaded, Eli, David, or Jonas runs it back to the barn and unloads the cornstalks into the silo. As soon as it's unloaded, they trot the horses back to the field and immediately get into position for the next load. The pace Levi and the other guys have set is definitely faster than last year, and way outside of my comfort zone for driving horses. Nevertheless, my job is to keep up, and thankfully so far, things are going okay.

Seven loads later, and we haven't stopped at all. Finally Eli says it's time for break. It's only now that I notice all of the fog has burned off. It is mid-morning, sunny, and at least 80 degrees. This is unusually warm weather for this time of year. Fortunately, there's a fairly strong breeze to keep the horses and us a little cooler. But both the horses, and people in this field, are sweating and panting hard enough. It is definitely time for a break.

A Tupperware container full of homemade cookies and doughnuts, all with maple frosting, sits on the ground at the edge of the field, nestled between two large thermoses, one with cold water and the other with pink Kool-Aid. Somehow, Katie was able to miraculously slow down one of the wagons back at the barnyard long enough to send out these refreshments. We're all a little tired, but the work is going very well, and the mood is upbeat as we munch and gulp away. David has been teasing Levi all morning about a small, padded, black vinyl seat on the corn binder. Now that there's a pause in the work, Levi explains the seat with exaggerated hand gestures and voice tones. "I found that little chair at the shop. I have no idea what it came off of, but I figured I could put it to good use. So this morning I came over early and bolted it on top of that hard old metal seat."

"Okay," David says, "we just don't want you getting soft on us."

The little vinyl seat does look comically out of place mounted on the antique corn binder, but it has to be more comfortable. Levi is more than willing to take a little ribbing to keep it.

Eli hauled three five-gallon white plastic buckets of water back from the barn on his last trip to the field before the break. He already watered his team back at the barn. David takes one bucket and waters his team. Levi takes another for the team pulling the binder, and Jonas grabs the last one for his team. Everything is going fine until Jonas's second horse decides he doesn't like this water and won't drink it.

Horses can be finicky and definitely stubborn, and it's not unusual for one to literally turn up his nose at the taste of water from a strange barn. Jonas keeps trying to entice the horse by putting a little water on his hand and rubbing it on the horse's nose. Finally he picks up the buckets and dips his muzzle in it. The animal rears back and absolutely refuses to drink any of it. It's a hot day, and it is important for Jonas's horse to drink and stay hydrated.

Jonas decides to let things bide for now. Chances are good that by noon the horse will be thirsty enough to drink any water put in front of him. It's worrisome, though. Jonas will watch him closely when he puts this horse into the barn for the midday break. The horse will have to drink then, or he could die working in the hot afternoon sun. If he still refuses to drink at noon, there's a harmless remedy. Jonas will simply take a dab of any common drugstore variety of mentholated cream and smear it on the horse's nose. The menthol masks the smell of the water, and the result is amazing. In a matter of seconds, a horse that has refused to drink will plunge his face into the same bucket and drink like there's no tomorrow. It's simple, it's cheap, and it works.

Break's over, and it's time to get back to work. Eli pulls his team into position next to the binder and gives me the reins. The palms of my hands are red and raw from the constant tugging of these thin leather control straps. I briefly consider repositioning the reins somehow to ease the pain, but with a quick "get up" Levi has started his team, and the binder is moving. I shake the reins in my hands, give a quiet command to the horses, and we are off. But something is desperately wrong. I can't steer the team, and I can't slow them down. The loader chute smacks loudly into the back wooden standard of the wagon. In unison Eli, Levi, and I scream, "Whoa!"

All five horses stop on a dime. Thankfully, neither the loader nor the wagon is damaged. Eli spots the problem, hops off the wagon, walks up to the team, and untangles one of the reins from a clip on the harness. A more experienced horseman would probably have had the presence of mind to stop the team verbally, before the loader and the wagon collided. Feeling more than a little sheepish, I announce to Eli as he crawls back on the wagon, "You can fire me if you'd like, you know."

"Fire you? No way. Any more trouble and I'll let you load."

His lighthearted and completely idle threat—we both know I couldn't keep up with the loader—restores my confidence. While I am not the best horse driver, I'm good enough. Besides, I'm the only game in town. There's simply no one else available to do this job today. Eli is ready. Levi starts his team, and I sharply flap the reins over the horses' backs and move them out with a strong "get up."

The rest of the morning speeds by without a major glitch or a break in the pace. A couple of times I'm able to grab a swig of water on the fly, but that's it. Just before noon, we stop for the morning. Levi unhitches his three-horse team from the binder and starts to walk them back down the road to the barn. I ride back with Jonas on the 16th, and last, load of the morning. He pulls the team and wagon up next to the silage chopper and stops.

It's beastly hot and I'm sweaty and tired, but I know that Jonas has worked a lot harder than me this morning. It takes all the will I have to say, "Jonas, let me take care of this load while you unhitch the horses."

He doesn't argue, "Well, okay, if you're sure."

"Yeah, go ahead."

Jonas gets down and walks back between the steel wheels of the idling John Deere 70 tractor. Climbing into the seat, he pulls the throttle down to maximum. The cylinders roar, and he releases the hand clutch for the PTO pulley on the side of the tractor. The long drive belt, connecting tractor to chopper, lurches forward, bringing to life the clattering cogs, sprockets, and gears of the rusty, old silage chopper.

With each corn bundle thrown on the metal conveyor belt, the machine groans and rattles as the butt-ends of the stalks hit the chopper blades and are cut into millions of ¾-inch pieces, before being blown up the long pipe into the top of the silo. As if in compassionate empathy, the tractor, too, groans with each load the chopper has to bear. The powerful roar of its motor swells and then subsides as the chopper struggles to cut stalks and then rests, waiting for the next bundle.

Alone on the wagon, I can set my own pace for this job. But mostly I keep my head down and feed bundles into the throat of the chopper as fast as it can swallow them. Finally, sweating like a worn-out pig stuck on an up-slope treadmill, I lift the last bundle from the wagon and throw it into the waiting jaws of the machine. Just as the chopper finishes digesting it, the tractor motor slows. Looking up, I see Eli on the seat, getting ready to turn it off. Tractor, belt, and chopper all rumble to a stop, and we are for a moment utterly surrounded and becalmed by soothing, restful silence.

Levi, David, Eli, and I take our time and meander up the cement walk to the back of the house and into the mudroom. We sit on various stoops, chairs, and ledges around the room, loosening the laces on high-topped leather work shoes, and then line the shoes up under the pegs for our hats. In turn, we each wash hands, arms, and faces in an old utility sink in the corner of the room.

Jonas comes in from the barn when we are all just about done and ready to go inside. He stayed in the barn to see if his horse had changed its mind about the taste of the water. David asks, "Did that stubborn horse of yours finally drink?"

"Yeah, he sniffed at it awhile and must have decided it was alright because he drank plenty. I think he finally got thirsty enough that it didn't matter what the water tasted like."

Everybody laughs a little, but really we're relieved. A little menthol on the nose wouldn't hurt the horse, but it's always best if they decide to drink on their own. Following Eli, we file up three steps into a kitchen saturated with wonderfully thick, exclusively homemade smells. Katie half turns from tending the stove and tells everyone to "just sit anywhere."

The expectations of my taste buds and cavernous stomach are tempered with a healthy dose of dread. I have a muscle disease called Essential Tremor that is somewhat akin to Parkinson's. I shake. Most of the time I can hide it, but at a dinner table, it's tough. Try eating a spoonful of chicken noodle soup with a startled gerbil duct-taped to your wrist sometime. Actually all of the people here today know about my shaking. It gets a little worse every year and waxes and wanes in intensity. Unfortunately, for whatever reason, it's much worse right now. For a fleeting moment, I consider excusing myself and saying I need to drive back to the office and I'll see them after lunch. That's lame and rude, and I won't do it to these kind friends.

Throughout my entire life and particularly in my professional career, I've taken pride in my ability to hide the tremors from almost everyone. However, as they've gotten worse, I've taken to simply telling people that I shake and not to worry about it. About four years ago, I was having dinner in the home of another long-time Amish friend. It was a shaky day and I just couldn't hide it, so I timidly told the family not to worry, I just have a little muscle disease.

With absolutely no artifice, my farmer friend looked across the table and said, "We noticed that 15 or 20 years ago. Thought maybe you were just nervous, but we didn't know."

I felt profoundly stupid. I'd been painstakingly hiding my inability to control my muscles for 20 years, and they knew all along. They were simply too kind to bring it up. All I could do was laugh and minimize it by saying, "No, no, it's just a minor hereditary disease that gets a little worse each year."

Again, he looked straight into my eyes with honest sincerity and said, "That must be hard. My father was a cripple like that. He had a deformed leg and couldn't walk right. I think he was always, kind of, you know, embarrassed by it."

My friend meant no harm. He does not have an e-mail address, does not watch TV, or listen to the radio and could not possibly know how politically incorrect the word "cripple" has become. But it is accurate and—probably because of the compassion in his voice—oddly comforting. I have been grateful to him ever since because he gave me a box to stuff this silly disease in. However, right now I've somehow got to control my shaking long enough to get through Katie's scrumptious dinner.

Katie is doing a little last-minute stirring and transferring large bowls of food over to the table. All the while she keeps a running dialogue with the whole group. Talking mainly about the weather and asking how the morning's work turned out. When everything is ready, she rustles us to the table with large inward swoops of her arms and a welcoming, "Come on, sit down, and eat before things get cold."

Eli sits at one end of the table and Levi at the other. I take the first place on the side next to Levi. David sits down to my right with Jonas next to him on the other end of the bench. Across the table, Katie picks up her little daughter standing next to her and puts her in a booster chair, overlooking an empty bowl and a spoon. Finally, Katie sits down next to Eli and we're ready to eat. Eli looks around the table making eye contact and then bows his head. After a few moments of silent grace, he clears his throat and prayer is over. As our heads rise, Katie takes charge again. "Well, just dig in," she says.

A huge bowl of steaming mashed potatoes—which happen to be my favorite food, bar none—is passed around. No problem here. I anchor my forearm on the side of the table to hold the bowl steady and confidently spoon a healthy portion onto my plate. Next comes a serving bowl filled almost to the top with succulent, silver-dollar-sized hamburgers in a lake of rich, hot, brown gravy. As the bowl moves from Levi's hands to mine, the placid gravy is magically transformed into a choppy, angry, churning pond about to slosh over its banks. Fortunately, Levi has the presence of mind not to let go, thereby saving both of us from what was sure to be a decidedly unpleasant gravy bath. As I release my grip, the gravy returns to its naturally placid state.

I feel my ears turning bright red as I glance into Levi's startled eyes and motion for him to just set the bowl down beside my plate. Dipping a now wildly shaking serving spoon into the gravy, I feel the table tense as each person slowly realizes that they may be the one, chosen at random, to have a steaming glob of brown gravy flung at their face. In an act of kindness mixed with self-preservation, David says, "Here, let me get that." Reaching across my plate, he picks up the bowl and says, "Just say when."

A collective sigh of relief drifts across the table. After a couple of spoonfuls, I nod and thank David. Levi passes a bowl of creamed corn directly to David. He scoops some on my plate without saying word. There's a dreadful, awkward silence that Katie mercifully breaks. "I baked the bread this morning. It's still a little warm." The bread is safe food, with little to no chance of any random flinging. She passes the basket around followed by butter.

Eli says something about the weather being good, and everyone agrees. The table becomes a hum of lively small talk. I put all of my concentration and effort into eating as fast as I can. My forearm is anchored onto the side of the table for stability. The arm slides down, bringing the edge of the table toward my wrist in order to move the fork to the plate. Then it slides up so the table is near my elbow and the fork hovers in front of my chest. Now I bend my head down and retrieve any food that hasn't already shaken off the fork. It's painfully slow going, and there's no way I'm going to finish with the rest of them.

Everyone is done and politely waiting on me to finish. Eli's daughter has crawled into Daddy's lap and is giggling as she plays with his thumb. I urge Katie not to wait for me, saying I'll catch up. She hesitates then walks across the kitchen and brings back chocolate cake, cottage cheese, a large bowl of cut fruit, and a pot of steaming hot coffee. Still working on the main meal, I pass on dessert.

David asks, "Coffee?"

At first I think he must be joking, but realize he is not, and the coffee does smell good. I ask him to pour half a cup and hope I can get it to my lips.

Dessert is over and I'm still only about two-thirds done with what's on my plate. The other folks around the table are trying to stretch out the last of their coffee. Still very hungry, my fork goes down, and I thank Katie for a delicious meal. Following Eli's lead, we bow our heads for a short silent prayer in which I earnestly thank God that this ordeal has come to an end. Dinner is over.

Eli is anxious to get started. He slides his chair back, grins at the crew, and asks the mock question, "You guys ready to get back at it?" There really is no choice. It's his farm and he's in charge today.

We all chuckle and Jonas says, "Not really, but there doesn't seem to be another good option."

13

Horsemeat for Breakfast

It's about six o'clock and I'm at home working on breakfast. I am totally focused on what is usually my favorite meal of the day, and my wife, Barb, has learned not to interfere. She calls me the "Breakfast Maestro" and will join me with her cold bowl of drippy, crunchy, highly processed cereal when I'm just about ready to eat.

It is not a shaky day so I go to work on a whole symphony of flavors. This morning the refrigerator has yielded one of my favorites: leftover mashed potatoes. I scoop two tablespoons into a Pyrex custard cup and pop it in the microwave for 50 seconds. Next I spin around to complete the petite green salad I have already started. Just some leaf lettuce, a little cucumber, some onion, a single cherry tomato (all from our garden), balsamic vinegar, a wonderful olive oil, cracked pepper, and a little salt, topped off with a couple of pieces of mixed dried fruit and just a few small strips from a slice of prosciutto.

The salad's done. A slice of local artisan bread is starting to brown in the toaster, and the microwave beeps. I pull out the hot mashed potatoes, grab another clean custard cup out of the cupboard, put a little water in the bottom of the cup, and pop it into the microwave. While it's heating, I grab an egg (bought yesterday from Mose Barkman) out of the refrigerator and pour steaming water into the teapot with a bag of Earl Grey. The second custard cup is boiling so I crack in the egg and put it back into the microwave to poach for about 50 seconds. Pour some orange juice and get out a jar of local honey for the tea. The microwave and toaster go off at almost the same second. Now all I need to do is flip the egg in the water to finish cooking it, drain it, dump it over the mashed potatoes, grind some black pepper and salt over the egg, butter the toast, add two dried olives to the plate, and—ahh—my little breakfast is ready.

As if by magic, Barb has appeared across the table with her bowl of cold milk, fruit, and cereal. I am perennially amazed that she can eat that stuff. It must be said, however, that she looks decidedly less frazzled than I feel as she serenely crunches away.

As is our custom over breakfast, we are talking and listening to the news on NPR. There's a story on the ongoing political insecurity and terrible loss of both American soldiers and Iraqi civilians. Really not much to say here. We've been over this sad ground for far, far too many mornings. Mostly we just shake our heads as our country numbly "stays the course."

There are a couple more stories about the economy, the deficit, and homeland security. Then an interesting, although very short, story on horsemeat dribbles out of the speakers. It seems the U.S. House of Representatives has passed a bill banning the slaughter of horses for human consumption. The story specifically addresses human consumption. Presumably if the bill passes the Senate, it will still be fine to grind horses up for dog food or those delicious kitty treats that cats adore. The message is clear: horsemeat is okay for pets, but keep it away from the table—and not only U.S. tables but all of the tables on this ethnically diverse globe.

Even though I knew this legislation was pending, and even though I know its chances of getting through the Senate and signed into law are extremely remote, my blood pressure still spikes. I calm myself with a large spoonful of mashed potatoes and egg and try to focus on the fact that this stupid bill will go nowhere. But its mere passage in the House means a lot of the damage has already been done.

It's hard to get reliable data, but probably somewhere around 30 to 50 horses leave Geauga and the surrounding counties each week, headed for a human dinner plate somewhere in the world. These are mainly younger horses that are, for one reason or another, simply not fit for farm work or recreational riding. Maybe the animal's feet are set too wide and it has an awkward paddling gait; maybe it's pigeon toed; maybe the hock joint (hind leg knee) is puffy and set at the wrong angle; or it's swayback; or maybe it's just plain too mean to be around. So the question is: what do you do with an unfit horse that nobody wants?

Obviously, the House of Representatives believes one of the best solutions is for everyone to take one of these animals home as a pet. Just back one of the SUVs out of the garage and put in a horse. If you're frugal, you can probably feed it for just $600 or $700 a year. Of course then there's the farrier to keep it shod and an occasional veterinarian visit. Oh, and don't get rid of that SUV; you'll need it to haul out 25 cubic yards of manure and bedding each year. That is, unless you adopt a draft horse; they poop about twice as much, so you may need to consider a larger SUV. Horses can live around 30 years. Still, some early funeral planning is helpful. Pick out a spot in the backyard where the backhoe can dig a huge pit to bury the aged equine. Then be ready to gather friends around the pit, join hands, and pray the decomposing carcass doesn't contaminate the entire community's potable water system.

Well, on second thought, it might be okay to allow people around the world to eat unwanted U.S. horses—and we'll all just try not to think about it too much.

Most of our local unwanted horses are eaten in French-speaking Quebec or Europe. Some might end up in Japan or other Asian nations—or almost anyplace else on the globe. It is only the uptight, predominantly British heritage of our forefathers that keeps horse off of most U.S. menus, while the rest of the world is happily perfecting recipes.

The human consumption market is extremely important to farmers and the horse industry, because it sets the economic floor, or lowest price, for horses in the United States. At almost any livestock auction where horses and other animals are sold, one or more meat buyers will be on hand. When a horse is brought into the sale ring and the bidding begins, the meat buyers will generally wait on the sidelines. Only after the other buyers have looked over the animal and decided not to bid—because it is for some reason unfit for pleasure riding or farm work—do the meat buyers start to bid. The meat market price typically sets the floor price at a livestock sale. Horses that are fit for farm work or riding will almost always be bid up above the meat price, by someone who wants a draft, buggy, or pleasure horse. The system works.

Again, this ill-conceived piece of legislation will probably not become law. Therefore, there will continue to be a much-needed market for the horses. But that does not mean passage of the bill in the House was harmless. No, with the passage of this arrogant piece of legislation the U.S. House sent a strong message to the horse-eating world. We—the people who brought you the Iraq War, the people who will do almost nothing about global warming, the people who manipulate global food prices for the benefit of our factory farms—have looked down our collective nose and decided that we don't like your values. Yeah, yeah, sure, the vast majority of the world sees no moral or ethical problem with eating horses; but we're so much better than that. Besides, we need to keep all of that scrumptious horsemeat for our pampered pets.

From time to time, when I'm in a cynical mood, I find myself thinking that the folks in Congress do almost nothing of importance. Ahh, but they do; even with this seemingly trivial bill, they have managed to offend and further alienate most of the rest of the world.

• • •

A couple of weeks have passed since the U.S. House passed the moronic bill on horse slaughter. Fortunately, as predicted, the Senate has not taken up the bill, and it has not become law. There's a festive mood on the Geauga County Fairgrounds this morning because the 27th Lake Erie Draft Colt Sale is happening today. Like most of the rest of this crowd of several hundred gathered in the livestock arena, I won't be buying or selling any of these giant workhorses today. I'm an observer, here to say hi to dozens of friends and to enjoy the excitement of a world-class draft horse auction. There are a handful of Yankees, but the bleachers and alleyways are mostly packed with Amish men, women, and children.

There is at least a chance I'll run into Eli Gingerich here today. When we were making silage a little over a month ago, he mentioned that he was thinking about possibly getting one more draft horse. Back when we did the original budget for his farm, we talked about the possibility of needing another horse. He has four draft horses, which is okay most of the time, but in the spring it's nice to be able to put together a five-horse hitch for plowing. It would be good to see Eli, but really, even if he is here today, I may not run into him; this crowd is pretty thick.

Looking across the crowd, I guess that maybe half of these people are from the Geauga County Amish settlement. The rest are from settlements all over the country, and probably a few are from Canada. Groups of neighbors from other settlements who rode in on the same taxi van generally sit together on the bleachers, forming small clusters of people who are dressed ever so slightly different from the clusters of folks from other settlements. It's hard to tell exactly where most of them are from. Across the way, there's a group of five young men without beards, which means they are neither married nor the head of a household. They're wearing blue vests with a variety of shirt colors and really wide-brimmed, stiff straw hats. Those hats look like they just might be visiting from the Lancaster settlement in Pennsylvania.

The guys next to them have black straw hats with short brims that come almost to a point in front—could be Old Order Mennonite or New Order Amish. We have a group of New Order Beachy Amish right here in the county. The Beachy Amish own and drive cars, but they sometimes still farm with draft horses. Over by the door there's a small group of older men in straight, dark-blue jackets and wide-brimmed black felt hats. They look familiar and very conservative. Unless I miss my guess, those are the "Nebraska People" from a small settlement only 15 or 20 miles from here over in Ashtabula County. They could be Swartzentrubers from down in the Ashland County area, but I doubt it. Swartzentrubers are extremely conservative and don't like riding in cars unless it's absolutely necessary, and there are draft horse sales a lot closer than this one. Undoubtedly, a fair portion of the crowd is from the settlement in Holmes County, Ohio. It's the largest settlement in the world, and it's only about 100 miles south of here, so it should be well represented.

Counting the front and back covers, the five-by-eight-inch sale catalog is 100 pages long. It lists not only the horses and their pedigrees but tons of other information. In the back there is a directory of northeast Ohio draft horse breeders and a list of consigners who have one or more horses offered for sale at this auction. Other pages give the rules and regulations, along with who's working on the auction floor today, and the sale "terms" including, "Strangers should bring suitable bank reference or certified checks."

There are also many, many ads. You can buy horse collars, ropes, halters, water cups, thermometers, heating stoves, and Belgian horses at Maplebrook Tack & Harness on Georgia Road in Middlefield. Feed, seed, and coal from the Dorset Milling Company. Mel's Shoes and More, over on Burton Windsor Road, is offering straw hats, gloves, socks, harnesses, and Horsemen's Pride minerals. The *Draft Horse Journal* out of Waverly, Iowa, has both one- and two-year subscriptions, and at least three local sawmills will buy standing timber. Byler's Belgian and Dutch Harness Studs and the Middlefield Banking Company, with offices in Middlefield, Chardon, Garrettsville, Mantua, and Orwell, both have full-page ads. The Middlefield Banking Company is locally owned and highly respected. It does a lot of business with the Amish community, and it's not surprising they would advertise at this event.

Most of the catalog is devoted to highlighting the horses. They are listed in groups and sold in order. The first group is made up of 6 Percheron stallions, followed by 12 Belgian stallions, then 25 geldings (castrated males), 13 grade stallions, 3 grade mares, 18 Percheron mares, and finally 63 Belgian mares. The grade animals and the geldings are unregistered. All the rest of these animals are, or can be, registered with their respective breed associations and can be used as breeding stock to produce more registered animals.

The mares might be used for breeding or farm work or both. Many farmers never have their grade draft horse mares bred because they lose a season of work during late pregnancy. However, almost all of these mares are registered, and they will likely produce valuable foals some time in their life. In fact, many of them are pregnant right now, and that increases their value. Most stallions are seldom used for farm work. They are just too darn unpredictable and dangerous to be let out of a secure enclosure. Geldings are obviously of no use in a breeding program, so they are true work animals.

The complete pedigree of the registered mares and stallions, back to their great-great-grandsires and -grandams, is listed in the catalog. Right now the two auctioneers—Lyle Chupp from Shipshewana, Indiana, the third-largest Amish settlement, and Andy Raber from Millersburg, Ohio, the largest Amish settlement—are getting ready to auction off horse #118. She's a Belgian mare from Port Dover, Ontario, named R&L Hazel B. Standing beside the two auctioneers on the raised platform at the north end of the arena, Steve Jones, the pedigree reader from Topeka, Indiana, intones into the microphone that the grandmother of this horse was the All-American Filly Foal in 1989, and her mother was the All-American nominee in 1998.

R&L Hazel B is trotting in front of the potential buyers surrounding the ring. A young beardless Amish man in a green shirt with the sleeves rolled up above his elbows holds onto the lead rope hooked to the harness under her chin and leads her back and forth. Another young Amish man, in a light brown shirt, follows along behind to help keep the horse moving. Hazel B towers over the Amish handler, her huge head swaying back and forth a good two to three feet above his. She is only swinging her long legs into a light trot, but the two hapless, sweating, short-legged humans are pretty much at a full run. Three "ringmen" are strategically placed inside the ring looking out at the audience. Two of these guys are Amish and one is a Yankee. Their job, once the bidding starts, is to watch for a hand to go up or head to nod, indicating a bid has been offered. When they see a bid, they shout so the auctioneer knows to raise the price once again, while the ringmen search the faces of the crowd for the next bid. It all happens pretty fast, and a horse can be sold in well under a minute, seldom more than two.

Hazel B appears to be a solid registered Belgian mare, well muscled with an easy gait. She's not flashy and certainly not a showstopper, but she could be a fine addition to the right breeding farm. The sale catalog says she was born May 18, 2004. There's no mention of her being bred, so the buyers will assume she's "open." As she passes mid-ring for the second time, Lyle Chupp shouts into the microphone, "Let's start this horse out at $1,200. Do I hear twelve hundred? Twelve hundred? Twelve hundred?"

The ringmen are silent; no bids are seen.

Lyle drops the price. "Eleven hundred dollars, give me eleven hundred. Eleven hundred? Eleven hundred?"

Still no bids.

Lyle's voice rattles on quickly, as he drops the price again and again. Finally, at $800 the Amish ringman at the far left side points into the crowd and in a loud, shrill voice yells, "YESSSSS!"

Lyle immediately reverses gears and starts going up. "I have eight hundred. Do I hear eight fifty? Eight fifty?"

"YESSS!" The other Amish ringman on the near right side of the ring has found a bidder.

Lyle asks just once for "nine hundred."

The Yankee ringman jabs his hand at someone in the middle of the right side of the audience and shouts a quick, "YEP!"

At least three people want Hazel B at this price. Lyle jumps to "nine fifty, nine fifty, nine fifty?" No one bids and in less than 10 seconds he drops the asking price to "nine twenty-five, do I hear nine twenty-five?"

The ringman on the far left has his eyes narrowly focused on the man who has been bidding. He recognizes the buyer's single short nod and immediately yells "YES." At nine fifty, the ringman on the near right calls a bid. The price goes up two more times and then stalls at $1,000.

Lyle calls for "one thousand twenty-five, one thousand twenty-five, do I hear one thousand twenty-five?" The ringmen and the auctioneers scan all of the faces in the audience, nervously looking for one more bid. "Going once, twice. . . ." Lyle strikes the wooden gavel sharply on the desk in front of him and says, "Sold, to the buyer on my right for $1,000."

Hazel B is trotting out of the ring toward her new home, as a middle-aged Amish man in the fourth row of the right bleachers holds up a cardboard sign with his bidder number on it. By the time the clerk writes down his number, the next Belgian mare, #119, passes Hazel on her way into the sale ring. It's all over in something less than two minutes.

Mose, a local Amish farmer who also has a dealership for new horse-drawn farm equipment, strikes up a conversation as I walk by his exhibit booth. Two other local farmers stop and join our talk, and I miss the sale of the next few horses. There seems to be a change in the tenor of the crowd sitting around the ring. There's a little more muffled noise, a little more excitement.

The pedigree reader is just starting to tell the crowd about horse #124 as I step up beside the bleachers to take a look. The reader tells the crowd that her mother was Woodland's Vivian and the stallion was UAB Captain's Commander. I don't even try to follow draft horse bloodlines, but many of the people in this crowd do, and they are obviously impressed. This mare's name is Nash Acre's Cindy. She's a four-year-old bred right here in Burton by a local Amish farmer. She is a big, well-muscled, blonde bombshell with a full white mane and tail. Her gait is easy and powerful. In short, she is stunning.

The microphone crackles to life as the auctioneer thunders, "Let's start this horse out at $3,000. Do I hear—"

"YESSSS!" The ringman on the far right already has a $3,000 bid and cuts off the auctioneer midsentence. For the next few moments the bidding is nothing less than furious. Jumping by $500 a crack. Then it abruptly stops at $6,000. No amount of auctioneer prodding or pleading can prompt another bid from the crowd. Nash Acre's Cindy is worth exactly $6,000 at this auction on this day. It's a good price and an exciting moment.

The auction catalog says that Baurley's Molly is "well broke to all farm machinery," and she sells for $1,100. Alpine Acres Rosie only brings $525. I couldn't see who bought her, but that's probably at or near the meat price. More than likely she is on her way to the slaughterhouse. Several other horses bring anywhere from $1,000 to $1,500. The red sorrel, Dutch Creek Lily, fetches $3,400. Two more horses sell near $500, again probably on their way to the packinghouse. The sale ends with the last three horses, each bringing about $1,200.

I never ran into Eli, but all in all this was a very good auction with a total of 141 horses. The prices were all respectable, and some were good. I had a great time seeing friends and soaking up the excitement of the sale, but the most important thing was that the market functioned properly this day. The floor, or bottom price, was set by the meat buyers, and somewhere around 20 of these animals will go to slaughter. For whatever reason, the crowd just didn't think those animals were fit for farm work or a breeding program, and few people are willing to take on a 2,000-pound draft horse pet. In a very few days, the meat horses will likely end up on family dinner tables in some other country. A country with its own values, customs, and mores, which are no better or worse than our own. Like it or not, most of the rest of the world views horses as livestock—edible livestock—and we simply lack the requisite moral authority needed to challenge the culinary belief systems of others.

Thankfully, the ridiculous House bill banning horse slaughter for human consumption did not become law. As a result, this auction was able to return fair prices to the small horse-producing farms, even for those animals that were unfit for farm work. Perhaps most importantly, we did not further alienate the rest of the world by questioning their family diet.

14

Tour the Manure

It's about twenty after seven, and the sun is busy burning the haze off of this morning. Marvin Weaver called me a couple weeks ago to talk about dairy manure, and that's why I'm on my way to his farm today. Marvin has always been a true innovator in the community. Sometimes to the point where he's raised a few eyebrows, but he always manages to stay just within the rules.

His current area of interest for potential innovation is the dairy manure handling systems on Amish farms in this settlement. He is, of course, right on target. When we talked, it only took a couple minutes for me to agree this was one of the more pressing problems on the farms. Back before the settlement allowed milking machines and bulk refrigeration tanks, the number of cows a farm could milk was controlled by the number of people who could be around twice a day to do the hand milking. Most farms had 10 to 15 cows, and the manure really wasn't much of a problem. Dad, or some of the older boys, took a few minutes with a pitchfork after milking and threw the manure into an old wooden manure spreader. It wasn't all that pleasant, but it didn't take long.

The situation changed pretty radically after most of the church districts in the settlement started to allow milking machines. All of a sudden, the number of cows a farm could have was not limited by the number of teat-pulling human hands available twice a day. Cow numbers went up dramatically over a period of one or two years. Instead of 10 to 15 cows, farms were milking 20, or 25, or even 30, still a trivial number of cows by Yankee standards, where hundreds or even thousands of cows may be on a single farm, but nonetheless a huge change for the settlement.

One of the unintended consequences of more cows was more manure, accompanied by more sore muscles and bad backs. It turns out pitching the manure from 10 or 15 cows is no big deal. It's not fun, but it's soon over. On the other hand, pitching the manure from 30 cows is a completely different stinking kettle of fish. Manure handling went from being just another job on the farm to an arduous, unpleasant, giant chore.

I'm really not surprised that Marvin chose to call me when he wanted to talk about manure. By training I'm an agronomist with a PhD in soil chemistry, and it is widely known that my PhD research and dissertation topic was horse manure management. Doing a dissertation on horse manure can lead to a great many jokes and some professional ribbing. But I always figured, heck, a lot of PhDs are horse manure—I just had enough honesty to put it on the cover. Besides, at the time, I couldn't think of anything funnier.

After talking about these manure concerns for a while, Marvin and I agreed that it might be a good idea to set up a little fact-finding tour down to the Holmes County Amish settlement. The Holmes County, Ohio, settlement—which actually encompasses parts of two or three counties—is about an hour and a half southwest of here, and it's the largest Amish settlement in the world. Milking machines have been common in that settlement for many years, and in general most of the church districts seem to be a little less strict when it comes to what farm machinery is allowed. That's not universally true. Some of the church districts are extremely conservative, but we reasoned we might pick up some ideas by visiting some of the more lenient ones.

We contacted Bill, one of the county agents who works closely with Amish dairy farmers in the Holmes County settlement, and he readily agreed to set up a tour for us. We decided to keep it small, just myself and three other people who could fit in my little car. We agreed on a date and decided to ask Eli Gingerich if he'd like to ride along. Marvin also wanted to see if his son Owen might be willing to go, which was fine with me, but Marvin didn't know for sure—his son's a little shy—so we kept a seat open for him just in case. As it nears eight o'clock this morning, I'm just pulling into Marvin's driveway. We've known each other for probably 25 years, and I'm looking forward to spending this day with him. He's an old friend.

It's a long one-lane gravel driveway with corn on the left and a great field of alfalfa on the right. Alfalfa loves dry roots, and the soil in this field is very well-drained sand. Actually the field is part of an old sand ridge left over from a time, some 12,000 years ago or so, when a tongue of Lake Erie covered the land just east of here. In any case, it grows great alfalfa.

There's a gravel pad midway between the house and barn where I pull the car to a stop. Not knowing if Marvin will be in the barn or the house, I start with the barn. Inside chores are done, the floors and manure gutters are all freshly cleaned, and a thin layer of ag slag has been sprinkled on the floor. Ag slag is a coarse ground limestone that sucks up moisture and provides some friction and better footing for cows, horses, and people. Most of the slag will be swept in with the manure at the next chore time and end up getting spread onto the crop fields. The slag is inexpensive, and the fields need lime, so it's a low-tech, common-sense fix for slippery floors.

The barn is empty. All the animals are already out in the pastures to spend the day eating grass. Marvin must be in the house. Meandering along the cement sidewalk that runs between the barn and the house, I'm not sure if I should go to the front door or the side door. Oh well, there's a 50 percent chance I'll get this right. Just as I reach to knock on the front door, a teenage girl steps out of the side one and says, "They'll be right there. They're just finishing getting ready."

"Thanks. I'll just wait up by the car." Should've guessed the side door, but the good news is she said "they," which means Owen has decided to come along. I am delighted that a member of the next generation of potential farmers is taking an active interest in what we are doing today. Standing back at the car, a small furry animal catches my eye. It's running around out in the pasture. It's at least 100 yards away, and I'm not sure if it's a groundhog or a mink.

Marvin steps out the side door and says cheerily, "Good morning, Randy, didn't mean to keep you waiting."

"No problem at all, Marvin. How are you this morning?"

"Good! Besides there's no sense in complaining. It doesn't do any good." He closes the gap between us in a few long strides.

"Now, did Owen decide to come along with us today?"

"Yes, surprisingly he did. He'll be right out."

"Well, good. I am well pleased that he is coming along."

Marvin looks out toward the pasture for a moment and quietly says, "So am I."

"Take a look at that animal out there in the pasture, Marvin, about 20 yards to the left of the cows." He strains his eyes, scanning the area looking for the critter. "Is that a groundhog or a mink?"

"I don't know. Your eyes must be better than mine. I don't see a thing."

"It's out there just to the left of the cows."

Marvin looks again but shakes his head. "I can't see it."

I am blessed with good distance vision, which sometimes can be a little awkward when other people can't make out what I'm looking at. Fortunately, Owen just came out of the backdoor and our attention shifts to him. Before he is halfway down the walk, Marvin raises his left arm and points out into the field. "Can you see that animal out there, left of the cows?"

Owen stops, squints, and studies the field. "There's something out there, but I'm not sure what it is."

After a few more minutes of looking and conferring, we conclude, based on the color of the pelt and the fact that it is moving around right next to a creek, that it's probably a mink. Actually, that was my conclusion, but the exercise took the tension out of the morning. Owen is relaxed and smiling. It's a good way to start this day.

"Owen, are you ready to solve this manure question?" He shakes his head no. "Well, why don't we go over and pick up Eli and see if he can."

He answers with a timid "okay." Marvin gets in the passenger seat, and Owen opens the backdoor and slips in behind his father. Eli's farm is only about 15 minutes away, but there's no good way to get there. It's all back roads. Fortunately, most, but not all, are paved. Marvin and I talk along the way about crops, the weather, manure, and local farming. Owen never says a word.

We wheel into Eli's driveway promptly at 8:30. He comes out the backdoor before I can even get the car turned around and plops himself down in the backseat behind me. "I just barely got ready in time. Had a cow decide to freshen this morning. She's a full week early, but it didn't seem to bother her that I had plans for today."

Marvin asks the ubiquitous question farmers ask after hearing about a cow freshening, "Heifer or bull?"

"Well, now, that's the good news, at least it's a heifer."

If she is sound, the heifer born on this farm within the last hour will be licked clean and nursed by her mother at least once. After that she'll be moved in with a few other heifers and be bucket-fed milk replacer for a while. Then she will move in with the older heifers and spend the next two years or so growing on grass in the pasture and a little grain and hay in the barn. When she is large enough, she'll get pregnant by artificial insemination. Like most local farmers, Eli and Katie don't keep a bull around; they're just too dangerous. Besides, genetically superior frozen semen is readily available and not outrageously expensive. Nine months after she gets pregnant, she'll throw a calf, come into milk, and be given a shot at becoming part of the permanent milking herd, right here in the barn where she was born this morning.

If, on the other hand, Eli's cow had given birth to a bull calf this morning, the story would be entirely different. Within a week, the calf would be sent to auction. There he would almost certainly be bought by a veal farmer, castrated, tied in a tiny stall way too small to turn around in, and live a few miserable months in a semi-anemic state, so at slaughter his meat will be a delicious shade of gray and not healthy blood red. But Eli's cow threw a heifer, so it's a good morning all around.

"Do you have enough room back there, Eli? Or do you want me to move my seat forward a little?"

"No, I'm fine, plenty of room."

"Okay, well let's take off."

Marvin was actually the last one to talk with Bill, and he agreed to meet us at the Ohio State University agricultural experiment station in Wooster at 10:00 this morning. It's just a few minutes after 8:30 now, so we should be right on time. The conversations in the car are lively and varied, but every few minutes they drift back to manure. As crazy as it sounds, that's what is on our minds. For a fleeting moment, I think that other professionals get to go to Power Point presentations in swank hotels and learn about the latest advances in electronic marketing. But no, not me, I'm driving an hour and a half in a cramped car to look at manure, and I wouldn't trade this day with anybody.

As we are passing the tiny town of Wadsworth, Eli mentions that he is "a little surprised we didn't think about going over to the Lancaster settlement in Pennsylvania."

"Well, that would mean a long day's drive over, and another day back, so it would probably take three days total." Marvin explains, "Besides they are all liquid systems over there, and we didn't know how much there'd be to see."

By "liquid systems," Marvin simply means that many of the Amish farms in Lancaster County handle the dairy feces, urine, and wastewater as a liquid slurry. Very little bedding is used so the slurry is kept liquid and will flow easily. Usually it goes from the barn through a pipe and then is stored in a large manure lagoon for several months or sometimes up to a year. These systems are common not only in Lancaster but on livestock farms across the United States. Forty or 50 years ago, they were state-of-the-art innovations in the vanguard of modern agriculture. Even today they are routinely installed on new or expanding livestock farms because they are relatively inexpensive and provide for fairly efficient movement of the manure. Unfortunately, liquid systems are yesterday's news, and they can present major problems not only for the farm but for the surrounding community.

The Lancaster settlement is the second-largest settlement, and in general the rules tend to be a little more liberal than the Geauga settlement. Lancaster started using milking machines back in the 1950s, almost 40 years before Geauga. As herd sizes grew, the farms gravitated toward liquid manure–handling technology. The Lancaster settlement continues to grow, and, as the next generations come on, some of the farms have been split up, so where there was one dairy herd, now there are two. That means more cows and more manure on less land. In round numbers, it takes about an acre and a half and sometimes up to two acres of cropland to use up the fertilizer nutrients in the manure from one cow. Many of these farms no longer have anything like that ratio. When more manure is put on a field than the crops can use, the excess nutrients build up in the soil, which can cause real problems.

When soils get overloaded, the nutrients have a habit of slipping off into little streams, and then bigger streams, and rivers where algae and some other aquatic organisms thrive in the fertilizer-rich broth and completely upset the natural balance of the water system. Sadly, still other aquatic organisms, like fish, can find themselves without enough oxygen and end up floating belly up. It's a mess, and a long-term environmental problem. Certainly, they are not the only contributors, but the farms in the Lancaster settlement have been implicated in degrading the water quality in nearby streams that stretch all the way out to the ocean.

It's a long drive, and we talk about the pros and cons of liquid systems for quite a while. Eli has never been to Lancaster. I've been there several times, and so has Marvin. He was once there in the spring when farms were emptying the lagoons and spreading the manure on the fields. "That whole valley can smell pretty rank, and it can last for weeks." Marvin goes on for a few minutes, emphatically talking about the stench.

Eli listens intently and muses thoughtfully, "That kind of odor could be a real problem where we live. Don't you think? I mean with all the nearby neighbors who don't have farms." Both Marvin and I readily agree. Owen stays quiet. He's listening to every word but so far hasn't offered an opinion on anything. In the end, we all agree that this visit to the Holmes County settlement will probably yield more useful ideas for us than a visit to Lancaster might have uncovered. Time will tell.

Eli and Marvin both have an abundant sense of humor, and the car is constantly filled with lively banter. One topic they keep coming back to is the differences in the various *Ordnungs*, or spoken rules of each church district, among settlements and among church districts within the Geauga settlement. Lancaster is vastly different. They are more "high" Amish, or more liberal; Geauga is more "low." Holmes is somewhat more liberal than Geauga but not as liberal as Lancaster. At least on some issues, Marvin's church district tends to be a little more relaxed than Eli's. There's no judgment in these discussions; it's just a way to characterize what may or may not be acceptable in a particular community. When I was new to in this job, I would not have been a part of these conversations. Now, after all these years, talking about the "rules" is commonplace and comfortable. But I still feel privileged by the community acceptance of my presence and opinions.

The time has gone quickly and we are already in Wooster. Up ahead is the main gate of the experiment station. It's getting hot outside and I think I see Bill standing by his car over in the parking lot. "Guys, is that Bill over there to the right?"

Marvin answers. "I'm pretty sure it is."

In the entire 90-minute ride, Owen has not said a word. I've gotten to know him a little over the past few years. He's a little quiet, much more open to talk one-on-one than in a group. When he does talk, it's worth listening. He's thoughtful, and though our conversations have been limited, he strikes me as real intelligent and completely likable. Given his personality, it's not at all surprising that he chose not to talk. He nodded from time to time and was interested in everything that was being said, but I'm sure being in the car with his father, Eli, and a loud old Yankee man was just a bit intimidating. Hopefully, he'll loosen up and feel more comfortable as the day goes on.

Bill waves as we get near, and I pull the car into the empty space next to his. Let the tour begin!

Bill shakes hands and greets each one of us as we pile out of the car. Over the years, Bill's gotten to know Marvin through different field days and meetings. A few years ago, he actually taught a session on milking systems for Geauga Amish farmers on Marvin's farm. So he knows Marvin fairly well, and, of course, he knows me from years of working together on various projects and educational meetings. Shaking Eli's hand, Bill comments, "You look familiar, but I can't place where we might've met." Eli explains that they met briefly at an educational field day about a year ago.

Bringing up the rear, the youngest of our group finally steps forward. "This is my son, Owen."

Bill is wearing jeans and a blue-and-white checked shirt. He's probably around five ten, maybe six foot, with black hair with a little bit of gray sprinkled about, stocky build, by no means fat, but stocky. Bill pumps the young man's hand with a loud enthusiastic voice, "Good to meet you, Owen, glad you could come along today." It's the perfect greeting. Owen's thin frame visibly relaxes. This should be a good day.

Bill turns back toward the rest of us, and I have a sense it's probably time to get started. "Well, Bill, what do you have planned for us today?" I ask.

"Well, I've made arrangements to stop by four farms, if we can get them all in before you guys need to head back. Thought we'd see two this morning, maybe have lunch in Shreve, and catch the other two in the afternoon."

"Let's see. Eli and Marvin, do you want to ride with Bill? And, Owen, maybe you can ride along with me, if that's all right?"

Everyone agrees to the suggested passenger arrangement, and we pile back into the cars. Bill wastes no time getting out of the parking lot and turning south toward the Wayne-Holmes County line. Owen and I follow 50 yards or so behind. Having Marvin and Eli ride with Bill will give them a chance to talk with the "expert" after each farm visit, and I'm hoping, even expecting, that Owen will break his self-imposed silence since there are only two of us in this car.

Bill's gotten a ways ahead and I need to push a little harder on the gas pedal to keep up. A lot of my colleagues now have GPS devices in their cars, and I am toying with the idea. If I had a GPS, I'd not need to keep up with

Bill. The university would happily buy me one in the name of efficiency, but I'm not sure I want it quite yet. There can be real joy and sometimes important work in being lost. When I was brand-new in the settlement, it happened almost every day. I would find myself walking through some field or barnyard up to an Amish farmer I didn't know to get directions. Always I would learn a little bit about this farmer, the farm, and as often as not, set an appointment for some future visit.

I don't often get lost in the Geauga Settlement anymore, but it still happens when I travel to other settlements. About a year ago, driving around another settlement, I got turned around and became hopelessly confused, irritated, and more than a little anxious. There was an Amish farmer plowing way out in the middle of the field and it took me a good 10 minutes to walk out to him. As I got closer, I could tell by his dress he was probably a Swartzentruber—the most conservative Old Order Amish sect. We don't have this group in Geauga, but I know these people really like to maintain separation from the larger world and I would have preferred finding another farmer. However, I was in a hurry and at this point committed.

As he pulled a team of five Percheron draft horses to a stop, I spread open my palms and said, "I'm lost."

Looking down from atop the plow he slowly shook his bearded head and intoned, "Aren't we all."

No squeaky electronic GPS voice could have possibly redirected my course or recalibrated my day so thoroughly. Suddenly, the day slowed down and there was again time to talk and get to know a little bit about this stranger on the plow. He was interested to learn I was from Geauga. Said he'd "never been to the Geauga settlement. Probably not likely to get there any time soon, but I've heard a lot about it." The Swartzentruber people try not to even ride in cars, and a several-day buggy trip to Geauga is definitely unlikely. We talked on for some time about farming in this settlement and then farming in Geauga. When we parted and I turned to walk back out of the field, I was even more behind schedule, but the exchange measurably enriched my day. All technology comes with a cost; something is gained, but something is almost always lost as well. Looks like my car is probably still not quite big enough to accommodate that GPS, not yet.

After just a few miles, I turn right following Bill into the long gravel driveway of the first farm. A tall man in his mid-40s, wearing a blue shirt and jeans held up by thin black leather suspenders, steps out of the barn as we pull up. Bill bounces out of his car first, followed by the rest of us, and steps over to the farmer to shake his hand. "Good morning, Levi." They talk a couple minutes and then Bill turns toward our group and gives a few details about each of us. Levi's red beard waves back and forth as he moves down the line shaking hands with each new person introduced.

I grab a box of disposable plastic boots out of the trunk and toss them on the hood of the car. Without a word, the group lines up and each person, except Levi, pulls a pair of the thin boots out of the box and slips them over his shoes. Levi probably would not have required the disposable boots, but putting them on is a simple precaution and a courtesy. All of us, especially the farmers, have been in other dairy barns in the last few days. The possibility of a tiny chunk of germ-laced manure stuck in the cleat of a work shoe and falling out to inoculate Levi's barn is an unnecessary and completely avoidable risk. In addition, the Geauga farmers aren't particularly interested in taking bits of this barn's manure back to their herds at home. At the end of the visit these boots will be left with Levi, so he can dispose of them. We will repeat this ritual before and after each farm we visit today.

Inside the barn, Levi, with some prompting by Bill, starts to point out the important features of this farm's manure system. Levi is jovial and easy to talk to, and within a few minutes the whole group, except Owen, is actively engaged in the discussion. The barn has a sloped center aisle with stalls for roughly 20 cows on each side. The whole barn has been cleaned within the last hour, and the cows are out on pasture, so it is easy for us to move around and look at the system. At milking time, the cows stand on rubber mats with their rear ends pointed toward the aisle. Almost no bedding is used and Levi jokes, "That aisle can get pretty messy. You have to wear boots."

After each milking, the manure is pushed out of the back of the barn with a motorized skid steer tractor. Those of us in the Geauga crew look around at each other for a minute, but nothing is said. We all know that a tractor-driven skid steer on a farm would be against the *Ordnung* of most, and quite possibly all, of the church districts in Geauga.

Once outside the barn, the skid steer driver does a 90-degree turn and pushes it into a 24-by-40-foot manure storage building. Out by the building, Levi points to three-foot-high walls of poured concrete and, 12 feet above the concrete wall, a trussed roof with asphalt shingles, held up by six-by-six treated-lumber posts. The floor of the entire building is concrete.

Marvin looks back toward the barn and then at Levi. "Why did you put the manure storage building at a 90-degree angle to the barn? Seems like it would have been a lot easier to put it directly behind the barn so you'd have a straight shot to push the manure."

Levi nods in agreement and takes a minute to gather his thoughts before answering. "Yeah, you're right, it would be easier. But I didn't want to block my view of the back pasture when I'm doing chores or milking. This gives me a chance to keep an eye out there and catch cows in heat. I also didn't want to block the natural ventilation through the barn."

What he explains seems logical enough. Catching "cows in heat" is one of those ongoing passive activities that dairy farmers on small farms need to be constantly attuned to. A cow in heat—meaning she is ovulating and ready to breed—is a hormone magnet if a bull is around. However, most of these farms don't have bulls. Even if they do have a bull, it is unsafe to allow it to wander around the pasture at will. So the bull is usually kept in the barn, and cows in heat are brought to him, or they are artificially inseminated by the farmer.

In either case, someone other than the bull needs to be able to detect when a particular cow is in heat. Normally, if she's not bred within a few hours, she won't get pregnant. If she doesn't get pregnant, she doesn't have a calf and she stops giving milk, which is patently bad on a dairy farm.

Nature is a wondrous, puzzling thing. For some unexplained reason, the "hormone magnet," which is clearly designed to attract bulls, also fires up the engines of other cows and heifers. From his vantage point in the barn, Levi can watch other females lurch up and forward with their front quarters to mount the cow "in standing heat." For a few seconds, the other female will ride her back, looking like an alarmed, wheezing, overstuffed couch with her rear hooves planted on the ground and the front ones dangling aimlessly about midsection of the cow in heat. From a procreation standpoint, this activity is a dead end, but, hey, like I said, nature is a puzzlement, and all the activity does help Levi identify cows in heat and get them bred when the time is right.

Turning our attention back to the manure storage building, Levi says that he believes it is really too big and overbuilt. But he used the government program to build it and had to follow their specs. Again, our Geauga crew furtively glances at each other, because none of the local church districts would allow a farmer to use the government program. The program Levi is talking about is government cost-sharing dollars available through the USDA Natural Resource Conservation Service (NRCS) to help farmers fund environmental improvements on their land. The basic thought is if

Levi better controls the manure management of this herd, the manure is less likely to end up in the creek, and that's a benefit to the entire community. However, the Geauga Amish settlement is historically very uncomfortable entering into close entanglements with the government, and our farmers simply could not use these government funds, even though they would save money and are readily available.

Levi is a gracious host and more than generous with his time. But we need to head on down the road, for there are three more farms we want to visit this day. We've picked up some ideas here and also seen some things that probably won't work in Geauga, at least not now. Back in the driveway, the plastic boots come off, and Levi holds out a brown paper bag for us to throw them in. We say our good-byes, and Bill thanks Levi one more time before we crawl back into the cars and head for the next farm.

Owen is much more talkative with only two of us in the car. In the course of a few minutes, I learn he is 15 and finished school "a year and three months ago." He works on the farm now and likes it, but he hasn't decided for sure that he wants to be a farmer.

I'm struck with how normal and completely appropriate it is for a 15-year-old not to be sure how he wants to spend his working life. "What part of farming do you like best, Owen?"

He answers definitively. "I like working in the fields, you know, the fieldwork, most." Then, almost in the same breath, he reconsiders and refines his answer. "But, actually, I like working with the cows too."

Again, the tenor of the discussion in the car is pretty much the same as it would be with any 15-year-old boy—one minute confident, the next not so sure. In fits and starts, his story develops the halting, exuberant expectation of the future that is the exclusive purview of a young person with an entire life stretched out in front of him. At some faraway level, I'm jealous.

The second farm is only a few miles away, and we are there in minutes. This time two men step out of the barn door as we drive up. Bill introduces the brothers, John on the left and Lester on the right. They are unmistakably brothers. Both look to be somewhere in their early 40s, with blond hair and fairly short-cropped blond beards. They are each about five eight, a little heavyset, but in good shape because of the everyday work on the farm. Lester has on a sky-blue shirt, John's is tan, and both have on the ubiquitous blue jeans held up by suspenders. Neither wears a hat, and they seem genuinely pleased with our visit. Bill again carefully introduces both of the farmers we are visiting to everyone in our group. After quickly slipping on our disposable boots, we follow the brothers into the barn to begin the tour.

Once inside, it's clear this barn has been recently remodeled. The barn structure above us is held together with old, hand-hewn wooden beams, but down here on the ground floor, where the cows are milked, everything is new. Whitewashed cement block walls with supporting steel posts, a clean concrete floor, and large window openings to let in light and ventilation give the entire room a bright, crisp, modern feeling. Lester points to the far end of the barn and says, "Why don't we start down there? We just put on an addition so we can add some cows." The whole group obediently follows Lester to the other end of the barn where a number of new tie stalls have been put in on both sides of the aisle.

Every one of us carefully looks up and down both lines of stalls, trying to mentally calculate the total number of cows that could be tied here for milking. Finally, after an awkward few minutes, Eli has the presence of mind to simply ask. "Lester, how many cows will the barn hold, now that you have the addition?"

"Forty-four."

Marvin quietly poses the question, "Why did you stop there? I mean why not 50 or 60?"

"Well, the way the old barn is designed we really couldn't add too much more. We thought about tearing everything down and starting new, but John and I talked about it for quite a while, and we think this should be enough. I guess we'll see."

The farmers in the group move around the barn looking at various features, while Bill and I are quietly caught up in a conversation about cow numbers. We are both a little troubled about 44 cows and two families. That's only 22 cows per family, and conventional wisdom says it's probably not enough. Way back in my college days, we were taught that a family farm needs about 30 cows per family to make a go of it. And in all these years of working with Yankee dairy farms, it seems that those who stuck somewhere near 30 cows per family seemed to do pretty well. Because of diversification and some other factors, old-style Amish farms have routinely gotten by with fewer cows, but this farm has all the bells, whistles, and expense of a Yankee herd, and we can only hope that 44 cows will be enough for both families.

Stepping over to where the farmers are clustered looking at the particular features of the tie stalls, Bill refocuses the group. "Now why don't you tell us about the manure system you put in here?"

Lester and John take turns explaining the features of the system. The manure is pushed out of the barn using a skid steer with a specially designed scraper attached to the front. They step out the backdoor, and we follow them over to the skid steer and scraper parked beside the barn. The scraper design is simple enough. Basically, it's a little wider so that more of the barn aisle can be cleaned with each pass. It looks like it should work just fine, and the brothers assure us it does.

Behind the barn, the manure is pushed into a small storage area with a roof, a concrete floor, and treated-lumber sides. John explains that every few days they use the same skid steer to load the manure into a spreader and haul it out to the fields. What they've shown us and described is a pretty straightforward, relatively inexpensive cleaning, storage, and spreading system for the manure. Most everything here would probably work fine in Geauga—except that skid steer. Unfortunately, it is plain difficult to imagine how you could make this system work without that skid steer. Still, the construction of a storage shed is interesting.

The morning is getting late, and we slowly start gravitating back toward the cars. Rows of incandescent light bulbs light our way as we walk back through the barn. I know the lights are powered by a diesel generator, but they would not be allowed anywhere in the Geauga settlement. Farmers in Geauga use kerosene lanterns to light the milking barn. Ohio law is quite specific, and the milk inspector will insist on one lantern for every four cows. The number of cows per lantern is a long-standing compromise that the state uses to accommodate the Amish prohibition against electric lights. It's true that some Amish areas—like this one—don't have a problem with generator-powered electric lights. But some other areas, like Geauga, won't use them, and one lantern per four cows still works just fine.

We are outside in front of the barn and it's just after noon. John holds a plastic garbage bag open for us to throw our boots into. After a few more minutes of discussion, thank-yous, and good-byes, we get back in our cars and head off in the direction of lunch.

Owen is positively talkative back in the car. We talk about both of the farms we've seen this morning. He is particularly interested in the skid steers and the cow stalls. I bring up the electric lights and he says, "Yeah, I noticed them too. I don't think anyone in Geauga has them, do they?"

Questions like that happen frequently enough nowadays. Because of my job, I get on many more Amish farms than most Amish farmers do, so it's logical enough to ask me what's going on around the community. However, I'm still always a little taken aback when an Amish person asks me what other Amish people will or will not use or do. If I knew Owen a little better, I might make a joke and say something like, "How in the world should I know? You're the one who's Amish in this car." But I'm enjoying the easy conversation with this young man, and I don't want to say anything that might shut him down, so I simply say, "No, they're not used anywhere in the settlement."

Owen thinks for a bit and looks down toward his feet. "I think these people might be a little higher than the people in Geauga, don't you?"

"Yeah, there's no doubt this is a more liberal area. Several of the things we've seen so far just wouldn't fly in Geauga." Again, I am pleased that Owen is so comfortable talking about the church rules with me. I suppose there's no reason he shouldn't be. He's heard his dad talk with me many times. Besides, on the whole trip down, Eli, Marvin, and I spent a good deal of time talking about what would, or would not, be allowed in Geauga. He also naturally assumed I would understand the Amish term "high" meaning more liberal. Of course I did, so our conversation didn't falter, and that's good.

We're just now pulling into downtown Shreve, and I am powerful hungry.

15

Manure Minutia and Lunch

Halfway down Market Street, Bill turns left into the parking lot of the Des Dutch Essenhaus restaurant. I haven't been here for a couple of years, but as I remember it's pretty good. It's clean and bright inside, and the manager immediately comes over to greet Bill and show us all to a table near the middle of the restaurant. The manager is not Amish. He's dressed in a checked shirt and black slacks. Most of these "Amish-style" restaurants aren't really owned or run by the Amish, but as a rule they tend to be pretty good with real comfort food.

A pretty, young, blonde waitress, dressed in a simple Amish-style light blue dress, complete with the traditional long white apron and white organdy lace bonnet, greets us, passes out menus, and asks what we would like to drink. About half of us get coffee and the other half iced tea. The waitress might actually be Amish. Young Amish people routinely work in local businesses. She might also be Mennonite, or just as likely she's a Yankee dressed in Amish garb to match the theme of the restaurant. I shouldn't use the term "Yankee" for a non-Amish person here in the Holmes County settlement. Here in Holmes County, if she is non-Amish, she'd be called "English." In any case, she is very pleasant and easy to talk to.

The sausage sandwich is starred on the menu as a "local favorite." When our waitress comes back, I ask her if it's as good as the menu says it is. She just laughs and says, "Sure." I'm about to order it when Bill breaks in and tells me I should get the soup and salad bar instead.

With my shaky hands and arms, menus are always a challenge. The first cut is to identify those items that have minimum potential for random flinging, and a bowl of soup with a hovering spoon doesn't make the cut—ever. Trying to gloss over a potentially embarrassing situation, I turn to look at Bill. "Well, I don't know, the sausage sandwich sounds pretty good."

As the waitress starts to write down my order, Bill persists. "No, you really need to try the soup and salad bar. It's excellent." She stops writing and looks back to me for a decision.

Feeling like a muskrat stuck in the steel grip of a leg-hold trap, I realize there's no way out, but to quietly explain to Bill. "You see the problem is, I have this little muscle disease. It's not Parkinson's, but it acts like it, and it's just real hard to eat soup."

Bill's voice rumbles through the entire restaurant. "Huh, all these years I thought it was Parkinson's."

I've learned to actually feel the red flush of embarrassment spread across my face, as I imagine a placard stapled to my shirt saying "Mr. Shaky." Worse yet, he just said "all these years." Didn't anybody get the memo? I have been trying very hard for a long time to hide this condition. So come on . . . at least act like you never saw it.

Defeated, I turn back to the waitress. "Sausage sandwich, please." She writes it down and finally the rest of the table can order. Eli asks for a half-pound cheeseburger with fries. Marvin and Bill get the soup and salad bar, and Owen orders a roast beef sandwich with mashed potatoes. The restaurant staff is fast and efficient, and the orders show up in a matter of minutes.

Our table settles into the quiet hum of small talk and chewing. Talking about manure systems in the middle of a restaurant doesn't seem quite appropriate, so we gravitate toward a variety of general agricultural topics. The manager stops by several times to chat with Bill, and make sure everything is all right with our food. The meals are simple but beautifully prepared, and my sausage sandwich with fries is delicious. The restaurant is perfect for our midday stop. We are all anxious to get on with the tour of the other two remaining farms, and lunch is completed fairly quickly. Individual tickets in hand, we move toward the cashier. Marvin gets ahold of Owen's bill and then leaves a tip for the entire table. As Bill is our host, I wrestle his check away from him and pay it. Bidding good-bye to the manager at the door, we are all ready for the next farm.

Before we get back into the cars, Bill takes a minute to explain that the next farm is one of the few certified organic dairy farms in the settlement. "He composts the manure there on the farm," he explains. "I thought you guys might like to see the whole organic angle."

Opening the car door, Eli says, "Yeah, that does sound real interesting. How far away is the farm?"

"Just a couple miles further south. We should be there in no time."

He's right. Owen and I barely have time to compare notes on lunch before Bill's car wheels into the wide gravel driveway of the next farm. Even though this farm is organic, the general appearance of the buildings, fences, and even the driveway is very similar to other farms in the area. Pulling up in front of what looks to be a large equipment shed, we both park, and, before we can emerge from the cars, the back screen door of the house swings open and the farm owner steps out.

Again, Bill takes the lead in carefully introducing everyone. Joseph is slender and around six feet tall with black hair sticking out from under a straw hat. I'm guessing him to be in his late 30s, maybe early 40s. Like the other farmers we've met today, he enthusiastically welcomes us onto the farm. A jet-black beard rims the bottom of a slender jaw, and his features are perhaps just slightly more serious about the face than the other three guys we've talked to this morning.

Joseph watches silently as we struggle into our boots, and then he points in the direction of the barn. Just as we enter the door, Marvin wonders aloud, "How many cows are you milking?"

"Right now about 45."

The question seems to hit the on switch for Joseph, and for the next several minutes he gives us a complete rundown on the various features of the barn as we walk around. He is now quite engaging, and the questions and conversation flow freely among the farmers. Our Geauga group is particularly interested in the organic aspects of the farm, and Joseph bends over backward to give complete explanations.

A common misconception is that all Amish farms are organic. They're not. Just like Yankee farms, a few are organic, but most are not. "Certified organic" means that the farm is inspected and certified by the state and has agreed to follow a rigorous set of standard organic practices. It takes a different set of crop and livestock management skills, as well as a different economic business model, to make a certified organic farm profitable.

Most of the basic organic methods aren't a huge problem to adopt on an Amish farm. The standards require that crops used to feed the cows are grown without commercial fertilizers, weed killers, or other pesticides. The cows can't be injected with artificial hormones to increase milk production, as is so often done on large dairy farms. Any feed additives are carefully controlled, as are fly-control methods in the barn and a number of other things. The regulations are a bit of a hassle, but on a small farm, and even on some large ones, it can be done.

One of the biggest questions for the farmer is whether it makes economic sense to become certified organic. On the upside, Joseph will receive a much higher price for any milk sold—usually in the neighborhood of one and a half or even two times as much as nonorganic milk. On the downside, any feed Joseph has to buy for the cows, heifers, and other livestock is correspondingly much, much more expensive because he has to buy it from other organic farmers. In addition, things like organic fertilizers are typically a lot more expensive than the regular non-organic fertilizers that most farmers use. He might also suffer a little less crop production due to following the organic standards. So the question for Joseph, or any farmer for that matter, is whether the added production costs outweigh the increased price of any organic product the farm ultimately is able to sell. In Joseph's case, he has decided the trade-off is worth it. But he is still distinctly in the minority for Amish and non-Amish farms. Organic products may, or may not, be more healthy or wholesome, but the overriding question from a farmer's standpoint is: are they profitable?

The farmers talk back and forth about organic production for probably 15 minutes or so, until Bill pulls the group back to our mission. "Why don't you tell us about the manure system you have, Joseph?"

"It's pretty simple really. I use a skid steer to push the manure straight out the back of the barn into a storage pit."

We all walk to the back of the barn to see the storage pit he's talking about. The area just outside the barn is a concrete pad. Maybe 30 feet behind the barn there is a ledge that suddenly drops straight down at least eight feet onto another concrete pad. A fence of stout, heavy metal pipe stands guard on our side of the ledge to prevent wandering cows—or an inattentive skid steer operator—from doing a fatal eight-foot header on to the rock-hard surface below. Joseph points over the ledge. "We can pile up the manure and store it right there for a few days, and then we use the skid steer again to push it into that compost pile over there." He points off to the right to a pile of manure that is approximately eight feet tall and 30 feet long.

Marvin is looking down at his feet, studying about a bushel of manure that didn't make it over the ledge. "Seems like maybe you're using more straw bedding than the other farms we've been on."

"Yeah, we do use more bedding. It soaks up the juices in the manure and helps everything compost better."

What Joseph means is that in order for a compost pile to work properly, it needs to be dry enough to allow air to move into and out of the pile. The extra straw bedding helps air circulate through the pile, and the air keeps the manure-eating microorganisms healthy. Studying the 30-foot-long pile, I confess to myself that I'm not all that impressed. I won't embarrass Joseph by asking, but I really can't figure out why he's trying to compost the manure anyway. It's not necessary. Composting is great for killing germs in manure that can cause people to get sick if you put it on vegetable crops. But in this case, the composted manure is going out onto crop fields that produce animal feeds. Manure germs die over time, and the length of time that this manure sits in the field while the crops are growing provides an ample barrier to kill germs and protect the herd.

The other dairy farms we've seen today and all of the Geauga farmers spread fresh manure on crop fields all the time with no harmful effects. So why bother composting? Part of it is probably just that the word "compost" is in vogue and it sounds so good. Again, there's nothing wrong with compost if a farm needs it, but this farm doesn't.

As our group slowly makes its way back through the barn toward the door, I'm not sure how much we've learned. Like all the other systems, this one needs a skid steer to work, and skid steers can't be used in Geauga. The composting is interesting, but probably not necessary. Still, learning a little bit more about the organic aspects of the farm was very worthwhile. Joseph is a great host, but I think it's time we try to get over to the last farm. Outside the farmers talk with Joseph quite a bit more about his experiences as an organic dairy farmer. A few minutes—and five pairs of boots later—we're on our way to our fourth and final farm visit.

Bill said this last farm is five or six miles northeast of here, so it is vaguely in the direction of home. That's good, because it's starting to get late and I want to be sure I get these guys back home for chore time. On our way out of the driveway, I ask Owen, "Do you think these folks might be Mennonite or just more liberal Amish?"

"I don't know. But they use things that would not be allowed back home in Geauga." It dawns on me that this is probably the first time that Owen has been exposed to other church rules. He seems fascinated and very willing to talk about it. The five or six miles go by quickly. Samuel is in the driveway cleaning out a wheelbarrow with a garden hose as we pull into his barnyard. He shuts off the hose and is over by the cars waiting to greet us before we can get the doors open. As he shakes each of our hands, he's animated and lanky with a compelling smile. I like him immediately.

In the barn he's anxious to show off a unique manure gutter-cleaning contraption of his own design. From the very outset, I'm certain I've never seen anything like it. It's all cables and pulleys mounted near the floor on both sides of the aisle with a hydraulically operated metal manure gutter cleaner hovering over each gutter. At Bill's urging—and it doesn't take much urging—he fires up the system to give us a demonstration.

Samuel pulls back on a lever on top of the gutter scraper on the right. The whole unit rattles to life, filling the air with the clanging, scraping, and pinging sounds of suddenly animated metal. With Samuel still holding the lever, the whole unit moves back about 10 feet. Then he pushes the lever forward and the cleaner drops into place and scrapes the first 10 feet of manure-filled gutter into a shallow pit behind the barn. Without stopping, he pulls a lever back again, this time moving 20 feet down the gutter. The lever goes forward again, and another 10 feet of manure gets pushed outside. He shouts over the noise, "The first 20 feet or so are harder because the heifer pens have a lot of bedding. It's easier once you get behind where the cows stand."

In a matter of minutes we watch Samuel clean the gutter on one whole side of the barn. Then he practically runs over to a switch on the far wall and shuts the whole system off. Before the din of the machinery has a chance to completely quiet down, he's standing in front of us. "Well, what did you think?"

I'm speechless, but Marvin and Eli are soon asking questions about pumps, pulleys, hydraulic lines, and switches. While the farmers talk, Bill and I step out the back barn door and look at the manure storage pit, which is about 3 feet deep, 12 feet wide, and 20 feet long. In a little while the farmers eventually get around to joining us, and I ask Samuel how he cleans the manure pit.

"Oh, that's no problem. When it fills up I just use a skid steer and a manure spreader to clean it out."

There it is again: that problematic "skid steer."

We talk for a few minutes more and slowly start making our way back to the cars. Just as we get outside, Samuel says, "I've been working on a new design for a piece of machinery to stuff large round hay bales into plastic bags for storage. It's in the barn out back. If you have time, I'd be happy to show it to you."

"Sure," Marvin says without any hesitation, and the farmers start to close the 200-yard gap between us and the barn that Samuel is pointing to.

Looking down at my watch, I say, "Hey, guys, you know it's a little after three o'clock, and we have a good hour and a half to get home. Are you okay with that, or should we leave now?"

Both Eli and Marvin brush off my time concerns and assure me it will be fine. There is no rush. Bill and I fall in behind the farmers, and we all spend the next 20 minutes or so looking at equipment for hay crops. Finally back in the driveway, we thank Samuel for allowing us to visit and Bill for putting the entire day together. Marvin gets back in the front passenger seat, Eli climbs in behind me, and Owen gets in the seat behind his dad.

As soon as we are safely out on the road, I turn halfway around to look in the backseat, "Well, Owen, you've seen four manure systems today. Which one is the best?"

He knows I'm joking but all three of us wait for his answer. "Oh, I don't know." Glancing into the rearview mirror I can see that he is smiling and, at least for now, staying engaged in the conversation.

Eli, Marvin, and I—with occasional input from Owen—easily fill the next hour and a half recounting what we have seen and discussing in great detail the plusses and minuses of each system. The fact that all four systems use a skid-steer tractor is troubling, especially to me. The farmers in the car are already figuring ways around the skid-steer problem. We talk about liquid systems, compost, bedding, and spreading. At first, I was concerned that the trip was of little value because of the skid steers, but the farmers seem untroubled. They have moved on and are building on what they learned today. A short section of the drive home is on an interstate through Akron. Surrounded for a while by other cars, I find myself wondering how many of these other folks have spent the last hour locked in a car talking about cow poop. My guess is not many.

The tenor in the car turns a bit more serious as we get closer to Geauga. Eli makes it sound like a joke, but he lets us know that he really does have to do something soon about all the manure. "The children are too small to help, and my back might not last all that long," he says.

Marvin isn't in such a rush because Owen is helping out right now. But like Eli, he needs to work something out in the next couple of years.

I drop Eli off at his house first and then Owen and Marvin. It's later than

I had counted on, and I hope it doesn't put them too far behind in chores. But they seem unconcerned. On the drive home, I quietly ask myself what was accomplished today. My sense is the farmers really did get some new ideas. It'll take some time to figure out what systems might work for these guys and what system might ultimately be allowed.

It's true, there are probably more edifying ways to spend a day than mired in manure minutia. But looking back all the way to sunrise this morning, I have a feeling this day was well spent. Right now however, I'm hungry. Wonder what's for dinner.

$$\bullet \quad \bullet \quad \bullet$$

Several months later I would once again be working with my old friend and colleague Bill. Only this time, he had just retired. Eli Gingerich had put me in touch with the Fishers, who were thinking about starting a new farm in the settlement. Eli and Katie are somehow related to Ada and Monroe Fisher. Anyway, Monroe called me and we set up a time for a farm visit. I did not know Monroe and could not recollect ever being on the farm, so the purpose of the visit was simply to get acquainted with this prospective new farmer, along with the farm buildings and land.

When I got there, the barn was in pretty rough shape. It had last been used as a dairy barn many, many years ago. The milk house, where the milking equipment is kept and the milk is stored, was a shambles. The stalls in the milking barn were very small. Undoubtedly, in its past life, this barn was used to milk Jerseys, Guernseys, Ayrshires, or some other very small breed. They were clearly too small for the modern-day Holsteins found on most dairy farms. To make matters worse, the farm didn't have a lot of pasture or crop ground. Monroe was pretty emphatic that he intended to milk cows some time in the not-too-distant future. So my job was to figure out how to help him get that done.

Clearly we needed some dairy housing advice. When he was working, Bill specialized in dairy housing and had quite a bit of experience working with the Amish. Bill is a good guy and a true expert in his field. With a little prodding, I was able to coax him out of retirement to visit Monroe's farm and make some recommendations.

On the appointed day, Bill showed up at my office right on time, and we drove out to meet Monroe together. It was a warm summer morning without a cloud in the sky. Monroe greeted us at the barn and was obviously pleased that we were there. He took plenty of time to show Bill around the entire barn and share some of his extremely tentative thoughts about how he might be able to transform this hand-hewn, hard-used old barn into a modern milking facility. Monroe is a carpenter and the extensive remodeling he described seemed plausible enough to me. We finished our tour and walked out behind the barn to talk about the possibilities.

The general mood was good, and things were going well until Monroe hitched a thumb in his suspender, looked toward Bill, and asked, "Now that you've had a look, what do you think about the barn?"

"Tear it down. Then you'll have plenty of room to put up a new loafing shed and milking parlor."

I couldn't believe those were the first words that came out of Bill's mouth. A "loafing shed" is basically a large roof held up by poles, with no sides, and a concrete floor, where the cows mill around all day waiting to be milked in small groups in the "milking parlor." Loafing sheds and parlors are designed for much larger herds than are ever found in the Geauga settlement. The initial shock on Monroe's face was quickly covered over with a mute, expressionless veil. In what was to prove a futile effort to save the day, I stammered, "Well, Bill, we really don't have loafing sheds in this settlement."

"Well, why not? Our guys down south use them all the time."

Then it struck me, in all the times I'd visited farms with Bill down in his neck of the woods, we always stopped at New Order Amish or Mennonite farms. Both of these groups are much more liberal in the technologies they are permitted to use, and the dairy herds tend to be much larger than the conservative Old Order Amish groups like here in Geauga. There are many Old Order farms down in Bill's area, but the ones we stopped at were always New Order.

Our visit was suddenly in a downward spiral. Monroe slowly shook off his disbelief and after a pause asked, "How many cows are you thinking I should have?"

"Oh, I'd probably start out with somewhere around 70 and then expand from there."

I was speechless, and that doesn't happen very often. Seventy cows is almost two and a half times the size of the largest herds here in Geauga. Again, Monroe gained enough composure to pose the question, "How would I take care of the manure?" Almost all of the church districts in the Geauga settlement, including Monroe's, allow only two manure-handling options: three-tanged pitchfork or five-tanged pitchfork. Five-tanged works better, but three-tanged could be used in a pinch. In any case, it's close to impossible for a family to clean up the manure of anything like 70 cows using pitchforks.

So what was Bill's answer? "Skid steer!" Ah, yes, the same skid steers that Eli, Owen, Marvin, and I saw over and over again on our tour of Holmes County. Those small, highly maneuverable little tractors that could push manure around a barn with the speed of the winged messenger god Mercury—and that were definitely not allowed in dairy barns in the Geauga settlement.

In a voice that can be best described as timid, Monroe quietly explained, "We really can't use those here."

"Well, why not?" Bill's booming voice indignantly demanded to know. "What's wrong with a skid steer?"

"It's just not allowed," was all Monroe could say.

"I still don't get it. What could be wrong with a skid steer?"

After a long and very awkward pause, I'd had enough. Taking a step forward to meet his eyes head-on, and in as jovial voice as I could muster, "Tell you what, Bill, why don't we send you into a Catholic school to talk about the latest birth-control techniques? Skid steers aren't used here because they are not allowed, and at least for now that's the end of the story."

Looking perplexed, Bill obviously wasn't buying it and muttered something under his breath about "still what he should do." I realized there was no more to build on here and changed the topic.

"Why don't we all step over there and see how the pasture fencing is set up." Bill was agreeable to looking at the pastures, and Monroe was visibly relieved to get out of any more discussion on the barn. We spent the next half hour talking about pastures and grazing, dairy nutrition, and crops. Barn remodeling didn't come up again, even though that's why we were there. The visit ended amiably with Bill and me climbing back into my car and driving off to Middlefield for lunch. We spent an enjoyable hour or so, talking mainly about his retirement activities and my looming retirement plans. Bill left for home around two, and I spent the rest of the afternoon writing and revising a long letter to Monroe.

The letter—with far more tact than is my custom—acknowledged that tearing down the existing barn and building a modern 70-cow facility was one option, but clearly there were other options to consider. The most obvious one was to milk Jerseys, Guernseys, or Ayrshires. After all, that's what the barn was built to accommodate. While most large farms today have Holsteins, there's nothing wrong with milking one of the smaller breeds.

In fact, sometimes there are real advantages. There's no question Holsteins produce more milk per cow. But Holstein milk tends to be very low in butterfat. The smaller breeds produce less milk, but it's high in butterfat. Dairy processing plants pay a premium for butterfat. So a gallon of Holstein milk is worth less than a gallon of milk produced by the smaller breeds. In general, each Holstein cow weighs somewhere around 1,200 pounds, while the smaller breeds top out in the neighborhood of 800 to 900 pounds. Not surprisingly, these petite little gals eat a lot less. A side benefit of the biological mechanics of eating less is that they also make a lot less manure, which is dreadfully important if your manure handling system is a five-tanged pitchfork.

So to sum it all up, big cows produce a lot of milk. Small cows produce less milk, but each gallon is worth more. The economics of each farm are different. In Monroe's case, the existing barn—with some fairly major modifications—could adequately house Jerseys, Guernseys, or Ayrshires. He has limited pasture and crop ground available to raise feed for the cows, and small breeds eat less. So the trade-off of less feed, less manure, and less milk—but at a higher price—starts to make some sense. Or he could tear down that old barn and go deeply into debt, replacing it with a modern dairy facility for 70 Holsteins, and further into debt trying to feed those big ladies.

Now in writing and rewriting the letter, I really did try, probably unsuccessfully, to hide my bias.

The next morning I drove back out to the farm and hand-delivered the letter to Ada. I knew Monroe probably wouldn't be there because he took the day off yesterday to meet with us and would need to work today. When Ada came to the door, she was as pleasant as the morning, and we talked a few minutes before I confessed how disappointed I was in yesterday's visit. Finally, I handed her the letter and asked her to give it to Monroe and tell him to call if he had any questions.

Back in the car with my own impending retirement filling the entire windshield, I realized I might never know what Ada and Monroe finally decide. The odds were better than average I'd be gone from this job well before they had time to start up this farm, or not.

16

Drafted Out of Retirement

Unbelievable! A few months ago, laws prohibiting the slaughter of horses for human consumption actually got passed. Surprisingly, it was not the U.S. Congress that got these laws passed but the state legislatures in Texas and Illinois—home of the last three horse processing plants—that were finally able to muster the sufficient stupidity needed to change their state statutes and ban horse meat for human consumption. It's not that the U.S. Congress wasn't trying. Both the U.S. House and Senate have been busily working on the "American Horse Slaughter Prevention Act," which would have banned horse slaughter for human consumption anywhere in the country. The result of all this important state and federal legislative action is that the last three horse processing plants in the country were forced to shutter their doors. And what about our country's yearly surplus of 100,000 or so unwanted horses? Must not have come up.

• • •

In April 2008 I retired and with almost no fanfare. My wife and I moved to the beautiful little town of Beaufort, South Carolina. It's October and we're back in Ohio to visit friends and to attend the 29th annual Lake Erie Draft Colt Sale. It's been two years since I've been to the sale. A lot has changed; a lot hasn't.

The biggest change for me is that I no longer live or work here anymore. It feels odd, yet comfortable returning as a retiree. In truth, I didn't want to retire. Even though I'd worked for the university for over 30 years—28 of them in the Geauga settlement—I was only 53 years old. Working with

Amish farmers is challenging, fun, and deeply rewarding. I liked my job. Ultimately, it was the frigid winters that drove me into retirement. My essential tremor muscle disease gets a little worse each year, and the shaking is strongly exacerbated by cold weather. In the end, this silly disease shook me out of Ohio, like a bowl full of quivering grape jelly.

Beaufort, South Carolina, is a great little town. The people are friendly, and it is warm enough to have palm trees, which was one of our criteria as we looked around the country for a place to live. Beaufort is home now, but it's great being back on the Geauga County Fairgrounds in Burton, greeting farmer after farmer as I walk through the crowded arena building. Today I'll spend time talking about draft horses and what's new in the Amish community. More than that, I'll reconnect with families I've known for so very long, and strive to achieve my goal of simply keeping in touch.

The sale catalog lists 131 draft horses, down about 10 from two years ago. But they added 76 "Crossbreds, Haflinger, Ponies & Miniatures" to be sold after the draft horses, so the total number of animals is up. The crossbreds, haflingers, ponies, and miniatures are usually sold at other auctions, and it's hard telling why they've been added to the sale. Crossbred simply means exactly what it says: two different breeds have been crossed to produce the animal. Haflinger is a warm blood, meaning that a roughly 2,000-pound draft horse has been mated with a 1,000-pound light horse, producing something hovering halfway in between.

There's been a strong demand for haflingers for several years now. They are particularly well suited for non-farm Amish families. These animals are just the right size for Dad to plow a big garden after work or pull a manure spreader, or for the kids to mow the lawn. They're not really big enough for heavy farm work, but they're fine for a non-farm rural Amish home, where Dad is "working out," or working off the farm. And since they're smaller, they don't eat quite as much as a full-size draft horse.

The ponies and miniature horses are basically pets for both the Yankees and Amish. Occasionally, a larger pony will be used to mow the lawn at an Amish home. Sometimes the children will ride them with a saddle or hitch them to a small two-wheeled cart and drive them around the yard. They're too small to be serious work animals on a farm, but they can be a heck of a lot of fun.

The scene around the sale ring hasn't changed at all. Lyle Chupp and Andy Raber are the auctioneers again this year. The ringmen are the same, and the audience around the arena is a dark-blue collage of ever-so-slightly different dressed Amish men, with a smattering of women and children interspersed in the crowd. It's late morning and the Belgian stallions, Percheron stallions, and geldings were all sold earlier. The Percheron mares are being sold as I make my way toward a gap in the crowd where I can watch and hear the action.

Numbers 61 and 62 are Grand River Lynda and Grand River Peggy. According to the sale catalog, they are a broke, well-matched pair of half sisters, and they are being sold as a team. In other words, they will be auctioned off together and will go to one buyer. They were bred and raised on an Amish farm right here in Burton, and at the end of this day they will both be at the same new farm in some other part of the county, state, or country, or even in Canada. They are not particularly big draft horses, but they are well matched and should work together very well. Doesn't take long for the auctioneer to sell them. They bring $600 each. It strikes me that's not a great price, but it's not completely terrible either.

The next few horses sell for between $600 and $900. The prices seem to be generally lower than they were two years ago. Of course, the general economy is in the tank and people are cutting back everywhere, even on draft horses. Silver Dollar Eady is a two-year-old, foaled in January of 2006. She only brings $350. I'm pretty sure that would not have happened two years ago. The U.S. meat buyers would have bid her up to at least $500. But there are no U.S. meat buyers here today. There are a few Canadian buyers, and they could still buy horses here, transport them to Canada, and have them slaughtered for human consumption there. However, because of the transportation costs, they are unlikely to aggressively bid on meat animals. I didn't see who bought Silver Dollar Eady, but the small farm family who brought her here walked away with at least $150 less than they would have two years ago. One hundred fifty dollars doesn't sound like much, until you realize it's a 30 percent drop in price.

Something else has caught my eye in the sales catalog; several of the "mares" are actually "fillies" well under a year old. Lone Valley Shirley is only four months old, and Winsome Lane Lily was born in March of this year. They each bring $350. It's not unusual to sell young horses at this sale. It just strikes me that there may be a few more this year. Could just be a coincidence, or it could be that families are getting out of the business and selling off all the horses. I don't know, and there is no time to check because this is only a visit to the Amish settlement. Quietly I remind myself that home is in South Carolina now.

J. D. B.'s Peggy's Elaine is broke, both single and double. Which means she is trained to pull farm equipment by herself or with another horse. She's a good-sized Percheron mare, mostly black with a few white marks. She's a little over two years old. The auctioneer points out—what anyone sitting near the ring could see—that her left hock is swollen. "But the vet checked her, and she's okay," he says. "She'd make a fine broodmare." The pedigree reader is very impressed with her bloodlines, which hail mostly from Michigan, although she was bred in Indiana. The bidding starts off at a respectable $1,200 and finishes at $1,500.

A six-month-old Percheron filly called Rock Islands Roxy brings the crowd to life and sells for $2,200. A little while later, Nash Acres Barb, a seven-month-old Belgian filly, brings only $300. UAB Daisy is a two-year-old Belgian mare that the auctioneer swears is broke so well that "the owner's 13-year-old son drives her." She sells for $1,000. Number 93, IHF Joanna, is five years old and broke to all farm machinery. Lyle Chupp yells into the microphone, "She's broke, she's bred," and tries to start the bidding at $1,400. But it slowly drops down to $1,100 when someone on the left side of the crowd raises his hand to bid. The ringman shouts, and the price slowly bumps its way up to $1,550, where Lyle drops the gavel and proclaims her "sold."

Six-year-old Southedge Joy from Jordanville, New York, is prancing into the ring as I turn to walk through the crowd and almost collide with Atlee Schrock's broad-brimmed, black felt hat. He knows that I now live in South Carolina and is startled to see me. "Why, Randy, what are you doing here?"

"Same as you, Atlee, just here enjoying the auction. We're visiting for a week or so, mainly to see friends, and I really did want to come to this auction. Gives me a chance to see a whole bunch of people all in one place. Anything new with you and the family?"

"Well, the big news is my son, Munroe, got married a few months back."

"That's great." I've always really liked Munroe. I spent a couple of days working with him harvesting speltz on his dad's farm years ago. He was just a boy then. If I recall correctly, he had just graduated from eighth grade and, therefore, was done with school. Lots of Amish young people take some time right after the eighth grade to work off the farm for several years. Most never come back to farming. But a few, like Munroe, do. For at least the past year or two, he's been back working with his dad. One of the last times I saw Atlee, he confided in me that he was keeping his fingers crossed, hoping that Munroe might decide one day to take over the farm.

Tentatively, with some trepidation, I ask Atlee, "Is he still working on the farm?"

"Yes, yes, he sure is." And then he adds, "She helps too, helps with anything—hay, milking the cows, out in the garden, anything." I've watched Atlee's red beard turn to gray over the years, but the excitement in his eyes and voice is unmistakable as he talks about his son and his new daughter-in-law. "She didn't grow up on a farm at all, but she's real interested in everything." With a muffled laugh, he shakes his head and goes on, "Why, last week we were butchering, and she even helped clean the chickens."

I am duly impressed. Even on a small farm, where every effort is made to kill the chickens humanely and not stress the animals, the entire process is still messy. Very often the birds are inverted and put in a metal cone that holds their wings gently back and exposes their head and neck through a narrow opening at the bottom of the cone. With a very sharp knife, the blood vessels in the neck are cut and the animal quickly bleeds to death. After the bird is dead, the carcass goes through a series of procedures, including scalding in hot water to loosen the feathers—yeah, it really does stink like lukewarm, sloppy, wet chicken feathers. The feathers are picked off, the body cavity is opened, and the internal organs removed. Some of these are saved; others are discarded or fed to the pigs. The entire carcass inside and out is washed and patted dry. Then it's time to move on to the next chicken. Apparently, this young woman with no previous farm experience actually *chose* to help. I am impressed.

"Even willing to clean chickens. Well, Atlee, she sounds like a very nice addition to the family."

"Yes, we are well pleased and can't be thankful enough."

"Good luck to you then, and say hi to Munroe for me."

Turning to step back into the crowd, a long-ago conversation with Crist Wingerd, one of Atlee's close relatives, leaps fully formed into my brain. Crist used hauntingly similar words and phrases as he talked about his son Mahlon's new wife. More than just the words, the pure joy of a new young couple contemplating taking over the family farm, bubbled unhidden and unfettered through each man's voice. And they were each very "well pleased."

Sunrise View Missy is being trotted up and down the ring as I return to the action and notice someone handing a note to the auctioneer. He adjusts the microphone. "We have an announcement. The buggy horses tied to the wooden fence east of this building are eating the rail. If you're hitched over there, please go out and move your horse." Some horses have a habit of gnawing on any wood in front of them, particularly when they're bored. The strange thing is, nearby horses who normally wouldn't even think of wood chewing often take it on as a temporary fad. Pretty soon you have the whole fun party of horses happily munching away on a rapidly disappearing wooden fence rail.

Trying mightily to hide my laughter—for I'm one of the few people here who would get this joke—I watch faces in the audience look to each other trying to figure out what's east and what's west, and trying to remember if they hitched the buggy horse to a wooden rail. It's an oddly Amish version of "we have a blue Ford pickup truck in the west parking lot with its lights on."

Lyle Chupp is busily auctioning off Sunrise View Missy when the growling in my stomach demands lunch, now. Stepping out a side door and starting off toward the lunch building, which is normally the 4-H rabbit and poultry barn, I run into Eli Gingerich, apparently also making his way toward a midday meal.

"Hi, Eli, you buy any horses today?"

"No, not yet. I bid on one mare but didn't get her." Then tongue-in-cheek, he smiles and asks, "How about you?" It's just a little good-natured ribbing. He knows full well that I don't have a farm, don't breed horses, and don't even live in the area anymore.

"Not hardly, Eli."

A portable metal barbecue grill unit, which must be 20 feet long and is stacked with mounds of hamburgers and hotdogs, sizzles next to the door of the rabbit and poultry barn. It's tended by a bevy of Amish men and young boys, flipping burgers or running for the door with roaster pans full of just-cooked meat.

"Hey, Eli, who actually puts on the lunch?"

"Normally, it's one school, but this is so big that two schools get together and do it. We did it last year, and it keeps you busy."

The 25 or 30 Amish schools in the settlement are all private, and they hold various fund-raisers to help cover the cost of running each school. So the mothers and fathers, along with older sisters, brothers, and even some of the older students, are the ones preparing lunch today. As we step in, there's a line of men in blue coats stretching from the serving tables in the middle of the room almost back to the door. A row of Amish women stands behind the tables serving hamburgers, cheeseburgers, hotdogs, potato salad, baked beans, and other surely delicious things that I cannot yet see from my place in this row of hungry people.

The line moves quickly, and in a very few minutes with a paper plate and plastic fork in hand, I ask the woman behind the table for a cheeseburger. Eli takes two and works his way down the serving line for a scoop of this or a ladle of that. Staring back and forth at the paper plate and plastic fork, I realize there is absolutely no way my rigorous hand tremor is going to cooperate and allow me to eat anything that employs a plastic fork. Settling for the cheeseburger and a Coke, I walk over to the cashier and pay. Eli and I find two chairs along one of the rows of eight-foot folding tables and sit down to eat—or, in my case, watch Eli eat. My cheeseburger is gone long before my hunger. Venturing over to the dessert table, I do find a sticky nut pie that will hold onto a plastic fork like glue. That's enough to tide me over. I can afford to lose a pound or two anyway.

On our way back to the auction arena, I ask Eli about the changes in the horse meat market and its impact on local farmers.

"It's pretty bad. There's really no place to send a horse that can't work. My brother-in-law had a horse that went lame all the time and just wasn't fit for farm work. He called the meat buyer, and the guy told him he'd pick it up, but he wouldn't give him any money until he found a place to get rid of it."

"What did your brother-in-law finally do?"

Eli shakes his head. "Well, he really just didn't have a choice. So he told the meat buyer to come on out and pick it up. I don't know if he ever got any money for it, but you can't afford to keep feeding it if it's never going to be able to work on the farm, and nobody else wants it."

In all likelihood, Eli's brother-in-law is simply out the $500 or so he would have gotten if the horse could have been sent to a meat processing plant here in the United States.

Back at the sale ring, the auctioneer is just finishing with another two-year-old Belgian mare. I don't catch the final price but it was something under $400. The prices just seem lackluster, particularly for the horses on the bottom end of the price range.

Prince's Ann is a young horse foaled on February 27, 2007. She's a red sorrel with a flaxen mane and a light tail. The sales catalog doesn't say she's broke, but the ringmen are having no trouble leading her around, so she definitely has possibilities. The pedigree reader wants everyone to remember she was sired by "Rose's Prince Charming, and her mother was Marks Delilah." The bidding starts at $1,800 and slowly works up to $2,500, where she is sold.

A couple of farmers stop by to say hi, and I completely miss horse #116. A. B. Belle's Bridget is an eight-month-old Belgian mare consigned by a farmer right over in Middlefield. But I have no idea what she sold for.

Crystal Springs Jolie catches her right forefoot on a clump of dirt and stumbles as she comes into the ring. She doesn't go down, and, as soon as her feet are back in order, her head snaps high into the air as she regally looks down on this crowd of mere humans. She hails from Shipshewana, Indiana, and was foaled in April of the year 2006. She is tall, magnificently muscled, and broke both single and double. The pedigree reader chants excitedly about her lineage. But she has already captured the imagination of the crowd with her long, flowing gait and sheer presence.

"Do I hear five thousand dollars?" Lyle Chupp almost dares the crowd not to bid. He drops down to "four thousand dollars" and finally to "thirty-five hundred dollars" before the ringman nearest the auctioneer's podium spots a bidder and shouts "YESSSS."

Lyle rumbles, "I have thirty-five hundred dollars, do I hear four thousand? Four thousand? Four thousand?"

"Yep." The ringman on the far right calls a bid.

"Forty-five hundred dollars? Do I have four thousand five hundred dollars?" Lyle pauses only briefly and says, "Okay, give me forty-one hundred dollars and let's get going, forty-one hundred dollars?"

The first ringman hollers "YESSS" once again. Another bidder jumps in at $4,200.

Lyle fairly coaxes a $4,300 bid out of the buyer on the far right, and it's all over. "Going once, twice, sold," and the gavel drops sharply. Every eye in the house is fixed on her alternately tensing rump muscles, as Crystal Springs Jolie flounces out of the ring without so much as a glance back at the humans. She leaves with the honor of being one of the most expensive horses sold this day. She deserves it, and everything about her demeanor suggests she knows it.

A few more horses sell for under $400. It's getting late and I think I'll go. Looks like the crossbreds, haflingers, ponies, and miniatures will have to sell without me. I doubt they'll mind.

So what really changed after the U.S. horse processing plants were forced to close, so that horses in this rich country couldn't be processed into meat for human consumption? Perhaps not much, really. A few Amish families went home with less money in the household budget. The Amish don't breed and raise horses as meat animals. However, in the past when an animal turned out to be unfit for breeding or farm work, the meat market provided some outlet and some money for an unwanted or unfit horse.

A few of these draft horses sold here today will be butchered in Canada, rather than in the United States. Horses in the southern part of the country are likely to be trucked over the Mexican line and slaughtered under conditions regulated by the "rigorous and watchful eye" of the Mexican government. I shudder. So with the closing of the U.S. horse meat–packing facilities, a few more jobs have been shipped to other countries. Veterinarians across the country are reporting an increase in the incidence of horse abuse and neglect. There are unconfirmed stories of unwanted horses simply being turned loose to fend for themselves in the hills of southeastern Ohio and western Kentucky. These are animals that have been cared for by humans for their entire lives. Releasing them into the wild is simply cruel. But with falling horse prices, no meat market, and the American economy in tatters, the owners may have little choice.

The international price of horse meat surely went up because most unwanted U.S. horses simply are not making it into the market. Somewhere on the globe a poor family undoubtedly went without meat this week because they could not afford it. Happily, with the Internet and global communications, they might be able to figure out which country it was that decided to impoverish them, even more than they already were. They won't understand why. But they'll know who.

The U.S. Bureau of Land Management is struggling ever more mightily to control unwanted wild horses in the western states. Horses are neither native nor natural to North America; they were brought over by early Europeans. According to a June 30, 2008, CBS News report, the Bureau of Land Management spent about $22 million in 2007 caring for around 33,000 horses in permanent holding facilities. Perhaps for this one problem there is an obvious answer. Since these horses are already in government custody, simply transport about 10,000 of them to Washington, D.C., for their contribution to the problem, maybe another 10,000 to Illinois for closing the last horse slaughter plant in the country, and let's give Texas 13,000 for those brilliant legislators who were able to close not one but two critically needed horse processing plants. These are, after all, government horses, and it is only fitting that they should be housed alongside the senators and representatives, under the respective state and federal capitol domes. Alas, even this solution is problematic. With that many equine posteriors in the same location, who could possibly determine which ones should report for the next roll call vote on the next carefully analyzed, important, compassionate, problem-solving bill?

While housing 33,000 horses in the halls of government fairly effectively deals with the horses currently held in confinement by the Bureau of Land Management, it does nothing to address the over 100,000 horses each year that were dispatched and processed in the three, now closed, slaughter facilities. What do we do with those horses? Advocates for the horse-meat-for-human-consumption ban often try to equate unwanted horses with unwanted cats and dogs. But a 1,000-pound light horse or a 2,000-pound draft horse is a whole different kettle of fish than a cute little puppy or kitten. Almost any family can adopt a dog or cat, but only a tiny sliver of the population has the space, money, or knowledge needed to adopt a horse. In addition, most cities and towns have ordinances that forbid stabling horses within town limits, so it is only the rural families that can even consider adopting a horse.

In the case of dogs and cats, programs to spay and neuter the animals make a lot of sense and are a good partial solution to reducing the number of unwanted pets. But the logic of this type of program breaks down when it comes to horses. We actually need a continuing supply of healthy horses to replace aging horses on farms and for recreation. The problem is, with our current level of genetic understanding, a fair number of horses are born with physical problems that leave them unable to successfully work on a farm or be used for riding. No one wants to breed horses that can't be used, but it happens every day in spite of our best efforts to prevent it. So the problem remains: what do we do with these horses?

At least part of what brought on all of this legislative activity were reports of animal abuse occurring at the horse processing plants. If these charges are true, the managers of the plants should be criminally charged, fined into abject poverty, and thrown in jail, for there is no excuse for animal cruelty. Focusing legislative and bureaucratic efforts on animal cruelty would have sent a strong message to other large processing plants for other livestock species across the country and would have started to address a truly important issue. Focusing instead on the trivial fact that these horses ultimately went for human consumption simply alienated most of the rest of the world and created—out of thin air and skillful rhetoric—a completely new problem for these United States. How in the world will we deal with over 100,000 unwanted horses this year, and 100,000 more unwanted horses next year and 100,000 more unwanted horses the year after that and, well, you get the idea.

17

The Milk Price Blues

It is hard to believe that I retired and moved to South Carolina just about a year ago. It's May of 2009, and this week we're back in Ohio again for a wedding and to visit so many old friends. It is a comfort to be back in the settlement and to drive up and down the gravel, dirt, and broken asphalt roads, past farm after Amish farm. Lots of horses are in the fields, hitched mainly to corn planters, but a few are hitched to hay mowers and even a few to hay rakes. Almost all of the horse teams are driven by farmers I know—some very well and some only in passing. There's not really much time, and it's hard to know when to stop and when to just drive by.

David Kempf and his family are working in the garden out by the road. There's no rush with garden work. The weeds you don't pull today will still be there tomorrow. So I'll stop here for a short visit.

"Why, it's Randy James." David makes this announcement to his wife as I drive in, but his voice rolls on across the garden and filters through my open window. Stepping out of the car, I am greeted by David's warm smile, a handshake, and two giggling towheaded toddlers smiling up in my direction.

"How are you doing this fine day, David?"

"Oh, pretty good I'd say. At least it's warm. We haven't seen much of you since you moved south."

"Yeah, we really don't get back very often. We have a friend getting married so we tacked on an extra week to see other folks. This is really the first place I've stopped. Since you are in the garden, I figured you might have a little time to talk." Pointing over toward the barn I look at David and ask, "How are the cows doing?"

"They are milking fine. They've been out grazing on all this new spring grass, and it has really helped production."

Cows on pasture always give more milk this time of year. Winters are harsh in these parts, and dairy cows spend several months mostly in the barn eating nothing but stored feeds. Usually their winter diet is dry hay, silage, and a mix of ground dry grains, minerals, and salt. The diet completely meets all of their nutritional needs . . . but it's not pasture. The lush green plants in a new spring pasture are packed full of protein, energy, and other nutrients. And judging by the way the cows attack it, it must taste pretty darn good as well.

"How many are you milking now?"

"Umm, let's see, 23 today; we dried two off yesterday."

"How's the price of milk? Since I retired, I really haven't been following it too closely."

"It's bad, real bad. This last check I got a little over $11. We're still making it, but it's tough right now."

"Wow." I'm momentarily stunned. Last year at this time the local dairy farmers were getting around $18 or $19 for every hundredweight of milk they sold; some of them were up above $20 with premiums for butterfat and quality. Now David says they are under $12 per hundredweight. That's in the neighborhood of a 40 to 45 percent cut in income. It's no wonder David says they're struggling. An awful lot of businesses could not survive a revenue loss of that magnitude. Fortunately, this is a small farm and not a large one. Small farms are normally much more resilient than large farms or businesses. They simply have more options to control costs or diversify their product line. I notice there is a flock of chickens scratching around the barnyard. I don't think they were there last year. In addition to supplying eggs for the family, there's undoubtedly enough left over to sell a few dozen to the neighbors along with an occasional dressed chicken. The garden, the chickens, and maybe a fattened hog will supply an awful lot of the grocery needs for this family this year. Even so, coping with a 40 percent income loss is going to be a struggle.

I stare at David for a moment, trying to think of something positive to say and finally mutter, "Well, milk prices are always volatile, you know. They go way up and then way down. Hopefully, they'll turn around real soon."

David is surprisingly upbeat and even manages a smile. "Yeah, that's what I figure, and we're getting by for now."

We talk on for 15 minutes or so, but with the staggering news about the milk price, my mind is drifting over toward the Gingerich farm. I wonder how they are doing. Clearly, it's time to visit Eli, Katie, and their children.

I find myself taking an indirect route, allowing time to quietly drink in the sights, smells, and gentle breezes for just a few minutes more. It's a little before 10 in the morning as I approach the farm from much farther south than I needed to be and turn into this very familiar gravel driveway. I pull my little car off on to a side driveway near the house, so as to be out of the way of the milk truck, should it arrive while I'm here, and then walk directly down the little path that leads to the barn. My bet is that I'll find at least Eli and maybe the rest of the family somewhere around the barn this time of day.

Katie steps out of the door in the older part of the barn, wearing a blue dress and a headscarf tied under her chin. As is so often the case, she is smiling and seems to be on the verge of breaking into laughter. Expecting a warm greeting, I am only very slightly surprised when, with a mischievous look in her eyes, she loudly announces, "You just missed it."

Now we do both dissolve into laughter. "Missed what?"

"That's what Eli said. He just now finished spreading manure and when you pulled up he said, 'Oh no, I'm done spreading, and he missed it.'"

Laughing still harder, I ponder what is it about my long career that makes Katie and Eli imagine I would be disappointed to miss two draft horses pulling a manure spreader that slings cow poop up into the air and onto a field? The truly funny part is that I am disappointed. Eli has been working on a new manure system, and I would have enjoyed a demonstration. Wouldn't anyone? Occasionally, in moments like this, I look back over all of those years and think I could've chosen a more edifying line of work. But I suppose that's all just manure out of the pit now.

Pushing past two Belgian draft horses, I step into the semi-darkness of the barn. "Hi Katie, how are you on this fine manure-spreading morning?"

"Real good. How about you? What brings you back from South Carolina?"

"I'm doing fine. We have a wedding up here, so we tacked on some extra days to see friends."

"That's nice. It's good to see you. I'm glad you could stop by."

In a brief, quiet pause it strikes me that, as with all good friends, the conversation takes off as if we last spoke just yesterday.

Eli appears from behind the draft horse closest to the wall. He is as boisterous as ever. We exchange greetings, and he is obviously also pleased that I stopped by. After a few minutes of general greeting, I wave to the two blond-haired children over near a horse stall and bend down to pat the ubiquitous dog, Chip. With mock seriousness, Eli suddenly asks me, "What are you going to do about these milk prices?"

He knows full well that, like him, there is absolutely nothing I can do about milk prices. I shrug my shoulders, avoiding his question, and say, "I've kind of lost track of milk prices, but I understand they're pretty bad."

"They are real bad." He nods his head seriously, and I notice out of the side of my eye that Katie is nodding too. "Last month our milk check was well under $12 per hundredweight, and I mean well under. We're getting by, but there's no money to spare."

Their faces show the wear of a troubled time. The milk check is by far the major source of income on this farm. They really don't have other farming enterprises going on the side, so the price of milk is critically important. If I were still working as the county agent, the milk marketing economist at the university would be supplying updates as to why price was so low, but, as it is, I have simply no idea. Turning to Eli I ask, "Do you have any idea why the price has fallen so dramatically since last year?"

"No one seems to know. I asked the milk hauler and some of the other farmers around, but nobody really even has a good guess."

I'm slightly peeved. It's no longer my job, but someone should have gotten information and future price predictions about the milk market from the economist in Columbus out to these farmers so they can plan for the future. Knowing how long they can anticipate low prices could be very helpful to all of the small farms. Correction, I'm real peeved. Oh well, there's nothing I can do about it. Hell, I'm sure they have a bevy of useless university administrators busily ignoring the problem at this very moment. It's probably a good thing I retired.

I stare at Eli a few seconds and say only, "Well, I'm sure it will go back up. It always does." Eli nods quietly and sort of shrugs. "Do you have time to show me this new manure system of yours?"

"Sure do. Let me finish hitching the horses to this load of horse manure. The boys are going to spread it."

Behind the horses is a heaping load of horse manure and bedding ready to go to the field. The manure is piled to overflowing in an old wooden box-style New Idea spreader that was probably built somewhere around the 1940s. This contraption is basically a wooden wagon with sides that are roughly three feet tall. It has rusty steel wheels and gears that run a set of paddles in the back of the wagon specifically designed to fling manure out across the field. The whole machine is ground driven, and the actual manure-flinging power comes from the movement of the wheels as the horses pull the spreader. Almost all of the farms in the settlement have a manure spreader like this, but I am a little surprised that it is a part of Eli's "new" manure system. Slowly it dawns on me that he may well have a second manure spreader specifically for the much soupier dairy cow manure.

Eli finishes hitching the spreader and says, "Well, let's go take a look at the new system."

By the time we walk over to the new part of the barn, the two boys are already rattling down the lane, driving the horses and spreader toward some distant field. This part of the barn is empty. Through the open barn doors, I can barely see the dairy herd grazing way back in the northeast corner of the pasture. "How many cows are you milking right now, Eli?"

"Thirty. I had to send two cows off for beef this morning. One had very low production, and the other had a bad case of mastitis that we just couldn't clear up. With milk prices the way they are, we can't afford to feed them if they're not producing pretty well." Eli pauses for a moment and looks vaguely out toward the pasture. "Particularly since the price of feed hasn't come down. They're out on pasture now, so that helps, but we still need to buy soybean oil meal and supplements for the grain mix, and those are expensive."

I have the distinct sense that Eli would have preferred not to have culled those two cows just yet. If the milk price were higher or feed costs were lower, he may have held onto them a little longer. Ultimately, all cows are eventually culled from the herd to make room for younger, healthier, or better-producing cows. However, in this case, the economics of the day forced Eli's hand, and he seems distinctly uneasy about it. He is still milking 30 cows. Anyplace else that would be considered a tiny number of cows for a dairy farm, but here in the settlement Eli's 30 cows are one of the very largest herds.

The two Holstein cows Eli culled from the herd this morning were undoubtedly shipped to the livestock auction over in Bloomfield. The auction is almost 20 miles from this farm, so Eli probably called one of the local truckers last night and made arrangements to pick up the cows this morning. There are a number of local truck drivers around the area who specialize in hauling livestock from farm to farm, or to livestock shows, or, most often, to the auction. Of course since these guys make their living driving trucks, they are all Yankees.

Once at the auction, a good cow is usually bought by another farmer who is expanding his herd. But the two Eli sent this morning aren't good cows, and they are headed for the beef ring. Unfortunately, they are not even good beef animals because they are older Holsteins, and their meat will be tough. Some time in the next few hours, each one will be driven into the auction ring and sold individually. A few local meatpackers will lazily bid against each other until the auctioneer drops his gavel and pronounces the animal "sold." The price will be low, for they are after all only low-quality beef. They will each be slaughtered later today or tomorrow morning. Most or in some cases all of the meat on the carcass will be ground into hamburger. Look for it at your favorite fast-food restaurant.

Eli is showing me where he cut a new trench in the concrete floor to shunt the manure out of the side of the barn. Unlike before, he uses almost no bedding now because the new system is a liquid system, and the manure won't flow if there is too much bedding. The cows don't really need bedding. The floor of each stall is covered with an individual cow-sized rubber mat, so the animals are kept both clean and comfortable.

We step outside and walk around the silos for my first look at the rest of the system. I'm not sure I've ever seen one quite like this—and I've seen a lot of manure systems over the years. The main feature is a gravel driveway dug into a hill that slopes away from the barn. There is a retaining wall made out of large concrete blocks holding back the hill, and the driveway appears to be at least eight feet lower than the barn floor. A boxy, close-topped metal manure spreader is parked near the center of the wall directly under a large, corrugated, black plastic pipe. A small metal door blocks the end of the pipe so the manure can't run out until Eli opens the door.

The odd-shaped metal manure spreader is fascinating—well, to me it's fascinating. There's a metal seat in front for the driver and a long wooden tongue to hitch the horses to. There're two small steel wheels in the front and two very large and wide steel wheels in the back. All four of these wheels are covered with a one-inch-thick belt of rubber. It must be ground driven and gets its power through those large rear wheels. At first I'm stumped as to why the wheels would be covered in rubber. But then it dawns on me that Eli has fields on both sides of the road, so the rubber is there to make the machine legal on the road. Pointing at the spreader, I ask, "Just how much did that contraption cost?"

"Forty-five hundred dollars."

Suddenly Katie is standing at the open barn door. "Do you have any plans for dinner, Randy?"

Dinner is the noon meal, and it is almost always the largest meal of the day. It is awfully kind of Katie to invite me to stay for dinner, and I know from experience that she is a wonderful cook. But my plan is to keep moving today and perhaps catch another farmer friend before noon. After a long moment of hesitation, I very reluctantly say, "Thank you so much, Katie, that's a great offer, but I'm afraid I'd better not today."

"Oh well, maybe next time." With that, she heads through the barn on her way back to the kitchen.

Turning my attention back to Eli, I still want to know more about the cost of the system and how it operates. "So what'd it cost to put in the whole manure system?"

"In round numbers it was about $16,000. But I did a lot of the work myself, so that helped hold down the cost."

"Okay, does that $16,000 include the cost of the manure spreader? Or is that separate?"

"No, that includes the spreader, so the total for the whole thing was about $16,000."

I'm struck that $16,000 is quite a bit of money for a farm this size. However, I'm surprised it wasn't more.

As we're talking, I remember that a year or so ago he was considering putting in another type of manure handling system. It had an underground tank to store the manure and a gasoline pump to pump the manure into a spreader. Eli had a complete set of plans drawn up for that system and was ready to begin construction, but for some reason the church elders put a stop to it. I'm curious to know why this system is okay and the other was not. I hesitate asking because I'm always a little reticent about getting into church issues. But I do really want to know. "So there is no church trouble with this system here?"

"Nope, with this system everything is gravity fed. There are no pumps and no underground pit. That took care of all the objections, so everything is fine."

As is so often the case, I am left a little confused by the logic behind this particular church decision. The *Ordnung* of each church district is a somewhat flexible set of spoken rules that can change over time. They are often renegotiated to accommodate, or reject, changes brought about by ever-encroaching modernity.

Another objection may well have been that Eli's proposed pit system was just too big of a shift from the traditional methods of farming used here in the settlement. The Amish truly value tradition in a way that is difficult for the rest of us to comprehend. Traditions have value in their own right, they are part of the fabric of everyday life, and they are only changed when there is a compelling reason to do so. It is easy for us non-Amish to throw stones at this one. For heaven's sake, why would anyone care, or want to maintain, a farming tradition that had to do with manure? Yeah, peering over our computer screens at these tradition-bound farm communities, it's temptingly easy to ridicule them for their quaint ideas and lack of progress. But there again, in terms of farm numbers, the Amish, with all their respect for tradition, represent one of the fastest-growing segments of U.S. agriculture today. Maybe it's best that we hold onto those stones or, better yet, take careful aim and fling them at some far more deserving part of our ultramodern farm industry.

I'm certain I will never know the real issues and factors that the church elders took into consideration in regard to this manure handling system. I doubt that Eli really knows either. In any case, it's here now and he's using it. The total cost of about $16,000 adds approximately $500 of capital expense per milking cow. In a herd this big, that's quite a lot, but it's probably doable, if they watch all of their other expenses carefully.

I wave my arm over the entire scene and ask, "Well, Eli, is it worth it?"

"Oh yes, I'd say so, yes, definitely." He nods his head decidedly up and down. "It was kind of expensive, but there's no way I could handle the manure from all of these cows by hand. I also think it does a better job spreading the manure."

"Do you mean it spreads it more evenly?"

"Yeah, when you get done spreading and look back, there is a uniform sheet of manure covering the whole field. Not at all like the old spreader where you had clumps and piles all over the place. I'm even cutting back on the fertilizer I use."

"If I remember correctly, Eli"—and I do remember this sort of thing— "you had just barely enough land to handle the manure from the herd, before you added any cows. Isn't that right?"

He looks at me for a moment with a puzzled look on his face that suddenly evaporates into a grin. "Oh, I keep forgetting you haven't been around. I was able to rent 20 more acres from the next-door neighbor. So I have plenty of land now."

"That's great. What's it in?"

"Half corn and half hay."

One of the problems we identified, way back when Eli was just thinking about starting a farm, was that if he ever got near his goal of 30 cows, he was probably going to need to find some more land to rent or buy. The land is important not only to keep his feed costs down—it's cheaper to raise dairy feed than to buy it—but also for a place to spread the manure. In round numbers, a dairy farmer needs to have available about one and a half to two acres of farmland for every dairy cow in order to utilize the fertilizer nutrients in the manure. When the right amount of manure is spread onto farmland, the farmer can save money by reducing the amount of expensive commercial fertilizer he has to buy. The nutrients in the manure are free plant food. But if the farmer doesn't have enough land and has to spread way too much on each acre just to get rid of it, the manure can quickly become a liability. The same manure fertilizer nutrients that can help crops grow when spread judiciously can become serious environmental pollutants when overapplied. When the manure and its nutrients are spread so thick that it runs off of a field, it can wreak havoc on fish and other wild critters and do long-term damage to the environment.

When a dairy farm the size of Eli's doesn't have enough acres, it can be a potential problem for the immediate neighborhood. When the dairy farm is 100 times larger with 3,000 or more cows, the impact on the environment from mishandled manure is potentially devastating. In any case, I'm glad Eli found his 20 acres.

To most folks it would sound silly, but one of my real passions is finding ways to reduce the cost of the commercial fertilizers a farmer has to purchase by using the manure generated on the farm. Replacing fertilizer with manure sounds easy enough, but in practice it takes some serious chemistry and math to get it done right.

"So, Eli, you can spread the manure more easily and uniformly over the field. Have you been able to really cut down on the amount of fertilizer you buy?"

In a strong and somewhat authoritarian voice, Eli proclaims, "Oh yes, I usually put down 150 pounds of triple 19 per acre through the planter for a starter, and this year I went to 150 pounds triple 10. Then I added some urea, of course, after the corn got up a little."

That is a substantial fertilizer reduction. Eli was using triple 19, which contains 19 pounds of nitrogen, 19 pounds of phosphorous, 19 pounds of potash in every 100 pounds of fertilizer, or 19 percent of each nutrient—hence the triple 19. This year he went down to triple 10, which has 10 percent of each nutrient, so that almost cut his starter fertilizer nutrients in half, and that should've cut the expense by something close to half.

Starter fertilizer is the stuff that farmers put down when they are planting the seeds. It's loaded into a metal hopper box mounted on top of the corn planter and is fed through long metal tubes down beside the seeds as they are planted. The urea that Eli talked about is broadcasted over the field with a broadcast spreader after the corn is up. Urea is strictly a nitrogen source. Corn needs a lot of nitrogen, and urea is 46 percent nitrogen. He probably used about 100 to 150 pounds of urea per acre. But that part of the fertilizer application did not change from before he had his new manure handling system. So his real savings are in the amount he was able to cut down on his starter fertilizer.

Saving *some* money on starter fertilizer is real good. However, as I start to match the number of cows pooping to the number of crop acres in my head, I'm not at all sure any starter fertilizer was needed. "Why did you decide to put down the triple 10 starter, Eli? I mean, did you look at the soil tests and calculate the amount needed or what?"

"No, not really, I've always used starter fertilizer so I thought I'd probably just better put some down."

Triple 19 or triple 12 or triple 10 starter fertilizers border on an addiction for most farmers. After all there's a starter fertilizer hopper box mounted right there on top of the planter, and we have to fill it with something. The equipment manufacturers didn't put the box there to look at. Never mind that all the university research says that starter fertilizers only help if the soil needs it, and instead of a "triple whatever" the fertilizer analysis should be chosen to make up what the soil lacks. On this dairy farm, I am almost certain that the cows poop enough phosphorous to take care of all that the corn could possibly need. So at the very least, that phosphorous number in the middle of the "triple whatever" starter fertilizer should be changed to zero to save money. It is all that I can do not to run back to my car, dig out my pocket calculator, and refigure this fertilizer recommendation. But, it's not my job, not anymore.

Eli shows no rush, but I'm beginning to feel like it's about time for me to go. Time to drive off toward some other farm for yet another visit. We wander slowly back through the barn, talking about manure, fertilizer, and other farm stuff. The price of milk has Eli worried. I can hear it in his voice and see it in his face. Yet his overall mood is, without question, optimistic. There is no doubt he truly loves to farm, and if at all possible will continue milking cows.

As we get over near my car, Katie comes out of the house and offers one more time, "You know, you're more than welcome to stay for dinner."

"Thanks, Katie, but I think I really should be going. Hopefully, next time I'll plan things better and able to take you up on that offer."

Turning back to Eli, I plainly ask, "Well, what's the near future going to bring? Are a lot of guys going to stop farming?"

"No, I don't think so. In fact, maybe just the opposite. A lot of guys right here in this neighborhood, who were never farmers in the past, are starting to grow things. Work in construction and the factories is way off, so people are growing beef, sheep, pigs, and vegetables, and quite a few put up little greenhouses where they are growing strawberries. It's a new thing. Hopefully, it will all work out for them."

"What about the larger farms. How are they doing?"

"Not so good from what I hear. You know Ray Smith over in Ashtabula County?"

"Yeah."

"Well, he's got over 300 cows, and he has to buy almost all of his feed. They say he has a huge feed bill and, with the price of milk, he just can't cover it. The small farms can always cut back somewhere or work off the farm a little bit, but when you're that big, you are committed. And with the price of milk, I don't know how long they can stay in business."

Three hundred cows really is not a big operation by today's standards. Farms of 3,000 to 5,000 are common enough, but 300 is 10 times bigger than Eli's farm, so at least to him it's big.

I nod in agreement with what he's saying. He looks back toward the barn, pauses for a moment, and then goes on. "The small farms around here will stay in business, partly because there are no other jobs. It's the large farms that are in real trouble. I don't see how some of them are going to make it."

Eli cannot know how profoundly I agree with him. Larger farms are less flexible and, by and large, less able to withstand serious economic downturns. All of the hype about farms needing to get bigger and specialize in order to stay in business is sheer nonsense. Large farms do not produce food more cheaply or more efficiently, and they certainly don't care for their animals better. There are virtually no "efficiencies of scale" in agriculture; there is simply "scale."

For a long moment, I consider sitting down right here in the barnyard and spending the rest of the day discussing the fallacies of the U.S. big farm complex with Eli. But it's a pleasant morning, and we both have things left to do this day. I quietly say my good-byes to Katie and Eli, wave to each of the children in turn, pat the dog, and drive away.

18

"It's What We Want to Do"

Quite unexpectedly, I'm back in Ohio only a few months after my last visit to attend the funeral of a relative. Before heading back to South Carolina, we are taking a few days to visit friends, both Yankee and Amish. Not surprisingly, I find my car pointed in the general direction of Katie and Eli Gingerich. Milk prices are near rock bottom, approaching a 20-year low, and I am concerned for them and for all of the other new small farms.

Everything looks the same as I pull into the driveway. It's about 11 o'clock and around 80 degrees. The white farmhouse is still on the left with the white barn on the right and the tool shed directly in front. There's a wire corn crib next to the shed, and in the background I can see some Holstein cows out in the back pasture. A few heifers are in the outside pen just west of the barn, and a blue pickup truck is parked near the milk house. That's unfortunate. It means some salesman or machinery repair person is here. It'll probably make it a lot harder to talk with Eli.

Farther up the driveway, Katie and three of her children come into view behind the house. She waves immediately as I park the car and get out. Walking up the path toward the back of the house, I can now see that they are all standing in or around a small vegetable garden that's maybe 15 feet wide and 25 feet long.

"Hi, Katie, how are things going?"

She smiles and then with a bit of a sigh says, "It's tough." I know she's talking about the terribly low milk price and how much it is hurting their pocketbook. Before I can say a word, she goes on in a voice that seems to shuffle back and forth between pleading and strong resolve. "But what else are we going to do? There are no carpentry jobs out there." Eli was a contractor with his own carpentry crew before they started farming. "Besides," she says with pointed emphasis, "it's what we want to do."

I will hear the same refrain over and over again in the next few days. Amish farm families acknowledging hard times brought about by low milk prices, which are totally outside of their control, followed by an understanding that the local economy is so bad that there are few, if any, other jobs or options. Then finishing up with a clearly articulated business and personal goal to keep the family farm afloat by whatever means are necessary.

"I'm sorry, Katie. I know these milk prices are really something, and it must be a challenge to make ends meet sometimes. By the way, where is the milk price right now?"

"I think this past month it was right at $12. It was lower last month, somewhere around $11.60."

That's only $12 for every hundred pounds of milk the farm ships. Last year it was close to $18 and maybe a little more with bonuses for quality. Any business or family would have a hard time coping with a third or more drop in monthly income, and the strain is obvious in the words Katie uses to explain the current financial realities. The Gingeriches aren't rich, but they're not exactly poor either. Amish farm families don't generally spend as much as their Yankee neighbors. Fortunately, on a small farm like this there are many ways to economize and restructure the business in order to survive. The trick is to make some changes quickly and then hope they were the right changes.

Eli and Katie's farm has no control over the price of milk or other commodities and only very limited control over the price of any other specialty agricultural products like maple syrup, honey, or vegetables. Likewise, the farm has almost no control over the price of inputs like fertilizer, fuel, feed, and seed. However, small farms like this one have a great deal of control over many other things, such as any hay, silage, or grain that is produced on the farm, equipment costs, profitable use of the manure, and, to some extent, animal health. These are real—and routinely overlooked—competitive advantages that very small farms are able to capture. Still, as Katie says, times are tough.

In vain, I search for something strongly optimistic and positive to say and finally settle for a tepid, "Well, hang in there. The price will turn around. It always does." To my surprise, Katie smiles and brightens a bit as she nods in agreement.

The heavenly aroma of a bakery is wafting out the backdoor of the house. Katie looks to her oldest daughter standing about 10 feet away and says, "Would you go check on those pies? We don't want to forget them." The daughter, who must be around 12, puts down the hoe she's using to weed the garden and traipses off toward the kitchen.

"Who's down in the barn with Eli?"

"Oh, that's the feed salesman. He's been here quite a while now."

The term "feed salesman" really doesn't do justice to many of the highly trained professionals who assist dairy farmers in designing a nutrient management program for each segment of the dairy herd and then sell the additives necessary to balance the diet. But "feed salesman" is at least partially accurate and is easier to remember than whatever title the parent company happens to be using this year. There is a lot of work involved in carefully balancing a ration using the farmer's own homegrown feeds and matching them to the available feed supplements. It's important work, and it takes a healthy amount of time to do it right. Since my time in the settlement is so limited with this visit, I think I'd better move on down the road to the next farm.

"Well, Katie, I don't want to interrupt the feed salesman, so maybe I'll try to stop back later."

Suddenly she looks truly distressed. "I'm sure Eli will be done soon. He's been looking up this way. He would be so disappointed if you left." Her message is clear, and I realize there is nothing I have to do today that is more important than spending time with Katie, Eli, and the family.

"Okay, then. Guess I'll stay right here and talk with you and the children." Their oldest son, Samuel, is standing nearby, listening to everything that's said, so I turn to him and ask, "How old are you now?"

"I'm 11."

"That's getting up there. Are you helping your mother with the garden this morning?"

Before Samuel starts to answer, I notice Katie slipping off into the house. Probably needs to check on the baking. The lad straightens up tall, hitches a thumb under his right suspender, and answers decisively, "Yes. This is a new garden, you know. Do you remember the building that used to be here?" I nod my head. I vaguely remember a building being there, but there are so many farms and so many buildings. "Yeah, we tore it down last year and then put this garden here."

"Well, it looks great." I'm not kidding. It really does look great. It's a true kitchen garden, right outside of the backdoor and stuffed with ripening vegetables.

Katie steps back outside and interrupts our conversation on the new garden. With both hands, she is holding a golden-brown loaf of bread wrapped in clear plastic. "This is for you and your family."

There are only a few things better in life than a gift of fresh-baked, homemade Amish bread. "Katie, that is so very kind of you. We will enjoy it. Thank you."

"Oh, you're welcome. I hope you enjoy it. I've been baking every week for a local farm market, but they were closed this weekend, so I have extra. This feels good because I can so seldom give it away."

Smiling, she holds the loaf out to me, and I take it gratefully. It's taken a moment for her words to sink in. On top of all her other duties and chores in running this growing farm household, she is now selling baked goods in order to help stretch the family budget. I am quietly and profoundly impressed with her strength of character. I make a feeble offer to pay, and she of course declines.

Turning away I say to her, "Let me put this in the car right now, so I won't forget it." What I don't tell her is that I already have serious designs for this bread. By tonight it will be re-gifted! My wife and I are having dinner with Bill and Suzanne—two of our Yankee friends—and the four of us will delight in Katie's fresh bread and a good bottle of red wine.

The feed salesman's pickup truck rolls slowly out of the driveway while I am stashing the bread in my car. I amble back up the path to the garden, and seconds later Eli is there greeting me. "I was going to call you, but I lost your card," he says. "The last time you were here, I put it in my pants but there was a hole in the pocket, and it fell out. So I lost it somewhere."

Katie looks a little perplexed. "We have it," she says with real emphasis. "I found it on the kitchen floor so I picked it up and put it in the book. It's in there."

"Oh well, I thought it was lost. Anyway, I'm glad you stopped by, and I really was going to call you."

"Was there anything in particular you wanted to talk about, Eli?"

"Well, yes, I think we need to diversify, wanted to talk about it a little, and see what you think."

I'm mildly surprised and cannot suppress a smile. When we first sat down to do a business plan for this farm, I had encouraged Eli to at least be open to the possibility of diversifying. While the main profit center of the farm might well be the dairy, it is always good to have other streams of income. At the time, Eli was at best lukewarm to the idea. His goal then was to get the dairy up and running and then maybe some time in the distant future consider adding some other enterprise. In any case, we did not include other farm enterprises in the original plan, and I'm pleased that he and Katie are thinking about it now but saddened that it is brought about by the current economic duress.

Many, perhaps most, modern dairy farms narrowly focus on only one thing—milking cows. They buy most or all of the feed for the cow herd, so they don't have to worry about growing crops and can focus on milking cows. Heifer raising is done by another farm under contract, so the dairy farm can focus on milking cows. A waste management firm is paid to dispose of the manure, so the dairy farm can focus on milking cows. By these standards, Eli and Katie's little farm is already fairly diverse because they themselves do most of the things needed to actually take care of the cows and calves. The monthly milk check is still the only major source of farm income, though, and that leaves them dreadfully exposed when milk prices plummet.

Katie's baking business is surely helping. But if they also had a few beef animals or could fatten out some hogs or raise vegetables, chickens, honey, maple syrup, or any number of other farm products, they would have other streams of income to augment the milk check. However, until now, they've stuck pretty much to concentrating on the dairy, and until now it's worked.

"Well, okay, Eli, there's a whole bunch of ways you can diversify a farm. Why don't we talk about some? If you don't mind, I would kind of like to see the barn, so maybe we could at least start to talk about options down there."

"Sure, that's fine with me. Let's go."

As we enter the barn through a side door, I ask, "So what are you thinking about adding to diversify the farm?"

"Well, we've always kind of had in the back of our minds," Eli pauses a minute and then goes on in a voice with more question than confidence, "maybe putting up a greenhouse."

I sincerely wish Eli and Katie had shared their possible future interest in a greenhouse back when we first set up the business plan for this farm. At the time, it would have been easy to add in a small greenhouse as a possible farm option. Oh well, that's all water over the dam. Geauga County has long had a thriving greenhouse, nursery, and landscape industry in the Yankee community, and in recent years quite a few Amish families here in the settlement have put up greenhouses and started profitable businesses. I can't think of any right offhand associated with a dairy farm, but the idea sounds plausible enough.

Putting up a greenhouse is about half the equation; the other half is deciding what to grow and how to market it. "A greenhouse could be a good idea. Have you thought about what you're going to grow?"

Eli nods and in a voice with slowly growing confidence says, "Yeah, I have a cousin over in Pennsylvania, and according to him it's flowers and vegetable bedding plants that pay the bills."

"I wouldn't argue a bit with anything you're saying, Eli. Greenhouses can be highly profitable, and right now with the severe downturn in the economy, a lot of people are expanding their gardens or putting one in for the first time in years. If you do decide to build a greenhouse, where would you put it?"

"Probably right in front of the barn. We have an area that's already level so we wouldn't have to do any grading."

"Sounds like you thought this through pretty well. Have you pulled together any numbers on construction costs or production and marketing costs or, for that matter, potential sales and profit?"

Eli smiles a little and says almost timidly, "Not much, yet. I'm really just getting started with the whole idea. I wanted to see what you and a few other guys thought before I went too far."

"Well, to me it looks like you've thought most of this through, and it could be a great idea. We don't see a lot of greenhouses on dairy farms, but I can't see any reason it wouldn't work. You need to pull together some more numbers, but I think the general idea has real potential." Eli seems genuinely pleased with my initial assessment. However, I do want to encourage him to do some more research into the idea. "How well do you know John Yoder over on Tavern Road?"

"Oh, I know John pretty well."

"Do you know him well enough that you'd be comfortable talking to him about getting started with a greenhouse?"

Eli nods emphatically and simply says, "Yes."

"Good. I think you should get over and see him just as soon as you can. He's been in the greenhouse and vegetable business for years, and I know he likes to see younger people getting started. He'd have a ton of numbers on the financial side and could answer just about any production problem you might run into. Anyway, I think talking to John would be the logical next step."

"Then that is exactly what I'll do. I should be able to get over there tomorrow or, at the very least, in the next few days."

When Eli does visit, I am sure John Yoder will take all of the time necessary to carefully explain both the pros and the cons of building and running a greenhouse. I'm also pretty sure that the economics will be good enough that Eli and Katie will be running a greenhouse by next spring. The new greenhouse and Katie's baking business are the first steps toward diversifying this small farm, but more could be done and I want to talk about other possibilities before I leave.

"Have you given any thought to raising free-range chickens?"

Eli's frame stiffens and his head turns slowly back and forth as he says with some finality, "The milk inspector won't let us have chickens running free near the cows. We do have about two dozen layers in cages out back, for our own use, but that's all."

"Two dozen?"

"Yeah, we eat a lot of eggs. Anyway, they got out once and just made a wreck out of the garden, so I don't see how we can have them just running around free."

"No, no. 'Free-range' doesn't mean that the chickens are completely free. It just means that, unlike most chickens today, they are able to walk around and do some foraging for food, outside on real soil. Usually groups of chickens are raised in portable pens with wire over the top so they can't fly away and are protected from predators. The pens are put out in pastures or fields and moved every day so the chickens always have fresh dirt to scratch."

Eli still looks mighty skeptical, but he does manage to show some interest. "What do they actually eat?"

"Mostly bugs, grubs, weeds, seeds, and worms. That's the beauty of it. You don't have to feed them very much. Most of what they eat, they gather with their own feet and beaks. Listen, there is a great book on all of this called *The Chicken Tractor*. I just reread it last week. The authors are Andy Lee and Pat Foreman. You can get it from the library."

Finally, a smile breaks over Eli's face. "What's a chicken tractor?"

"It's what they call the cages."

"Why?"

"I don't know. Read the book." Actually, I do know but that's taking us too far off the topic. The cages got the name "tractor" because, if they are built right and put between rows of crops, the chickens will cultivate out the weeds with their scratching and pecking.

This is going better. Eli is laughing a little so I press on. "I know it sounds funny but you really do need to look at the economics of this. In Ohio it is perfectly legal to home slaughter and process up to 1,000 birds a year and sell them to your neighbors without any kind of government inspection or permit. The average bird weighs about seven pounds, and free-range chickens normally sell for somewhere in the neighborhood of $2 per pound."

Quickly doing the math and his head, Eli looks directly at me and with a growing smile says, "Wow, now that's not too bad."

"Yeah, and they pretty much feed themselves."

We wander over to the backdoor of the barn as we talk, and for the first time I can see the rest of the herd. It looks like the older heifers must be out with the dairy herd because there appear to be well over 30 black-and-white animals scattered far out in the northeast pasture. We talk a little bit more about milk prices, crop yields, and how much the cows are milking right now. But I'm still anxious to talk more about diversification.

"You know, Eli, the chickens don't have to be broilers. Five hundred layers could pay a lot of bills."

Laughing heartily, he is barely able to say, "The egg market is flooded."

It's infectious and now I'm laughing too. "Yeah, what in the world is going on? I notice as I have been driving around that there are 'eggs for sale' signs all over the place. It looks like about every third farm is selling eggs."

"Sam Mullet did it." Sam is another young farmer who lives about a mile away and has sold eggs from his own flock of chickens ever since he started to farm about five years ago.

"Why is it Sam's fault?"

"Every year he would sell 1,000 or more chicks to the neighbors around here. I told him he was going to put himself out of business."

"Well, you can get peeps [baby chickens] through the mail. For that matter, you can order them from the feed mill over in Middlefield. They get a batch in every spring. So Sam's not the only place you can get little chickens."

"I know, but he made it easy. Finally, this year he told me he's not selling another one to anybody."

Deciding now to let go of the discussion about the profit potential to be found in the egg business, I reluctantly admit to myself that Eli's probably right: Sam did kill the egg market, at least in this neighborhood. There is a PhD dissertation's worth of research here to fully examine the dynamics of this tiny egg market, where most of the customers come in on foot or buggy. The transportation issues alone would be fascinating, not to mention Sam's tremendous, albeit unintended, market influence. Unfortunately, any graduate student who would take on this research project would undoubtedly be under the tutelage of a Department of Agricultural Economics in some College of Agriculture at a major university. Therefore, the preordained solution to the market difficulties would obviously be to "get bigger and specialize."

As we amble out of the side door of the barn, Eli says it's time for lunch and asks if I will stay. Without any hesitation, I agree. I'm looking forward to spending more time with the Gingeriches today. They are not only fun but inspiring, and I definitely will make the time to join them around the dinner table.

19

Chinese under the Maple Tree

As we step into the kitchen, Katie turns away from the counter where she is cutting vegetables, and in a voice that is more directive than questioning says, "You are staying for lunch—aren't you?"

"I'd love to, if you'll have me."

"Sure, I was expecting you to stay. We're having Chinese. Is that all right?"

"I love Chinese." I do love Chinese food, but I have to admit this is the first time I can remember eating it in an Amish home, and I've had a lot of meals in Amish homes.

Through the screen door I catch a glimpse of two children setting plates on a picnic table out on the lawn under the shade of a maple tree. Eli and I step out on the side porch to wait for lunch. We're in our stocking feet because we left our barn shoes in the mudroom at the backdoor. That's just fine. The day is warm and the ground is dry; we don't need shoes.

"Have you given any thought to growing produce, Eli?"

"I have, but I'm not sure how well it would work in with the dairy. We have two fair-sized gardens here, just for our own use, and even that seems to conflict with the farm fieldwork. I mean, when you feel like you should be working in the garden, you should be out in the field too. I help out where I can, but really it's Katie and the children who mainly take care of the gardens."

Produce would go a long way toward really diversifying this farm and increasing the farm income. However, on this one, Eli is probably right. The peak labor times for vegetable and field crop production on the dairy simply overlap. When it's time to harvest zucchini, it's also time for second cutting hay or thrashing oats or cultivating corn or any number of other summer jobs. I may be forgetting somebody, but I only remember one dairy farm that got seriously into the produce business. After a few years, that farm ended up reluctantly selling the cows because of the conflicting summer labor requirements of the two farm enterprises. Both were profitable, but there was no way for the family to keep up with all of the summer work.

No sense beating a dead horse, so I willingly concede the vegetable point. "It's true. The real work for produce happens right when you need to be in the field working on the crops for the dairy. So I can understand your reluctance, and I really can't say that I know of a dairy farm that is also a successful produce operation."

Starting to feel like a bit of a nag, I hear myself nonetheless press on with yet another marvelously clever diversity scheme. "What about pigs?"

Eli leans back almost to the point of tipping and says, "Feeder pigs are very expensive." Feeder pigs are simply young pigs, weighing generally anywhere from 30 to 100 pounds. One farmer buys the feeder pigs from another farmer and then feeds them out to market weight and sells them for meat.

Translation: Eli doesn't want to have pigs. That's a shame. A few pigs can really round out the income sources for a dairy herd. If nothing else, feeding out one or two pigs and butchering them in the fall helps reduce the family's annual food budget. The rule of thumb is about one fat hog is needed per family per year. Pigs also make use of some feeds that the dairy cows can't. If allowed, they will even root the undigested kernels of corn out of the heifer or cow manure and eat that. Besides all of those wonderful attributes, pigs happen to be my favorite farm animal.

It is obviously no use. I can tell by his demeanor that he does not want pigs on this farm. If he were open to it, we could even discuss getting a few sows and a boar so he could start a little breeding operation. After the sows farrow (give birth) they could raise the shoats (baby pigs) all the way up to market weight and then sell them.

Ahh, "market weight"—whatever that is now. Without question I over-analyze seemingly trivial things and as a result often spoil my dinner or, more to the point, my wife's dinner. Thirty years ago when I was a brand-new county agent, the average "market weight" of a "fat hog" was around 200 to 230 pounds. Now it's somewhere between 300 and 330 pounds. Oh, and they are no longer "fat hogs" ready for "slaughter," they are "market animals" ready to be "harvested." Along with massaging the English language, the hog industry also figured out that if you increase market weight slowly, people probably won't notice. Since pigs still have the same number of bones as they had 30 years ago, more meat and fat have to be packed around each bone, so the pork chop you—or your children—eat today is about 50 percent bigger than the one that would have been on the plate 30 years ago. And guess what—we're getting fatter.

Oh well, there really is no reason to grapple with the ethics of the mega-hog farms or the giant hog industry today. Eli has made it perfectly clear that he is not going to feed out a few pigs, at least not this year.

As if on cue, Katie and the children burst out of the kitchen door with large bowls of steaming food and head for the picnic table. Without any prompting, Eli and I gladly follow. He takes his place at one end of a bench with Katie at the other end and two children between. The other two children and I sit on the opposite bench. When everyone is seated and quiet, Eli says, "Let's have grace." In the few moments of silence that follow, I have time to reflect on how truly blessed I am to be here with this young farm family, out here under a tree in the middle of the American heartland. Eli clears his throat and the silent grace is over.

Almost immediately Katie says, "I do hope you like this." She passes a heaping bowl of hot rice my way. Then she stands and starts to ladle big scoops of the richly aromatic chicken stir-fry over the mound of rice on my plate . . . Chinese-Amish style. "Say when."

"That's just fine, Katie. This smells great."

She works her way around the table, serving each person and finally herself. As she sits down, we all dig in. It really is delicious, with loads of chopped fresh vegetables that were still in the garden not more than an hour ago, along with canned chicken and a mildly spiced sauce. That's "canned" chicken that Katie put up herself in a mason jar a few weeks ago. The chicken spent most of her days providing eggs for the family and quietly clucking with the rest of the hens out behind the barn. Today she provides one more meal, and I am grateful to have this chance to share it. Fresh homemade bread, butter, jam, and a just-from-the-garden salad round out our meal. A pitcher of cool water, with the beads of sweat forming on the glass, sits at the edge of the table ready to refill our glasses when needed.

What little conversation there is around the table for the first few minutes is largely limited to how good everything is. After a few mouthfuls, the chewing pace slows down and Eli introduces a new topic. "Hey, I read a very short article in the *Plain Dealer* the other day that said 'cap and trade' was going to put small farmers out of business. It was really just a headline. Then it said to learn more about it go to the *Plain Dealer* website. So just what is this cap and trade stuff, anyway."

He is smiling as he asks the question, but the frustration in his voice is clearly apparent. The *Plain Dealer* is the dominant newspaper in most of the counties around Cleveland, and a healthy percentage of all the small farm owners in the entire readership area are Amish. For the newspaper to announce their cherished way of life is in peril by cap and trade—whatever that is—and then to direct them to a website that they obviously cannot access is simply irresponsible. The near-record high cost of cow feed coupled with abysmally low milk prices have given these families quite enough to worry about, and they do not need the *Plain Dealer* piling mystery catastrophes onto their emotional load.

Time to vent a little shared frustration. "First, let me say there are some very good reporters at the *Plain Dealer* who have taken the time to understand agriculture and the farm community fairly well. However, it is a *Cleveland* newspaper, and most of the folks there know as much about agriculture as that asphalt road running past your mailbox knows."

"Well, I know that." Eli is laughing now but there's still a hint of concern in his voice. "But do you understand this whole cap and trade thing?"

"Honestly, I haven't kept up with the current debate or any pending legislation. They have been talking about cap and trade for at least 20 years, and I've kind of lost interest until something concrete happens. The basic idea is that the amount of carbon that each business or industry puts into the atmosphere is capped at some level. Then if that business ends up putting less carbon into the atmosphere than they are allotted, they are allowed to sell, or trade, the remaining tons of carbon to some other business that is generating more than they were allotted."

Both Eli and Katie have a fairly confused expression on their faces, and I'm not surprised this whole concept is difficult. "Does that make any sense at all?"

"Well, some," Eli exhales heavily. "I mean, I've read quite a bit on it over the last few years, but I still don't understand all of it. Like how are they going to sell all of this carbon?"

"I don't understand all of it either, and remember I haven't really tried to keep up with this topic for a few years. But I believe one of the proposals is to set up some form of an electronic auction so that the people who need to put more carbon into the atmosphere could buy the rights from the people who had excess carbon in their allotment."

"They don't plan to actually ship carbon around the country, do they?"

"No, they're just selling the right to pollute the atmosphere with some number of tons of carbon dioxide."

"And the carbon dioxide is a greenhouse gas, right?"

"Yeah, that's right." Eli is leading this discussion, but Katie is following along with real interest on her expressive face and occasionally nodding agreement or understanding.

Stifling a silly grin, I am suddenly struck with the incongruity of this entire scene. Here I am sitting around a picnic table on a lovely sunny day, with a charming Amish family, eating Chinese food, and talking about global warming and greenhouse gases. The technical nature of the conversation itself does not surprise me. While Amish people complete their formal education at eighth grade, most continue to educate themselves through avid reading, and I have learned never to assume that they are unaware of current events and issues.

Something is pushing on my foot. Looking under the table, expecting to find a kitten or someone else's foot, I'm momentarily puzzled to find a metal pot slowly inching its way forward onto my foot. Directly across the table, Daniel starts to giggle uncontrollably. I jokingly chastise him for the prank, and soon the entire table is laughing along with us.

As soon as things settle down, Eli is back on track with his questions, but thanks to Daniel the mood is measurably lighter. "I still don't quite understand how this cap and trade thing is going to hurt small farms. I mean, do farms generate a lot of carbon dioxide?"

"Well, yeah, they produce some. I suppose how much probably depends, at least in part, on the size of farm and also on what type of farm it is and on what farming practices are used."

Eli leans back a little. "I do remember reading something about dairy cows and greenhouse gases a while back. But I don't really remember the point of the article."

"Yeah, I vaguely remember a study that was done a few years ago that looked into the amount of CO_2 that was released into the atmosphere through cow burps." The whole table is chuckling a little over this one. "It was picked up by a lot of the media because it was funny, and there was kind of a 'so what' aspect to the whole study. If I remember correctly the researchers took all of the cows in the country, or maybe the world, and calculated how much carbon dioxide they would burp out on an annual basis."

Katie chimes in, "That's kind of silly, isn't it?"

"Well, yes and no. I suppose the researchers were trying to get a handle on how much carbon dioxide different parts of agriculture generate, and cows would be a pretty good place to start, as far as the livestock portion of agriculture goes."

Through her laughter. Katie now emphatically asks, "But why pick on cows?"

"Because that big first stomach of theirs, the rumen, generates a lot of carbon dioxide, and the cows stand around and burp it out all day long. Most other animals don't have a rumen, or at least aren't so big, so they generate less carbon dioxide. Of course all animals, including people, exhale carbon dioxide. Cows just have more to get rid of, that's all."

Eli adds, "Doesn't the manure have something to do with it too?"

"Yes, it's organic matter, and all organic matter puts carbon dioxide into the air as it breaks down." This stuff is complicated, and I am not at all sure that my explanations are improving the understanding of the topic around this table. However, they seem to be truly interested, and it is a fascinating topic. "And you don't want to concentrate just on livestock. That's not the only place that carbon dioxide is generated on the farm. One of the big culprits is plowing."

"Plowing?" Eli looks surprised.

"Yeah, plowing. There is solid research that says every time you plow a field, you release a whole bunch of carbon into the atmosphere. That's probably not the major reason, but it is one of the reasons there is so much interest in no-till farming. In fact, some of the cap and trade schemes theorize that farmers could be paid to convert to no-till so that the carbon would stay trapped in the soil."

Pondering all of this for a moment or two, Eli finally looks back at me and says, "So who would pay farmers not to plow? The government?"

"No, the thought is that businesses who needed to put more carbon into the air than they are allotted under the 'cap' would pay the farmers." Pausing for a long drink of water to gather my thoughts, I add, "Take, for example, a coal-burning electric utility company that puts lots of tons of carbon into the air every year. That utility company could spend a lot of money to clean up its processes, or it might find it more economical to pay a bunch of farmers to convert to no-till. Then the company can 'trade' the tons of carbon that it paid farmers to leave in the field for the carbon that belches out of its smokestacks. Does that make any sense?"

Eli nods pensively, "Well, yes, it's making some sense. But it still sounds like this cap and trade thing is going to mainly hurt small farmers because the cows and the manure are still going to put out carbon dioxide."

"Yeah, that is true, but a lot of what happens on this farm actually traps carbon dioxide. Any time a crop is growing or soil is left undisturbed, carbon dioxide is trapped. Plants breathe in carbon dioxide and breathe out oxygen, and the carbon is what goes into building the plant. So all of the pastures that you seldom, if ever, plow build up a little bit more carbon every year, and the cow pies [manure] that fall in the pasture are pretty quickly taken up by plants or added to the soil carbon." The children are starting to glaze over, but Eli and Katie still seem interested so I go on. "A big thing on this farm and a lot of others around here are the woods. Trees suck up a lot of carbon and keep it trapped for a long time. You have what? Maybe 12 acres of woods here?"

Eli leans back a bit and mutters, "Yeah, that's about right."

"Well, it's not quite 12 acres," Katie says.

"Okay, but it's in the neighborhood of 11 or 12 acres, right?"

Eli and Katie nod and quietly say yes in unison.

"Well, however big it is, it traps a lot of carbon. And it is very possible that on this farm more carbon is trapped every year than is released to the air. So you might well be a net carbon collector. That is generally not the case on large farms. You know, if you have 2,000 cows on a concrete barn floor, store all the manure in a huge pit, and grow no crops, a lot of carbon gets generated and released into the air as greenhouse gas." I should stop right there, but I can't help adding, "And that's just another of the many, many reasons why large dairy farms should not be allowed to exist in this country."

Katie and Eli chuckle a little at my emphatic tone, and it's time to wind this conversation up. "Anyway, the bottom line—at least as I see it—is that small farmers probably have little to worry about any cap and trade program that might someday be implemented."

Katie stares blankly at my empty plate for a few seconds and then, as if startled by something she momentarily forgot, draws a quick breath and offers, "We have more. Do you want some more?"

"No, I'm full Katie. But thank you."

"We have dessert."

"Well, now, I might have saved just enough room for dessert. What do you have?"

"Pie—pumpkin pie!"

"That sounds way too good to pass up."

Katie and her oldest daughter slide down the picnic table bench to the end and stand up. Each one gathers an armload of dishes from the table and heads back across the lawn toward the kitchen door. Turning back toward Eli, I casually ask, "What are your plans for this afternoon?"

"We're thrashing out the last of this year's oats over at Jonas's. There're only six more acres and we'll be all done."

"How are the yields running?"

"In general, not too bad. I averaged just about 90 bushels an acre."

"Yeah, that's pretty good." Actually, 90 bushels per acre is good but not great. When there's an excellent growing season, it's not unusual for farms around here to average 100 bushels and sometimes a little more. Ninety is okay but it probably means that Eli will need to buy a little bit more feed this year, and with the terribly low milk prices, that's not good, not good at all.

Nodding his head, he leans back a little then goes on. "Most of the fields were fine, but this last one of Jonas's has been a mess all season. We had Les out, and he said it was the worst infestation of cereal leaf beetle he'd ever seen, and he said Jonas should spray it with some special insecticide."

Les is my former assistant who still works here in the county, and cereal leaf beetle is an insect that occasionally causes some damage to growing grain crops. You can generally find a few cereal leaf beetles in about any oat field if you look really close, but I've never seen an infestation that warranted spraying. In fact, it's very rare to spray an oat crop for anything. However, Les knows his bugs, and if he said it needed spraying, I'm sure it did.

"So did Jonas ever spray the field?"

"He did, but not with what Les recommended. That stuff costs nearly $450 a gallon. Why, you can almost buy the oats for that." Probably a bit of an exaggeration, but not much. I nod my head in general agreement, and Eli goes on with the story. "Jonas went and talked to the guys over in Middlefield, and they suggested a substitute. Even that was $160 a gallon, but it will keep for three years, so it's less expensive and hopefully it did about as good a job."

"Oh, I'm sure it did." The "guys over in Middlefield" are the crop advisors at the local farm co-op. One of their jobs is to stay up-to-date on the current prices of a wide variety of agricultural chemicals and then help farmers like Jonas figure out the least expensive way to take care of the problem. Still, if I understand Eli correctly, Jonas used about a third of the gallon on his six-acre field, and that works out to almost $10 an acre, not counting the time, expense, and bother needed to hitch up his buggy and go to Middlefield to buy the stuff and then hitch a team of workhorses to a field sprayer, mix the insecticide with water in the sprayer, and then finally apply it to the field.

The kitchen screen door slams shut and Katie appears tableside with a fresh-baked pumpkin pie in her hands. A few seconds later her daughter sets a plastic carafe of steaming hot coffee, three cups, sugar, and cream on the other end of the table and then skips back into the kitchen. She reappears seconds later with a tray full of miniature pumpkin pies. As her daughter carefully places an individual pie in front of her siblings, Katie explains, "I baked those little pies for the children. I thought they might get a kick out of each one of having their own pie." Daniel gazes down at the mini-treat in front of him, giggles with delight, and attacks it with two sharp jabs from his fork.

Once again I am struck with how wonderfully thoughtful and loving Katie truly is. She laughs with Daniel and then cuts a large wedge of pie for me, another for Eli, and finally puts a smaller piece on her own plate. Coffee is passed around, along with a pitcher of cool water, and for a few sugary moments this table is silent.

Completely sated, I interrupt Eli's last few bites. "I understand milk prices are still real bad."

"Yeah, you can say that again." In between bites, he good-naturedly recounts the same gloomy economic report that Katie gave earlier. Last month milk prices were at a disastrous $11.60 per hundredweight; this month they are only slightly better at $12. For the last three months, the farm milk check has been $5,000 per month less than what it was last year. In round numbers, that's roughly 30 to 50 percent less money than the farm was receiving one year ago. It's a distressing report and an anxious time, but amazingly both Eli and Katie are pretty matter-of-fact about the situation and, at times, even optimistic and cheerful as we talk.

"I hope we remember this in the future." Katie is looking at me but she's talking to herself and the rest of the table. "It's taught us some things. We've learned to cut back in the house and with the cows."

With a full laugh, Eli chimes in, "It has taught us some things, but I would like to buy some Cheerios or Oreos once in a while." It's a great line and we all enjoy the moment. Underneath the humor, he has found a way to support his wife's words and lighten the mood, if only slightly.

"Things will be better in a month or two," Katie adds in a guardedly optimistic tone. "We have a steer running with the heifers, and he'll be ready to eat pretty soon. It will be a lot easier when we have meat again."

The steer she's talking about was born a bull calf, right here on this farm, about a year ago. He was castrated, or steered, sometime before he was a month old. It's always advisable to steer bull calves while they are still very young; older bulls can get downright ornery about the procedure. In fact, older bulls—particularly the dairy breeds—can get downright ornery about darn near anything. Bulls are by nature big, unpredictable, and a constant threat to any nearby human life. That's why they get castrated young. Steers are more chilled out, mellow, and way safer to be around. In this case, safe enough to spend all day out in the pasture munching grass, while surrounded by a tribe of sweet young heifers.

"Does this steer have a name?"

Daniel pipes up and definitively answers "Ace."

On average, half of the big Holstein moms in a dairy herd give birth to bull babies, and half have heifers. The heifers will all be raised on the farm and will eventually replace aging dairy cows in the milking herd. Almost all of the bull calves will be sent to the community livestock auction before they are one week old. Once there, they will most likely be bought and trucked to a veal farm, where they will be allowed to live out the remaining weeks of their short lives, until they are large enough to be processed into light gray veal cutlets, veal shanks, and other tasty bits. Okay, that's quite enough on the veal business for right now. The practices this industry uses in the United States are repugnant.

In contrast, the steer that Katie is talking about was held back from the auction and raised on the farm as a beef animal. He almost undoubtedly was given his name by the children, and he's spent his whole life growing up as part of the heifer herd. Which, any way you shuffle the cards, is far better than the hand dealt to the veal farm internees. Normally, on a small dairy farm like Eli and Katie's, one or two bull calves a year are selected to be steered and raised as beef to feed the family. If, in a given year, the farm has excess feed, several calves may be fattened out and sold as beef, helping to diversify the family income. Usually, an animal destined to fill the family larder will be selected in the early fall as a newborn calf. That way, the animal will be grown and ready for slaughter the following fall as the weather turns cooler. It is so much safer and easier to process meat in cooler temperatures.

If we all get up from this picnic table right now, I'm sure we could pick out Ace in one of the far pastures. Some time in the next couple of months, when there is a break in the fieldwork, butchering day will come. The unknowing steer will casually stride into a familiar, thick-bedded stall, and lower his head to an enticing bucket of sweet grain. Seconds later a single, carefully aimed, rifle slug will shatter through his brain, and Ace will be dead long before his carcass settles into the straw. Harsh, but humane. He will have had a good life and a dignified death.

In the next instant, the still warm carcass will be drawn into the air by a block and tackle to sway, head down, above the floor. Deft hands and a sharp butcher knife will open the veins in his neck, allowing the warm blood to drain out of his body and onto the floor. In the busy next hours, family, friends, and neighbors will fall in to cut, saw, grind, and peel the animal into human-sized portions. Katie and the other women will spend the afternoon putting cubes of beef into light green mason jars and sealing them up in a pressure canner for meals yet to come.

But some of the meat will be eaten right away. That evening, after milking and other chores, the whole family will sit around the supper table, and in a moment of reverent, silent prayer they will thank God for this steer's life. There steaming on a plate is a small part of the animal that they fed, watered, and watched grow out in the back pasture. Katie will understand, Eli will understand, and in their own way each of the children will understand the enormous sanctity of this meal.

Would we could all eat so well.

The children are starting to fidget on the hard wooden benches of the table, and there's much more to be done before this day is over. Our conversations around this table have been meaningful, informative, and pleasant. But most of all it's been a time for old friends to reconnect. I can hear the reluctance in Eli's voice as he says simply, "Well, it's time for prayer." Three children and three adults quietly bow their heads for a moment of silent prayer. Eli softly clears his throat as the prayer, the meal, and our time together comes to a gentle close.

20

We Always Do

Back on the road again, traveling north, I pass three "Eggs for Sale" signs and one "Broilers for Sale" sign in under two miles. Eli is right. This egg market is definitely flooded. Most probably the farm with broilers for sale started out in the egg business and soon learned there were already too many hens and too many eggs in the neighborhood. The obvious solution to this business predicament is to break into a new market by liquidating your hen assets as quickly as possible and converting them into broiler assets. The broiler business model is substantially different from the egg business model, but almost none of these farms have over 100 hens, so no marketing or feasibility studies are needed to make the conversion. The advertising campaign was finished the day they tacked a sign out near the mailbox saying "Broilers for Sale." No new licenses are required, the feed costs are the same, and the tax ramifications are trivial. Perhaps most importantly, no new manager salaries were put in place to eat away at the efficiency of the operation. There will be no waste. If a particular broiler is found to lack a buyer, the family will enjoy it with some mashed potatoes and garden vegetables.

No megafarm—or other large business for that matter—has the ability to shift into or out of production enterprises to meet market demand as swiftly and seamlessly as these very small, diversified Amish farms, and that is yet another secret of their success. But, of course, that flies in the face of everything we so firmly believe, and the collective wisdom will likely remain "get bigger and specialize." I hope nobody tells Eli or Katie.

About 20 minutes later, a familiar set of white farm buildings materializes down the driveway on my left. Neither Marvin nor his son, Owen, looks up as I walk in the open door at the back of the barn. Fully half of the initial 30-yard gap between us is closed before Marvin jerks up his head and stammers, "Well, hello, Randy. This is a surprise."

"Yeah, I was passing by and thought I'd stop in and see how you folks were doing." Owen is standing quietly in the soft shadows of the barn and smiling. He must be in his late teens now, a little taller, but still shy. No sign of a beard, so he must not be married yet. Actually, at his age it would be a real surprise if he was even thinking about marriage. Most Amish young people don't get married until somewhere in their 20s. "And how are you doing, Owen?"

With a pronounced slow nod of his head, as if to emphasize a carefully reasoned, well-tempered response, he looks at me and earnestly says, "I'm good." That's it, no embellishments, but I really didn't expect more. After all, he is a young man, and young men—whether they are Amish or Yankee—tend not to be overabundant in words shared with elders. Perhaps he will loosen up as the conversation goes on.

Turning now back to Marvin, I say, "I understand milk prices are really bad."

"Yeah, they are, but you know things are pretty bad all over—at least here in this area. Timber prices are down, so the sawmills are slow. A lot of people are laid off. And there's no new construction, so most of the carpenters don't have any work." He pauses for a long moment as if waiting for a response—or maybe he's just collecting his thoughts—then goes on in a voice filled with coarse gravel, "A lot of people are suffering around here. Maybe it's okay if we suffer a little too."

Marvin's few sparse words lay bare a deep-seated sense of community and an empathy for the troubles of those around him, qualities that are so very common in the Amish community and so very rare in our own. I truly don't know how to respond. After a few moments of awkward silence, I lamely mutter, "Well, I suppose that's right."

Owen quietly resumes tightening the bolt he was working on. Marvin shifts gears and announces, "We're adding three new stalls."

Focusing now on the work the two of them are doing, my eyes pick up on some fresh concrete and a cleanly cut PVC pipe. The pipe runs over the top of all of the stalls in the barn and supplies the vacuum pressure that runs the automatic milking machine. It's apparent that until today the pipe was sealed off and plugged at this end. Since they are expanding, a new section of pipe needs to be added to service the three new tie stalls. Expanding the pipe is not a big job, but it needs to be completed before chore time tonight or else the entire barn will be without the vacuum needed to run the milking machines.

Marvin is busy bolting a blue, round-bottomed, automatic watering cup to the front of one of the stalls. All the cow has to do is put her nose in the cup and it automatically fills with water. The cups are placed between each stall, so no cow is ever more than a nose length away from water, and no cow in this barn ever has to go thirsty.

"Marvin, are you going to buy three more cows or did you raise some heifers?"

"Well, actually, I paid my neighbor to raise these heifers for me. He had room in his barn along with extra feed and pasture, and we are pretty tight around here as far as space for the cows goes. So I took these heifers down to him almost a year ago, and now they're about ready to freshen. All in all, it worked out good for both of us."

"Now with these three new stalls, how many do you have in total?"

"Thirty-four."

I know for sure 34 cows make this one of the largest Amish dairy herds in the settlement. It's still a very small herd by Yankee standards. It's even a small number of cows compared to the herds in more liberal Amish settlements, where the *Ordnungs* permit much more technology and modern innovations. But in the middle of this very conservative settlement, 34 head of dairy cattle is a lot. One of the big limitations on herd size is simply handling all of the manure. By fits and starts, over the years, Marvin has slowly pushed on the edges of the local rules and been able to partially mechanize his manure handling system. That partial mechanization, along with milking machines and bulk refrigeration tanks, has allowed this herd to grow to its present size.

Strolling up and down the aisles, looking at the two long rows of empty tie stalls, I can't help thinking how much better these cows have it than their sister dairy cows, milling around in huge confinement barns on some megafarm. These tie stalls are empty because the entire herd is out behind the barn in one of the pastures munching sweet grass and waiting for the next milking time. Late this afternoon they'll come back into the barn to be milked and fed. Then, if the weather is clear, they will probably go back out and spend the night in the cool pasture. I move back over toward Marvin. "This barn is about as full as it can get, isn't it?"

He laughs. "Yeah, we had to tear out a box stall to put these in."

Box stalls are simply large, square, wooden enclosures, usually built at the far end of the barn and used to raise heifers—which might explain why Marvin is paying his neighbors to raise heifers for him.

Only half joking, I point to the far end of the barn. "I suppose you could knock out that back wall and put some stalls in there, Marvin."

With a quiet smile he says, "We're thinking about it."

This farm is one of the first to use rotational grazing, one of the first to put in a bulk refrigeration tank and milking machine, and probably the first Amish farm in these parts to milk over 30 cows. As a rule, change comes slow in this Amish community, but by and by it does come—when needed. It won't surprise me a bit if that wall is gone and they are milking over 40 by my next visit.

"Other than the lousy milk prices, how's the season going so far?"

"Pretty good," Marvin says without any special emphasis. "The cows are milking good this year because it has been cool. They're comfortable, and there's been very few flies."

"Before I retired, there were quite a few guys getting into farming. With the low milk prices, is that still going on?"

"Oh yeah, I know of several young guys starting up. Milk prices are low, but so is everything else. Some of them feel this is a pretty good time to get into the dairy business. I guess they think it can't get much worse, so if they can make it now, things will be better in the future."

He has stopped working on the watering cup and seems to be focused on our talk about the young farmers. Owen starts to clean the end of the PVC pipe, getting it ready to glue on the new section. But he too is listening intently. That's no surprise. I know he would like to farm, and maybe even take over this farm, as his dad moves into retirement mode.

"Well, Marvin, do you think these new guys getting into dairy farming is a good idea right now?"

"Yes, I do. I'm pretty optimistic about the dairy business, and all farming really, around here. I wasn't always optimistic, but I am now. Actually, the whole community has changed over the past few years. There's a lot of support for young farmers, and that wasn't always the case." He pauses, searching for the right words to help explain his point and then looks me square in the face. "Well, you remember what it used to be like," he says.

"Yeah, I remember. It's much better now."

Marvin's head moves slowly up and down and he quietly says, "Yeah, much better."

We both remember. There was a time only a few years ago when the farmers in this settlement could be counted on to complain about how hard farming was, regardless of whether times were really bad, really good, or somewhere in between. Complaining was a bad habit, and it discouraged most of the young people from even entertaining the thought of starting a farm. But that's all changed, and it truly is much better now.

"So how many cows are most of these young guys starting off with?"

"Well, it varies, but the last two or three that I've seen got started with around 14 to maybe 18 cows. That's not enough. I'd really like to see them get started with about 30."

"Can't argue with you on that, Marvin, but, you know, they can get started with 15 or so and get a cash flow going and then keep the heifers and gradually get bigger. That also gives them a chance to work out some of the bugs while the herd is still small."

Marvin nods his head in agreement and then goes on to talk about how he would like to help these young guys get started. He does help them whenever he can, but he'd really like to help them cut feed costs. According to Marvin, the local feed salesman who works with many of the Amish herds does a good job. He's honest and likable, and the cows in the herds he works with really produce. The trouble is the feed products he sells are expensive, and they end up nearly doubling feed cost. Feed is one of the largest monthly expenses for these dairy herds, and holding down the cost is one of the real keys to running a successful farm.

Animal nutrition, and particularly dairy cow nutrition, is just plain hard. There is no simple, homespun, common-sense way to approach the topic. First off, a cow's digestive system is completely different from ours. Like sheep, goats, and termites, old Betsy over there, poking her head in the door to see what's going on, comes equipped with a rumen and three other stomachs. This rumen allows her system to break down cellulose in grass and hay and turn it into food. Basically, the rumen is a large vat where the feed she eats sloshes around, fermenting and producing various gases. Then these gases get absorbed by the rumen wall, and that's where she gets most of her energy. Does that make any sense? Of course not!

Yet understanding each cow's nutritional needs is the easy part. The hard part is matching the quality of the feed the farmer grows to what he needs to buy. Each farm is different. Right now, in the haymow above us in this barn, Marvin may have some first cutting hay that's only 11 percent protein and some third cutting hay that tops out around 22 percent protein. Based on last year's conditions, the corn silage in his silo may be either very high or low in protein and energy. Add to that the need to balance things like neutral detergent fiber, crude proteins, bypass proteins, total fiber, acid detergent fiber, total energy, vitamins, minerals, and salt, which all are designed to keep the cow healthy while producing a prodigious amount of milk, protein, and butterfat. Sound complicated? It is, and it can easily overwhelm a young dairy farmer with a million other things on his plate.

Probably 25 years ago, I teamed up with another ag agent in a nearby county to put on a series of basic dairy cow feeding schools. He was really good at dairy nutrition. We set up "kitchen meetings" in various Amish homes across the settlement. The first one got off to a bit of a rocky start when the other agent pulled out a slide projector and started looking around for a place to plug it in. But he was up to the challenge. When the laughter finally died down, he went back out to his car where he found a paper flip chart and two magic markers and gave a good talk. After a few years he moved on to another job. By then most of the folks at the university had become absolutely enamored with huge dairy farms and, therefore, lost interest in the little ones. After a time, I pretty much stopped trying to bring dairy nutrition schools to the settlement.

Because of his years of experience and study, Marvin is able to calculate customized rations for his herd. High-producing cows get one ration, low producers another, and still other rations are needed for heifers and dry cows. He buys the feeds that the herd needs from a local supplier and saves a ton of money. The cows do well, and he likes the idea of supporting a local business. So for him, it's the way to go. However, for the novice, the local feed salesman provides a valuable service.

Marvin, Owen, and I settle into a round of casual talk about the weather, milk prices, local farms, the neighbors, politics, cows, crops, and nothing in particular. With some prodding, Owen makes a comment or two, but mainly he listens. After 20 minutes or so, Marvin brings up the topic of the community lending fund and the committee that oversees it. The fund was just getting started in the last few years that I lived here. Each of the four large Amish settlements—Holmes County, Ohio; Lancaster, Pennsylvania; Shipshewana, Indiana; and now Geauga—have similar funds. Essentially, people in the settlement invest in the fund, and under the direction of a local committee the fund makes loans at very favorable, long-term, stable rates to young Amish couples buying their first home or farm. It's another concrete way for these communities to provide support to their young families.

Some of the committee members recently asked Marvin if there were any benchmark financial numbers they could find to help them guess whether a new farm had a chance of making it and whether they should make the loan. "I'd like to find a good 'debt per cow' number for them to use. Do you have any idea what they're recommending now?"

"No, Marvin, I don't. We used to have some general recommendations, but that was years ago. And I never really trusted them anyhow. Each farm is so different, and you really have to analyze them on a case-by-case basis."

"I know, but we're just kind of looking for a ballpark number."

"Tell you what, I'll look around when I get back home and send you a note with anything I find. But I'm not optimistic."

Simply put, the "debt per cow" number tries to answer the question of how much debt a dairy farmer can reasonably handle. It is calculated by taking a farm's total amount of debt and dividing it by the total number of milking cows. Then the global question is, how much debt can each cow carry and still generate enough income from her milk to pay all of the other farm bills and take care of the farm family income needs too? Sounds simple, but it's not. It makes a considerable difference if the farm is milking 20 cows and not 2,000. The cost of feed varies dramatically if the farmer buys it all or grows most of it. Many Amish dairy farms also earn income from things like maple syrup, eggs, beef, and who knows what else, so all the debt should not be carried by the cows. Then, of course, there's the ever-volatile price of milk.

As promised, when I get home I'll spend some time looking through some old references and a considerable amount of time searching the Internet. But I very much doubt that I will unearth anything the committee can actually use. Most of debt capacity analysis for dairy farms is based on debt per 100 cows. There's just very little out there designed to help small, diversified farms deal with debt-management questions. At the end of the day, there are no shortcuts to sitting down face-to-face and pushing numbers around a sheet of paper until that next anxious, young Amish couple looks at each other and decides it is time—or not time—to buy those cows.

Where did the day go? Started out early this morning with the intent to make one or two short visits and then to drive over to the state hunting grounds east of Farmington to spend a lazy afternoon fishing the ponds for yellow perch, bass, bluegill, and maybe a bullhead catfish or two. Six or seven visits later, I'm still here in the middle of the settlement, and it's late afternoon, pushing dusk. Everything is a trade-off. The fish will wait for another year. Some of the old friends I saw today may not.

It's midsummer and the corn, clover, and alfalfa fields are a rich vibrant green. Hasn't rained in a while and the wheat-stubble fields, farm lanes, and dirt roads are dry and dusty. The waves of heat coming down from the sun are just intense enough to put a little spring in the thin-paved asphalt roads, so tires and buggy wheels leave a slight depression as they pass by. Don't need a calendar to tell it's Thursday. There are weddings all over the place. Weddings are always on Thursday in this settlement, unless there are too many. Then occasionally one is held on Tuesday. Never heard anyone say why they are on Thursday, but that's the tradition, so that's when they're held. Weddings are a big deal with all the sisters, brothers, aunts, uncles, cousins, neighbors, and friends that a big, extended family can muster. Many come from the surrounding neighborhood. Others hire taxi vans and come in from across this settlement or from far-flung settlements across the country.

This end of Nash Road is unpaved dirt and gravel. Right now there's a sea of walking people, horses, and buggies on the left side because the wedding down the way is starting to break up. There are at least 10 black buggies filled to the brim with people inching their way down the road. One of the buggies has two horses hitched in front, which is a bit of a surprise because, unlike some other settlements where two horses are the norm, the buggies in this settlement are always pulled with one horse. In fact, the buggies here don't have a doubletree, so there's really no way to effectively hitch two horses. The driver waves as he passes, and the riddle is solved. The second horse isn't really pulling anything; she's a young mare in training, loosely tethered beside the horse that is actually pulling the buggy. Trotting along beside her older companion gives her time to become familiar with the road, traffic, and the whole idea of pulling a buggy. The older, road-confident horse pays little mind to the young mare, but its steady influence, along with the leather tethers, will keep her from doing anything really stupid, like jumping out in front of a 4,000-pound SUV as it roars by equipped with a young driver frantically texting her girlfriends. This and other patient training techniques will slowly turn the mare into a reliable and safe "buggy horse." Over time, her understanding of the job and the family's confidence in her abilities will make her a regular member of the local buggy-pulling horse crowd.

Just ahead an unbearded Amish man in his late teens or early 20s is riding on a sulky and pulling out of the driveway where the wedding was held. The horse is a sleek, young, chestnut Standardbred gelding with his head punched up in the air, nervously moving his muzzle back and forth to test the limits of his steel bit, leather reins, and the human driver. Now there is an animal to be mindful of as you drive past. Hard telling what a high-strung horse like that is likely to do.

Amish guys in their late teens buy these powerful, headstrong horses as soon as they are deemed not quite good enough to bet on at the local professional racetracks. Hitched to a light sulky, which is little more than two wheels, an axle, and a thin seat for one, these animals can almost fly down the road. The whole rig—sulky, horse, and driver—is roughly the Amish equivalent of a hot sports car and a Yankee teenager. Oh, and, yes, they do sometimes get together on Saturday night for a little street racing; and yes, they do occasionally have a wreck; and yes, now and again, they are pulled over by the cops. But it sure looks like it would be a heck of a lot of fun.

A group of six or eight teenage girls is ambling barefooted along the side of the road. The faster buggies, sulkies, and taxi vans rumble by, kicking up a small cloud of dust as they pass. Shuffling along behind the girls is a group of teenage boys, also barefooted, but more animated, with a scuffed up baseball getting tossed about the group. Can't hear, but I'm sure they are teasing the girls in front of them, and the girls are happily teasing them back. It's all good fun and important work in this whole business of growing up.

Past the wedding party now so there is time to safely look around. The farms and entire agricultural community seem to be thriving. There are pastures full of dairy cows and heifers where I have never seen them before and several small fields of vegetables, most of which will end up at the local fruit and vegetable auction in Middlefield. The picnic table along the side of the road has a variety of vegetables and what appears to be a basket of fresh-picked wild elderberries for sale under the shade of a pin oak tree. At the edge of the table is a cardboard price list and honor dish with some bills held down by a rock and some small change. Customers simply stop by in their car or buggy, pick out what they want to buy, and make their own change. No need to worry about thieving; it won't happen, not here in the settlement.

Pulling up to the corner where Nash and Newcomb Roads cross, I see a tiny four-wheeled cart pulled by a miniature horse. Two boys are on the seat and the back is loaded with empty cardboard vegetable boxes. The farmers hereabouts fill these boxes with whatever vegetable is ripe and then either hitch a team to a flatbed wagon or hire a Yankee neighbor with a pickup truck to get the boxes over to the wholesale auction. The auction prides itself on being a source of high-quality, very fresh local produce. Usually the vegetables get to the auction within a few hours of being picked. Sometimes they're picked the night before and kept cool for delivery the next morning, but that's about as old as anything is allowed to get before landing on the auction market floor.

As they round the corner, one of the boxes rumbles off the back of the wagon and comes to rest at the edge of the road. Twenty yards later the little pony is pulled to a stop and the boy on the left hops down and runs back to retrieve the fallen box. The boy on the right is the driver, and he stays in his seat holding the reins. In automobiles, the driver sits on the left at least in part to keep an eye out for oncoming traffic. In buggies and pony-drawn carts, one of the biggest hazards is for the wheels to slip off the side of the road onto the soft berm and flip the vehicle over into the ditch. Sitting on the left would make it hard for the driver to see across the horse and judge the edge of the road, so buggy drivers sit on the right. Besides, it's the tradition.

With the vegetable box back in its stack and the passenger back in his seat, the driver flicks the reins and they are off again. The little pony is doing a fine job pulling the cart, but he's a bit comical to watch. He's a paint with big brown splotches randomly distributed over a mostly white body. His head's high and his ears are alert as he prances down the road, but he can't be much more than two and a half feet tall at the withers (ridge between his shoulders). It's hard to take him seriously, even though he obviously takes himself very seriously.

In just a very few years, these little carts have become quite popular. You can see them all over the settlement, mostly on the unpaved back roads, but occasionally on asphalt. Inching past the boys now, I suppose these carts are really no more dangerous or unpredictable than a kid on a bicycle. Of course, you virtually never see a kid on a bicycle around here because the church districts in this settlement don't allow bicycles.

Probably has something to do with the relative speed and ease with which a bicycle can take a person out of the community and into the larger world. That's just a hunch, but these folks make everyday decisions based on whether some new thing will pull the community together or apart. These two young boys are responsible for this spry little animal and will soon drive him back to the barn where they will unhitch, water, feed, and probably comb out his mane. It's hard to imagine how a bicycle could possibly improve things in the slightest. There is clearly a lesson in there somewhere for us Yankees, but more than likely we'll go on missing it . . . we always do.

21

Moving On

Another year has gone by. It's July of 2010, and I'm spending this day quietly driving around the settlement to reacquaint myself with the landscape.
In no particular hurry, I'm slowly winding my way over toward the north
end of Hosmer Road and the farm that belongs to Monroe Fischer and his
wife, Ada. Well, at least I think it still does. This is one of the last families I
worked with before retiring. And I don't think they actually started to farm
before I left. But my memory is getting a little fuzzy. I believe a year or so
after I retired, on one of my trips back to the settlement, someone told me
that they had indeed started to farm, and on this trip I'm making it a point
to stop in and catch up. The driveway is just up ahead on the left.

The sign on the mailbox says FRYERS FOR SALE in bold black letters. The two-story white farmhouse is on the right, a small greenhouse and
massive vegetable garden line the driveway to the left, and straight ahead
are the dairy barn and a half-full corncrib. The old barn's been painted and
the milk house rebuilt. I don't see any cows, but the fence is in good repair.
Somebody is obviously farming here—hope it's still Monroe and Ada.

The backdoor opens before I can knock, and I'm greeted by a pretty,
dark-haired girl in a blue dress with a white apron. She looks to be about
16. Can't say I recognize her, but that's not unusual. She starts the conversation before I have a chance to say a word.

"Oh, my mom and dad will be very pleased to see you."

"Well, hello. I'd like to see them too. Are they around today?"

"They're here, but they're down the road in a field, shocking oats."

"That's fine. Tell me where the field is and I'll drive down and find them."

The girl pauses for a long moment, as if to get her thoughts together before trying to explain exactly where the field is. Then she happily announces, "Let me just get in the car and show you where it is. Is that okay?"

"Sure, hop in."

She immediately pulls open the door and slides in the front passenger seat. I swing the car around in front of the barn and head back out the driveway. At the road I pause just long enough to ask "right or left?" She points to the south and we are on our way.

We barely have time to start any sort of a conversation before she points to a mud driveway on the right. "It's right here," she says. The field is a good deal less than a mile from the house, and I suspect she was about ready to start walking to it to help shock the oats when I showed up. Riding is better than walking, so it worked out good for both of us. The trip was so short that I never did get her name. As soon as the car stops, we both get out and start walking.

Ada and Monroe are quite a piece away, near the other end of the field, and they don't notice the car when it pulls in. Both are busy picking up small bundles of oat stocks, called sheaths. They lean them together to form rows of small teepees, or shocks, about two feet across at the base and tapering up into an explosion of ripe oat heads. More than likely the oats were cut earlier today or sometime yesterday, using a binding machine pulled by horses. The binder cuts the stocks of oats off near the ground and gathers them up into small bundles tied together with "binder twine." The twine is the same thin hemp rope used to hold hay bales together, but in this part of the world it's still often called "binder twine" rather than "baler twine," even when it's holding hay bales together. That's because horse-drawn binding machines substantially predate tractor-driven hay-baling machines.

The shocks will be left standing in the field to dry for about two weeks. When the oat grains in the seed heads are dry enough to be stored in a grain bin without rotting—around 14 percent moisture—Monroe will contact the other farmers in the threshing circle and call them together to set up the threshing machine and haul the shocks in to be threshed out. Once set up, the threshing machine remains stationary and is powered by a long leather belt spinning on a pulley that juts out from the side of the motor of an old tractor. The shocks of oats are then fed into the jaws of the threshing machine, where they are rumbled, rattled, shaken, and sieved into a pile of bright yellow straw on one side and bushels of plump grain on the other. Because of the cost of the machinery and the labor required for the total operation, threshing machines—much like Eli Gingerich's corn loader—are almost always owned and operated through threshing circles. The threshing circles generally have anywhere from three to six farms and, among other good things, create a time for the farmers and families in the community to work together.

Monroe and Ada are still well over 100 yards away, near the middle of the field, when Monroe raises a hand to the front of his broad-billed straw hat to further shade his eyes from the sun and try to make out who just got out of the car with his daughter. When the gap closes to about 50 yards, a look of surprised recognition spreads across Monroe's face. "Well, hello, Randy. What brings you back to these parts?"

"Just want to see how you folks are doing. Heard you started to farm a while back."

He offers a warm handshake, and Ada almost bubbles a cheerful "hello."

Because they had not yet started farming before I left, I don't know this family nearly as well as many of the other farmers, and I am touched by their overtly warm welcome. We make small talk for several minutes, catching up on friends and the community in general. The field we are standing in looks to be about six, maybe eight, acres. Monroe tells me he was able to rent it this year from a Yankee neighbor who is no longer farming. The oat crop is planted with alfalfa and some sort of grass, so I assume he has a long-term lease or at least a verbal agreement. An alfalfa hay crop generally lasts five years or so, and farmers don't put it in unless they're pretty sure they will have the land for several years. "What do you have seeded down, Monroe?"

"Alfalfa and timothy."

Alfalfa is a legume, which means, like clover, it's part of the bean family. All legumes bear their seeds in pods, but in hay crops, like alfalfa and clover, farmers are after the plants and leaves, not the seeds. In fact, the goal is to never allow an alfalfa plant to bear seeds. Young alfalfa plants are very nutritious and particularly high in protein, so the plants are cut early, dried, and made into high-quality hay for the cows. The timothy is a grass that is grown and harvested along with the alfalfa. On small dairy farms like Monroe and Ada's, the timothy helps fill in where the alfalfa does poorly and also speeds the drying process for the hay.

But it's clear this simply is not a good stand of alfalfa and timothy. The young plants poking up through the soil are few and far between, and they are yellow and spindly. Not a good sign. Bending down to pull one sickly alfalfa plant out of the soil, I laugh and apologize for "maybe pulling up half the crop."

Munroe takes the joke in stride. Ada sighs and says, "Maybe Randy can tell us what went wrong."

Actually, I do have a fair idea of what probably went wrong. Throughout the field and particularly at the edges where the oat plants aren't as thick, there is an infestation of sheep sorrel. This little weed has dark green leaves about an inch or so long. It's easy to recognize because each leaf looks like a child's mitten with a thumb on each side. The leaves are sour but edible, and not bad sprinkled lightly in a salad. Unfortunately for Monroe and Ada, sheep sorrel is also an "indicator" plant. Back in the days before modern soil tests were available, this was one of the plants used to judge just how acid, or "sour," the soil in a particular field was. If sheep sorrel is present, you can rest assured the soil is too acid and needs lime to raise the pH or "sweeten" it. In this field, the oats look to be a pretty good crop, and the timothy is not bad either. But both timothy and oats are grasses, and grasses by and large really don't care how acid the soil is. Alfalfa—which is the most valuable crop in this field—is real particular when it comes to soil acidity, and it simply cannot thrive if the soil is too acid. My hunch, based on the sheep sorrel weed infestation, is that this field is way too acid for alfalfa and needs several tons of lime spread on each acre.

"Monroe, do you know what the pH is on this field?"

He shakes his head and says quietly, "No, not really."

"Do you have a soil test on it?"

"No, we just got this field early in the spring, and there wasn't time to do a soil test."

We talk several minutes about sheep sorrel and my hunch that the field is too acid. Lime is expensive, and farmers hate to add it to rented fields, but alfalfa just won't grow without it. It's perfectly understandable that Monroe didn't have time to do a soil test since the field came up for rent so quickly. And since Monroe is the new farmer, he may not even know how to take a soil test or interpret the results once they come back from the laboratory. All of this type of thing is part of the steep learning curve each new farm family faces. In this case, it's a setback, but not a disaster. We talk some more about the window of opportunity in the first two weeks of

August when the alfalfa can be reseeded and just how to go about getting it done. He and Ada ask some questions and seem generally comfortable with the recommendations and the plan, so we move on to whatever the next topic might be.

"So how many cows are you folks milking right now?"

Munroe glances at Ada for reassurance on the number and says, "Right today I think it's 22, isn't it Ada?"

She nods and simply says, "Yes, that's right."

This sounds like a simple question, but it really isn't. In a dairy herd, cows are continually "freshening" and having a new calf so they come into the milking group. Meanwhile, other cows are pregnant and late in their lactation so they are "dried off" and move over to the dry cow lot. The actual number of cows being milked on any given day changes all the time.

"I couldn't see the cows when I was up by the house. What breed did you finally decide to milk?"

Monroe answers decisively, "Jerseys."

I try to suppress a smile but cannot. Inwardly I am delighted. Apparently Monroe looked at his buildings, pasture, and cropland and made the determination to milk one of the small breeds, rather than Holsteins. I ache to know if my letter was at all helpful in the process. I ache to know if my advice was important. I want to ask, but that would be prideful. Instead, I mutter, "Well, that's probably good" and change the topic with "How long have you folks been milking?"

He again looks toward Ada to be sure he has the time frame right. "I think it's just about two and a half years." Ada nods her agreement and Munroe goes on. "Prices were real good for the first few months, but then the bottom dropped out in 2009. In truth, it wasn't enough to cover all the bills. Then things got better in 2010, and it's still getting better."

"What are you getting for milk right now, Monroe?"

"We're pretty close to $24 a hundredweight, which I think is pretty good."

"I should say so. That's better than what I hear most folks are getting. Of course, with the Jerseys you're getting a pretty good premium for butterfat, right?"

"Yeah, the butterfat premium really helps, and we're keeping our costs down quite a bit with the rotational grazing."

"When I was up near the barn I didn't see the cows, but it did look like the fences were divided up for grazing. How's that working?"

Monroe laughs out loud. "It was working just fine, but now that it's gotten hot the cows want to stand around all day under the trees instead of eating. But I suppose they're doing more eating in the evening or early morning. Don't you think?"

"Oh, I'm sure they are. Just try not to let them stay under one tree too long and make a mud hole out of the place." He explains that because it is rotational grazing, the cows don't stay in one paddock long enough to turn it into mud.

Ada and her daughter have been talking quietly at the side and interrupt Monroe for a question. It's something about the other children, after they get home from school, and chore time tonight. In the pause I bend down to pluck a sheep sorrel plant out of the dirt and start to nibble on the leaves.

In these sporadic visits back to the settlement, time has a way of becoming jumbled. The sharp, sour, green juice of the plant pulls me back 25 years or so to another conversation about cows, pasture, shade, mud, and trees. It was some time during my first few years on the job when Andy Byler called to say he was having a terrible problem with mastitis. Most of the girls in the herd had very sore, inflamed udders. Their milk was stringy and clotted and couldn't be sold. He had treated a few of the cows with antibiotics, but the problem just seemed to be getting worse. We set up a time for a farm visit the next day, but I had no idea what might be wrong.

The next day we walked through the barn. Things were clean and dry, and there was no reason to think the mastitis germs were being spread from cow to cow in here. Still clueless and not very optimistic about finding an answer, I suggested we at least take a look at the pasture. It was midsummer and hot. The cows weren't hard to find. They were all standing or lying in the shade of the only tree in the middle of the pasture. The place where the tree was growing was in a low area, and it was wet. The cows had churned the soil into a soupy mess. As they walked around, their teat ends got dragged through a watery film of mastitis-laced slime. I think we both probably recognized the problem at the same time. I looked at Andy, pointed at the mud, and declared, "Well, there's the problem."

We both stood there looking at the mud for a few long minutes, until Andy broke the silence with, "What do you think I should do?"

"Got a chain saw?"

"Well, yes."

"Then cut that tree down."

He did, and the cows got better in about two weeks. Sometimes the simplest solutions really are the best. Cows don't really need shade in the cooler northeast Ohio climate, but if a shade tree is around, there're likely to be under it.

Monroe's voice seems far off as it pulls me 25 years out of the past back into our conversation today. "Like I was saying, the cows don't really stay in one place long enough to turn it to mud."

I'm still struggling to wash away memories of the past and get my bearings, so I just look at Monroe and agree that he probably won't have a problem. Time is short, and there are many other people I'd still like to say hello to on this trip, so I start to move to close out the visit. Monroe and Ada are in no hurry, the day is pleasant, and I do have a question or two more for them. "Would you do it again? I mean, if you had it to do over, would you start the farm again?"

Immediately, in unison, they both say yes.

"Do you think you might keep farming, now that you've had a taste of it for a couple of years?"

Then Ada says yes again, and with a touch more seriousness she adds, "We want to." She looks toward Monroe for support. He is nodding his head in emphatic agreement. She looks back to me and goes on. "It's a good place to raise the children. They enjoy it. Even the little 18-month-old plays out in the barn at chore time."

In my mind, it is easy to envision this family working together at evening chores because I've seen it so many times: each child busy with his or her assigned tasks. The jobs aren't just made up to keep the children busy and out of trouble. They are important to the life of the farm. An older son or daughter might be helping with the milking, while another is feeding the calves, and still another might be throwing bales down through a large square hole in the floor of the haymow in the upper story above the cows. And there is teasing, laughter, and play—all under the watchful and often amused eyes of mom and dad. There is little doubt that indeed it is "a good place to raise the children."

Monroe holds his peace while Ada is talking. As she finishes she looks back to him, and he says it all. "If someone was to give me a million dollars, I think I'd just go on farming like this. Can't think of anything I'd like to do better."

We talk a few more minutes, but the most important things have already been said, and it's time to leave. "Well, it's been great seeing you folks. I'm glad things are working out okay for you. Guess it's time I better get on down the road before you put me to work shocking oats."

Monroe quickly declares, "These oats can wait."

"There's no rush. We have time," Ada says. "It is so nice that you took the time to stop by."

Again, I am touched by their warm expressions. But the reality is those oats can't wait for long. They need to be shocked so the grain heads are off the ground where they can dry out. It's time to go.

Back in the car I remind myself, once again, that this is no longer my job. Whether or not Ada, Monroe, and the children stay on the farm shouldn't matter to me. It's not my job. But it does matter, and it is impossible for me to explain why or how much . . . it does matter.

Eli is mowing the front lawn as I pull in the driveway. It's a little before 11 o'clock and the morning is sunny. It's been almost a year since I last visited Eli and Katie. He pulls the chestnut-brown Standardbred buggy horse to a stop as I walk across the yard. I know I've seen this a thousand times, but for some reason this morning the sight of a buggy horse pulling a gang of three bright-red rotary mowers, with Eli walking behind holding the reins, strikes me as oddly comical. It's not, of course. The horse is simply pulling whatever it's hitched to, as it has its entire life, and Eli is simply mowing the lawn because the grass is too tall. But for whatever reason, I am unable to suppress a few measures of laughter as we heartily shake hands.

"How have you been, Eli?"

The beard on his chin waves back and forth a few times as he slowly nods his head and says, "Good . . . real good. What about you?"

"I'm just fine. Don't know how things could get much better."

We fill each other in about our respective lives—small talk really. After a very few minutes, Eli looks down blankly at the reins in his hand, as if he has forgotten why they are there and stammers, "Let me finish this one pass. Then the lawn will be done and I'll meet you back at the barn."

"Okay, I'll pull my car on up near the tool shed and then walk over there."

Turning away to go back to the car, I hear a quiet "get up," and the air fills with a low metallic rumble as the mower lurches back into service.

As the car rolls to a stop in front of the shed, Chip, the family dog, lifts himself off of the back stoop of the house and ambles over. He's moving slower these days and might've put on a little weight. But he's still timid and hangs his head low between his shoulders begging to be petted. A few pats on the head and we are friends all over again. He turns and stares intently at the backdoor, where a few seconds later Katie emerges and heads our way. She's wearing a traditional blue dress and white apron with a small white cap covering her jet-black hair. Today she's barefoot, and as her face comes into focus her warm smile and twinkling eyes almost seem to precede her on the path. It's wonderful to see her again. I produce a gift of southern pralines, pecans coated in sugar, that my wife, Barbara, has sent along for the family.

Katie's eyes get even brighter. "Oh! You brought some of those to us last year, and they are wonderful! The children just love them, and we can't get anything like that around here."

"Well, I'm glad you liked them. Barb thought you might."

"Yes, we do. Please tell her thank you for us."

I hand over the jar and quietly ask, "How have you been Katie?"

"Better." Then in a still softer voice, "Definitely better."

"Yeah, I know last year must have been very tough. Milk price has gone up some though, hasn't it?"

"Oh, yes! It's not quite as good as a couple years ago, but it's much higher than last year. Well, you know, last year was terrible."

"Yeah, I remember. But I didn't have to live through it like you folks did. Where's the price of milk now?"

"We got a few pennies over $17 a hundredweight this past month. So that's pretty good."

"Pretty good" is an understatement. In 2008 the price of milk hovered around $18 per hundredweight, and then by the summer of 2009 it fell to near $11 per hundredweight and stayed there for many months before it finally started to turn around. So for most of a year, Katie and Eli and all the other small dairy farms had to find ways for their growing families to get by with about 40 percent less income. It was tough. A fair number of the super-big, "efficient" factory farms, milking thousands of cows on concrete pads, simply had to fold their tent and go bankrupt. Small farms like the Gingeriches' generally fared better—not good, but better. Some non-farm Amish families even saw it as an opportunity to buy cows and heifers cheap and start up new small dairy farms with the hope that prices would someday rebound. Their gamble has paid off. Prices are much better now.

Walking toward the barn, Katie and I are catching up on the news in the settlement and talking as old friends do. She suddenly stops and turns toward me. "You know times were hard last year. We lived on potatoes and canned beef, but we didn't suffer." She pauses a moment and goes on in a voice punctuated by optimism and confidence, "Really, we were all right."

"I know Katie. . . . I know." There's really nothing more to say. We turn and walk on toward the barn door. Katie is just starting to show me a new calf, born last night, when Eli appears at the door with the buggy horse, now unhitched from the mower.

"I'll be right with you two, as soon as I get this horse put away."

As we walk toward the next stall to look at two more calves, Katie, as usual, asks me to stay for dinner, and I readily accept. In a couple of minutes, Eli shows up in the aisle behind us and asks in his normal full voice, "What'd you think of those calves?"

"Well, they look fine to me, Eli."

Katie interrupts before our conversation goes any further. "I need to go in and start dinner. Why don't you two go ahead and tour the barn here for a few minutes and then come on up to the house."

Eli answers for both of us. "That sounds good."

There's really not much to see in the barn. The aisle way is swept clean, and the cows are all out on pasture this time of day. Still, it feels good to walk from one end of the barn to the other talking with Eli. After a short time, we find ourselves walking back up toward the house. Without taking off his heavy leather work shoes, Eli leans his head in the side door, exchanges a few words with Katie, and turns back to me. "She says dinner is not quite ready yet. Why don't we go sit out back?"

"That's fine. The sun feels good out here." As we walk around to the backyard, I'm thinking of a few years ago when Eli had just transitioned out of being a carpenter and started this farm. Back then he called the midday meal "lunch" because most of the time it came out of a lunch-bucket. Dinner was at night after the taxi-van brought him home. But on this and the other dairy farms in the settlement, the main meal of the day usually happens around noon, and Eli has adapted to calling it "dinner." It's a subtle shift in verbiage, spoken by a man now long accustomed to spending his days working on the family farm, and for some reason it delights me to hear it.

As we settle into two folding lawn chairs behind the house, Daniel, mischievous as ever, and his tottering younger sister break out of the backdoor to join us. He gets to the child-sized bench swing just in time to shorten the chain on one side, so when his sister sits down she is badly off plumb and leaning about 30 degrees starboard. Confused, she gets off. Daniel points to the swing chains as if he solved the mystery and carefully readjusts them. This time when the little girl sits down, she is leaning 25 degrees port side.

Eli doesn't raise his voice, but his words are saturated with a father's tired exasperation. "Daniel, stop that."

The boy shrugs as if the game has gone on long enough anyhow, levels the swing for his sister, gives her a little push to get the swing started, giggles, and runs back into the kitchen. She sits contentedly, swaying her legs back and forth with the motion of the swing, and hums a quiet baby tune to herself, while Eli and I strike up our conversation again.

An Amish farmer a couple miles down the road suffered a bout of illness and couldn't work for a time this past spring. Naturally—for it is no great surprise in this community of faith—farmers from the surrounding neighborhood showed up one afternoon to work his fields. "Never saw anything like it," Eli says, shaking his head slowly back and forth in still-lingering wonderment. "There were 44 horses, five two-bottom plows, and several single-bottom plows. We plowed 14 acres that afternoon."

"That really sounds like something. I would've loved to have seen it, Eli." A 14-acre field is almost too small to bother with on a 3,000- or 4,000-acre Yankee grain farm, but it was likely more than a third, and maybe as much as half, of all the crop ground on his neighbor's farm. The two bottom plows that Eli talked about have two plowshares mounted beside each other on a metal frame. When pulled through the field, usually with a five-horse hitch, it turns over two furrows of soil at a time. The single bottom only turns over one furrow, so it's much slower, but it's pulled with fewer horses. Everything's a trade-off.

The equipment and the horses are impressive. However, in my mind I'm slowly formulating a question to draw Eli into a conversation about the amazing, and sometimes overwhelming, quiet power of the Amish community in this settlement. Does he understand how remarkable and different it is from the larger Yankee world? Does he appreciate it? Can it sometimes be smothering? As I open my mouth with a half-formed question, the backdoor swings open and Katie calls out, "Dinner's ready." Our talk will have to wait. Here, as everywhere, hunger trumps philosophy.

Eli helps his little daughter off the swing and holds her hand for a few steps until she breaks free and runs on her short, wobbly legs to the picnic table in the side yard. We all reconvene around the table under the shade of a tree where I've often been before. Eli and the children are taking their places. Katie points to the spot on the bench directly in front of me and says, "Sit right there. That's fine."

Everyone is seated now. Daniel is tickling his brother with a serving spoon from the kitchen. Eli's eyes roam the faces around the table until his gaze stops and centers on Daniel, and he quietly commands, "Let's have grace."

After grace, Katie invites us to "just dig in." She retrieves the serving spoon from Daniel and passes a big platter of fried fish fillets my way.

"This looks good. What kind of fish is it? Something you caught, Eli?"

"No, no. I didn't catch it. It's supposed to be walleye. At least that's what the man who brought it around to sell said. I guess we'll see."

Door-to-door salesmen are almost a thing of the past in the larger community, but here in the settlement they are very common. Transportation is always a challenge for Amish families, so local individuals, stores, and shops will load up a van with everything from dress fabric and flour to horse medicines and tools and drive these back roads looking for sales. The fish we're eating might have come from a local store or maybe just a guy who had a particularly good day fishing Lake Erie. In any case, it's good! A true garden-fresh salad with creamy dressing makes its way around the table, followed by boiled potatoes, homemade bread, butter, and sour cream. There's a large, sweating pitcher of cool water waiting to refill our glasses.

The table falls into a few minutes of active silence as food is passed, silverware scrapes, and bread gets buttered. After a time, Katie breaks the quiet and nods in the direction of their oldest daughter. "Next year is Regina's last year of school." Since Amish children finish school after the eighth grade, Regina's probably 12 or 13 right now.

I look her way, click my tongue and in a feigned serious voice, and ask, "Gittin' kind of old there, aren't you, Regina?"

Uneasy with the attention, she blushes as she looks down at the table and shyly mutters, "Oh, I don't know."

Sometime after she finishes school next year, Regina will probably get a job off the farm. She may work in a store or roadside market. She may get in a taxi each morning with a group of other girls and head off to the Yankee side of the county to clean houses. She may work in a sit-down restaurant or at the McDonald's drive-through window in Middlefield.

As she gets a little more into adolescence and young adulthood, Eli and Katie will encourage her to experience all there is in the outside world. There will be boys and dating and get-togethers and parties. She'll probably get married somewhere around her mid-20s. Exactly when is her choice. But sometime in her early 20s or just before she gets married, she will face the decision of whether or not to be baptized and become Amish. Children living in Amish homes are not "Amish" until they make the decision to be baptized as adults.

Because she will have fully experienced what the outside world has to offer, Regina will know exactly what it is she's giving up if she joins the church and becomes "Amish." But she has also grown up in this community and understands the close bonds, security, and wonderful opportunities she will lose if she chooses not to join the church. Exact numbers are hard to come by, but Amish elders estimate that when Regina's great-grandmother cooked in this kitchen and when her great-grandfather ran the farm, about 50 percent, or at most 60 percent, of the children grew up to join the church. Today with all of our technology and worldly temptations, things have markedly changed. Now somewhere well over 95 percent of all the young people in this settlement stay in the faith and very consciously make the decision to become Amish. Almost certainly, Regina, too, will weigh all of her options and one day join the church.

Thinking we have probably embarrassed Regina quite enough, I turn toward Eli and ask, "How are the crops looking?"

"Good, real good. Jonas Burkholder just took off a field of speltz and got 112 bushel an acre, along with about 70 bales of straw an acre. The corn and the second-cutting hay both look good. I'd say it's been an exceptional growing season, at least so far."

"Yeah, driving in I thought things looked pretty good all around, and that speltz yield is outstanding." A hundred bushels of speltz an acre is really good, and anything over that is very unusual. So the growing season so far must have been great. "What about cow prices, Eli? Have they moved up at all?"

"I really can't tell you. I haven't sold or bought anything for several months. We had a nice springing heifer we almost sold this past winter."

Katie jumps into the conversation and says emphatically, "But we didn't. Not after we heard the price."

Eli nods his head in agreement, "No, we did not. A cattle jockey—well, you probably know him—Novy Doan?"

"Oh, sure, I know Novy." Can't say I know Novy well, but I've run into him many times over the years while visiting Amish farms.

Eli goes on. "Anyway, Novy stopped by when we were thinking about selling her and said he could only pay $700, even for a springing heifer, because farmers just weren't buying when the price of milk was so low. I told him no way." Eli chops the side of his right hand into the palm of his left for emphasis. "Old cows are worth $500 for beef, and $700 for a good springing heifer is just way too low. He wouldn't budge, so we ended up keeping her and adding her to the herd. It all turned out okay. She's a pretty good cow, and now with the price of milk up a little, we can use the extra production."

I do get a kick out of Eli's animated retelling of the story and fully understand why he was unhappy about the price offered for this heifer. A springing heifer is a young female cow that is about to have her first calf and start producing milk for the first time. Normally, a good springing heifer is a very valuable animal because she is likely to have several more calves and spend many years in the herd going through successive lactations. The "old cow for beef" that Eli threw up to Novy is a cow that's no longer profitable in the herd and that's sold for low-quality beef, generally at a very low price. But last year wasn't a normal year. As farms closed down over low milk prices, the heifer market became flooded, and the $700 Novy offered Eli was probably the best he could do.

"Well, sounds like it all worked out for the best in the long run."

Eli nods in agreement as Katie pronounces, "Yes, in the long run, I guess it did."

In the back of my mind I'm remembering some conversations we had about the possibility of putting a greenhouse on this farm. But it was supposed to be over near the cow barn, and it's not there. "Hey, weren't you folks considering putting up a greenhouse last year? Whatever happened to that idea?"

Eli draws up a little in his chair and says, "We did talk about it, but in the end we decided to go to three-a-day milking instead. We did it for about six months and that was enough."

I am shocked, "You did? I don't think I've ever seen a farm this size go to three-a-day milking." Milking a herd of cows three times a day, rather than the normal two, generally increases total milk production by around 10 percent or a little more. But it requires a giant change in the labor schedule. Instead of milking once at five or six o'clock in the morning and then 12 hours later in late afternoon or early evening, cows on a three-a-day schedule need to be milked about every eight hours. Just like people, cows like to sleep in the middle of the night, so that usually means someone needs to be there to do the milking at around 5:00 in the morning, then again at 1:00 in the afternoon, and yet again at 9:00 at night. On the dairies with 1,000 or more cows, they do it all the time, but they use three shifts of hired workers to do it. On this farm the total labor pool is made up of Katie, Eli, and the children, and I can't imagine how they did it.

Eli quickly rationalizes the decision. "The cows ate a little more, but we had plenty of feed and it gave us more milk to sell, even if it wasn't worth much."

Katie adds, "One of the big things is we didn't want to take on any more debt. So we worked a little harder . . . well, a lot harder. I would just finish dinner and then go down to the barn to help with milking before I even did the dishes. It was a lot of work, but we got through it. We're all glad to be back to two a day now though."

Once again I am humbled by the hard work and tenacity this family displays every day. The dinner hour has stretched out way past where it should. There's still a half-day of farm work left to be done, and I should be going. Eli draws the meal to a close with another silent prayer. Chip walks me to the car and gets one last pat on the head before the door closes. That big white barn over there holds Gingerich cows and horses, Gingerich hay and grain, and Gingerich hopes, prayers, and dreams for the future. Watching it grow tiny in the rearview mirror fills my entire being with melancholy. I hate to leave.

On a cold gray winter morning, a young Amish man named Eli called and nervously said, "We are thinking about starting to farm. . . ." That was more than five years ago. The business plans and farm budgets we drew up together and carefully reviewed over the kitchen table with mugs of hot coffee have worn well. Over the years, the plans have been revised and changed and revised again. But looking back, it's clear they have passed the muster of time.

Katie and Eli have weathered the storm. They've pulled past one of the worst economic downturns dairy farmers have seen in a generation. The farm is on solid financial ground, the herd is healthy, and this year's crops look good. They did it through hard work, planning, business innovation, flexibility, and what can only be called grace. They have earned the right to proclaim, "We are farmers."

Their young family is flourishing. During the school year, the children who are old enough to be "scholars" walk a little down the road and around the corner, carrying kid-sized lunch buckets to the two-room Amish school. When not in school, they play and work with both of their parents on the farm. They spend each day growing under the protective eyes and, usually, patient guidance of their mom and dad. Once or twice a week, they walk a mile down the road and spend some time with grandma and grandpa. They are farm kids, and most of the time they're having fun.

Life doesn't deal many sure hands, but the odds are pretty good—barring some catastrophe or personal tragedy—that one of these children, or another yet to be born, will some day years from now take over this farm. Likely the son or daughter will spend many anxious hours with their new, young spouse, poring over budgets and farm plans until they gain the confidence needed to timidly announce to the world they are thinking about starting to farm.

As the new family takes over, Eli and Katie will slow down a bit and partially retire to a small house here on the farm or one just a little down the road. Their years will be surrounded with children and grandchildren and children after that. Starting this farm was a huge personal gamble; it took real courage. According to all of the ciphers added up in my ledger, this gamble paid off very well. It has been an honor to share even a tiny part of their story. Somewhere out there in the future, our paths may cross briefly again, but for now, as the barn behind me fades from view, it's time to move on.

This road meanders deeper into the settlement. The afternoon is sunny, and I think I'll stay on it a while. The field on the left has rows and rows of shocked speltz drying in the sun. Beside it is a field of newly mown alfalfa hay, and across the road is about five acres of waist-high corn. I pass several buggies, a team of two dappled Percheron draft horses lazily pulling an empty hay wagon back to the field, and of course one of the ubiquitous baseball diamonds carved out of the corner of a crop field—the Amish folks around here do love baseball.

At first, it looks like very little has changed, but slowly I start to notice some differences. That's really not surprising at all. A careful observer sees that this community is continually evolving, continually changing, as the years move forward. This year, for some odd reason, family cows are back. House after house has a single Guernsey, Jersey, or Ayrshire tethered in the lawn. These little brown or brown-and-white cows are about two-thirds the size of the big black-and-white Holsteins found on most dairy farms, and they give a lot less milk. Even a decent Holstein might produce 10 or 12 gallons of milk a day, which is more than enough to leave any family swimming in milk. On the other hand, a run-of-the-mill Jersey, Guernsey, or Ayrshire gives just enough milk for a family or two. That still doesn't explain why they are suddenly here. In all of the years I worked in this settlement, family cows were a rarity. So what's changed?

Slowly putting two and two together, I remember we are in the middle of a terrible recession. Amish people who were carpenters, masons, factory workers, and plumbers are out of work. With little or no money coming in, the family cow has returned to stretch precious food dollars. It's a little depressing, but my mind immediately jumps to the possible educational opportunities and the classes I could put on. Then jerking harshly back to reality, I remember that it's not my job . . . not any more.

At the next stop sign, I turn due south and begin my sojourn home. It will take a while to actually get out of the community. The settlement is more than twice as big as it was some 30 years ago when I first came here. There are more families, more farms, more schools, more church districts, more cows, more crops, and more farmland. By any measure this humble Amish settlement is hugely successful, and there is no reason to imagine that it will do anything except thrive and flourish in the years to come. The future is brilliantly sunny for the Geauga settlement and its people. Thinking of Katie and Eli, their children, and the settlement, I pass the last big white Amish house, and the road pulls me once again back into the Yankee world.

Afterword

It's all here, stretched out in front of me like a hellish prison for gentle
cows. Thousands of black-and-white cows milling aimlessly about on
rock-hard concrete floors, covered with a soup of runny, loose feces and
steaming urine. But this farm is not unique. In fact, it's the norm for modern, large dairy farms. The bleak, short lives of the cows in front of me are
little different from many thousands of their sisters on other large dairy
farms. Indeed, most of the dairy cows in these United States live out their
lives in huge, covered metal sheds like this one. And most of the milk, butter, cheese, and ice cream that we gobble down each day gets its start in
the stench and filth of floors like this.

A single cow wandering up the aisle toward me has caught my eye. Her
ear tag identifies her as cow #3076. She's probably looking for an empty
stall to collapse into. To save money, these barns are nearly always built
with many fewer stalls than there are cows. Therefore, #3076 may spend
a fair portion of her day or night looking for a place to lie down. If she gets
too tired, she may give up and flop her carcass down in the runny manure
of the aisle floor. If she does find a stall, it will be a little longer than she
is and about twice as wide. Two curved pipes will delineate the sides. The

floor of each stall is raised about six inches above the aisle floor and covered with rubber mats. Cows always walk headfirst into a stall, so except for a few inches in the back covered in manure, the stall floor is relatively clean and dry.

I've always hated using numbers rather than names for cows. Of course, if you're going to treat them like this, a numbering system certainly provides some emotional distance and allows them to be efficiently reduced to mere "animal units." The simple act of assigning a number to a living creature reduces its moral standing and helps dehumanize it for those responsible for its care.

Just for a moment, I silently rename cow #3076 and call her Elsie after the gentle brown cow that lightly danced through many of the TV milk commercials of the 1960s and 1970s. But this big-boned, brooding, black-and-white cow, with the horns cut off—or burned off—of her drooping head, bears little resemblance to the doe-eyed Elsie. Except she is almost certainly gentle. Were I to walk down onto this floor, I could easily push my way through this herd of beasts, even though each is several times my size and weight.

Hundreds of years of careful breeding and close association with humans have led to the modern, very docile dairy cow. In the past, when a farm family milked and cared for one cow or a small herd, a mean cow could not be tolerated. Someone in the family might get hurt. A young cow who kicked, butted, or horned a person once too often was soon removed from the gene pool—and added to the family larder. So docile cows got to have many docile cow babies, and mean cows got to be supper. The end result is that being "gentle" is in a cow's genes. She truly can't help herself, even if we choose to treat her poorly.

Cow #3076 is still slowly making her way toward this end of the barn. Just now cow #923 strides down the aisle. She's a tall first-calf heifer with small patches of black hair on her sleek, well-conditioned white body. She's in good flesh with a swelling udder tightly attached to her frame. She bumps poor old #3076 out of the way, and the old girl ends up directly behind cow #1448, who unfortunately just stood up to relieve herself.

Sadly, #3076 hardly seems to notice. She just resumes her unsteady sojourn toward this end of the barn. She is close enough for me to get a really good look at her now. She's not a pretty sight. Her big, round eyes show too much white, as they seem to fairly pop out of her head. She's emaciated—so thin that the skin stretching over her side forms deep valleys between the rib bones. Her face is mostly white, except for a two-by-four-inch apostrophe of dried brown manure fused into the coarse hair of her sunken forehead. The brown patch starts up near where her left horn used to be and sweeps across her face, down almost between her eyes. Hard telling how long it's been there, but it doesn't look like she's even tried to scrape it off.

Her pink udder is immense and looks to be near bursting full. The udder is so big that it barely fits underneath her broad belly, and with each step a big hind leg slowly pushes forward and kicks it out of the way. It sloshes back and forth and hangs so low and loose that the four teat ends almost drag in the manure soup.

She's favoring that front right leg with a decided limp each time she takes a step. Could be her knee or hoof or foreleg or all of them together that are causing such pain. She's limping now, and like as not she'll be completely lame before long. For a moment I have to turn away and hide my disgust. I am a guest at this farm and it would be discourteous for me to offend or lecture this particular farmer. After all, this farm is not unusual. The scenes here are repeated thousands of times in huge factory dairy farms across the United States every day.

Soon this emaciated, dirty, lame old #3076 will be loaded onto a truck and sent to slaughter. She'll meet her end on the packinghouse kill floor. What little meat there is on her scrawny carcass will most likely be ground into hamburger. But sizzling under a thin sheet of yellow cheese and a pickle in some fast-food restaurant, she'll eat okay. Maybe a little tough but okay.

Don't count my Elsie out completely. She's not dead yet. Number 3076 is not lame enough to cull out of this milking herd. She will continue to be a contributing member of the dairy industry until the pain in her legs makes it almost impossible for her to walk. After that, hopefully without her knowledge, and certainly without her consent, she will experience a major career shift. The minute she limps onto the cattle truck and starts her trip to the kill floor, she will officially leave the dairy industry and become a valuable part of the U.S. beef industry.

The conditions in the cattle truck might start to suggest that her new role in the beef industry is not a management position. If her chauffeur is following the American Meat Institute guidelines for animal spacing, she should have around 20 square feet, or maybe even a little more truck floor space, just for her. Well, not just for her; that's an average number, so each of probably 30 or so cows on the truck will get that much space. Then it's off for a quick ride to the slaughterhouse. Maybe not so quick.

The National Market Cow and Bull Beef Quality Audit says that in 2007 the average ride to the slaughterhouse was about 9 hours, or 409 miles. The real distances varied anywhere from 22 miles all the way up to 1,050 miles. However long the trip, Elsie will likely stand the whole way, along with all of her jostling truck mates.

The Executive Summary of the 2007 National Market Cow and Bull Beef Quality Audit is an impressive document—not an easy read, but interesting. Researchers from no less than seven universities—Texas A&M, North Dakota State, California Polytechnic State, Penn State, the University of Georgia, the University of Florida, and West Texas A&M—conducted the studies that went into the report. The whole thing was coordinated by the National Cattlemen's Beef Association's Beef Quality Assurance Program and funded by the industry-supported Beef Checkoff program.

I know from personal experience that trying to get a large group of researchers from different universities to function as a team is very much like herding feral cats. The mere fact that all of these faculty members were able to work together on a common project is a remarkable achievement in its own right. Very similar audits were conducted in 1994 and 1999, so it is now possible to look at trends in the beef industry over about a 12-year period.

These folks visited 23 meatpacking plants in 11 states for the 2007 audit alone. In round numbers, they examined 5,500 live animals, 5,000 carcasses during processing, and another 3,000 carcasses hanging in the coolers. That's a lot of meat. They interviewed government inspectors, meat packers, processors, and finally end users like restaurants. The researchers identified lists of things that could be improved and then worked with the beef industry to come up with specific suggestions to correct problems. They tracked industry progress in addressing the problems across the 1994, 1999, and 2007 audits, and in many, but not all, cases they found real improvement.

One segment of the beef industry—"dairy cows for slaughter"—is a persistent laggard in the whole improvement effort. Unfortunately, "dairy cows for slaughter" happens to be the division of the industry that Elsie will soon transfer into. The problem is that in some ways the picture for "dairy cows" that enter the beef industry is plain grisly and getting worse by the year.

In the audit executive summaries of beef quality, the animals going to slaughter are usually broken into four categories: beef cows, beef bulls, dairy cows, and dairy bulls. Sometimes the category "all cattle" is included, which is just a total of the four groups. It's important to remember that these audit summaries deal only with "cows and bulls." The results for the much younger "steers and heifers," which make up the bulk of the beef industry, are found in other audit summaries. So these particular summaries look only at the older cows and bulls. Now, because of the way the dairy and beef industries are currently structured, most of the animals represented in these summaries are from large or very large dairy and beef farms.

Therefore, much like darling Elsie, the vast majority of the dairy animals represented in the summary spent their entire adult lives as animal units at some huge dairy farm. In other words, these animals spent the most time under the direct "care" of dairy farm managers. And the National Market Cow and Bull Beef Quality Audits directly reflect the quality of that "care" and track its improvement, or degradation, over time. These slaughter-time studies provide a fascinating peek into the past lives of millions of hamburgers, hot dogs, and bologna sandwiches.

The data in the executive summaries of these audits reveal a dim outline of the quality of life these animals experienced. Unfortunately, some of the really tantalizing details are omitted or obscured in the executive summaries, which are released to the public and the press. The summaries are quick to point out areas where the industry has improved and also areas where improvement is still needed. However, for some reason Elsie's category of "dairy cows" is conspicuously absent in most of the written analysis. She and her sisters do show up in some of the charts and graphs presented in the documents, but they are almost never discussed.

The 2007 audit reports that 69 percent of all cattle observed in the holding pens—this is where cattle are kept just before they are sent onto the kill floor—had no visible defects. Of course that means that 31 percent had a defect that was severe enough to be picked up simply by looking at the animal. Seventy-two percent of the beef cows and a whopping 76 percent of the beef bulls had no visible defects. In other words only 24 percent of beef bulls are visibly defective. That's great news.

But what about cow #3076? How did Elsie's sisters look on the death pen runway? If only 28 percent of the beef cows and 24 percent of the beef bulls were defective, how is it that 31 percent of all the cattle were defective? The obvious answer is that more of the dairy bulls and dairy cows had to be visibly defective. So in the case of dairy cows, were Elsie's sisters 40 percent or 50 percent or 60 percent defective? We don't know.

Today these holding pen girls are much cleaner than those that passed before them. In 2007 only 59 percent were spattered with mud or manure. That's way down from 1999 when 98 percent of the dairy cows came in with at least some covering of manure or dirt. It's not that their lives are any cleaner—they still live every day in filth—it's just that the farm system managers have decided it's a good idea to hose these ladies down before they get to the slaughter facility.

Elsie is so thin it hurts my eyes to look at her. Mercifully, there is no agonizing data in the 2007 report to tell us how many other dairy cows meet their end looking this way. I really should have let this one lie right here without knowing. But curiosity got the best of me and I went back to the 1999 audit report. Tucked away in the middle table, there's a line item called "light muscled" dairy cows. In layman's terms, "light muscled" just means scrawny. The numbers aren't good. In 1994 a little over 11 percent of the dairy cows going to slaughter were "light muscled." Just five years later, in 1999, fully 72 percent were "light muscled." That year, well over two-thirds of these cows met death with their hides draped over a bony frame where thick muscle and rich fat used to be. Again, the 2007 audit report omits any direct reference, and we do not know how many dairy cows walked to the kill floor in a "light-muscled" condition.

What about that lame right foreleg? How unusual is Elsie's lameness? The authors of the summary never really seem to get around to discussing lameness in dairy cows. They do discuss lameness in beef cows and beef bulls, but not dairy. However, the data on lameness is presented in a table that's not discussed anywhere. Still, it's sitting there, quietly waiting to be discovered.

Actually, the table presents data on the percentage of cattle that were "not lame." So 84 percent of the beef cows in 2007 were not lame. At this point, I must confess some irritation with the authors' presentation of the results. Obviously, the question being examined is, how many animals are "lame" by the time they get to the slaughterhouse? If 84 percent of the beef cows were not lame, then 16 percent had to be lame. The 16 percent lame figure is, of course, the number anyone looking at this report should be reading. Had I pulled a stunt like this in presenting data in my days as a grad student, my advisors would have rightly laughed me out of the room and maybe out of the program.

By the way, 11 percent of the beef cows were lame in 1994, 27 percent were lame in 1999, and 16 percent were lame in 2007. So fewer beef cows in 2007 limped onto the kill floor than eight years earlier. That's good news. But more of them limped onto the kill floor than in 1994, and that's bad news, at least for the cows.

Beef bulls didn't fare too badly in 2007. Only 31 percent limped in to be butchered. That's down from 36 percent in 1999, but up from 27 percent in 1994. Dairy bulls might be the real success story here; only 22 percent of these animals were limping onto the kill floor in 2007. That's down from 29 percent in 1999 and 24 percent in 1994. Hooray for dairy bulls.

The news isn't nearly so good for dairy cows. Elsie's division of the industry has been on a steady downhill slide. In 1994 a mere 23 percent of the dairy cows showed up lame at the slaughterhouse door. Just five years later, the number of lame dairy cows had ballooned to 39 percent. By 2007 almost half, or 49 percent, of these miserable old gals hobbled to their death on legs racked with persistent, debilitating pain. Hell, Elsie's aching leg isn't even unusual anymore. It's the norm.

Cow #3076 will undoubtedly be culled from the herd in the very near future because she will be simply too lame to get around. After a quick shower—the only one of her life—she'll drag her thin, sore body onto a cattle truck, where she will join the beef industry. In the holding pens, her limping gate won't even be noticed because every second dairy cow waiting for death will be just as lame as her. A few will have abscesses on their legs, a few will have maimed udders, a few will have lumpy jaw or cancer eye, but the most common ailments of these aging animals are surely lameness and emaciation.

We in agriculture know why these poor cows are going lame. We can produce long lists of contributing factors. The reasons are many and varied—as are the excuses. The bottom line is that too often the inhumane housing, feeding, and management systems in huge dairy production farms are just plain unhealthy for cows. There's plenty of blame to go around: from the land grant universities and agribusiness companies that helped develop the management products and systems for large dairies; to the veterinarians, feed consultants, milk, and meat processors who have quietly observed the general decline in animal health on these dairies; to the farmers themselves who must surely understand the impact of their actions on the innocent animals in their care. For my part, I am profoundly sorry that in a moment of intellectual caprice, I saddled this one wretched, dirty, scrawny, lame cow with the hauntingly gentle name of Elsie. In the future, I will try to think of her only as animal unit #3076 . . . if I think of her at all. When it comes to the animals on megafarms, numbers really are better than names, after all.

Not all Amish or small non-Amish farms name the cows. Some do and some don't. But on small farms, each animal is an important part of the fabric of the entire operation. Not a pet or a member of the family, but not a stranger either. And her place in the herd is light-years away from that of any sequentially numbered animal unit. We could do better on large dairy farms. After 30 years of learning each day from a thriving, thoughtfully modern community of Amish farmers, I know we could.